# BLACK
# UTOPIAS

UT

Duke University Press   *Durham and London*   2021

# BLACK
# OPIAS

Speculative Life and the Music of Other Worlds    JAYNA BROWN

© 2021 Duke University Press
All rights reserved
Printed and bound by CPI Group (UK) Ltd, Croydon, CR0 4YY
Cover and text designed by Courtney Leigh Richardson
Typeset in Futura Std and Warnock Pro
by Copperline Book Services

Library of Congress Cataloging-in-Publication Data
Names: Brown, Jayna, [date] author.
Title: Black utopias : speculative life and the music of
other worlds / Jayna Brown.
Description: Durham : Duke University Press, 2021. |
Includes bibliographical references and index.
Identifiers: LCCN 2020030935 (print) |
LCCN 2020030936 (ebook) |
ISBN 9781478010548 (hardcover) |
ISBN 9781478011675 (paperback) |
ISBN 9781478021230 (ebook)
Subjects: LCSH: Philosophical anthropology. | Philosophy,
Black. | Utopias. | Racism. | African Americans—Attitudes. |
African Americans—Race identity. | Utopias in literature.
Classification: LCC BD450 .B67 2021 (print) |
LCC BD450 (ebook) | DDC 128—dc23
LC record available at https://lccn.loc.gov/2020030935
LC ebook record available at https://lccn.loc.gov/2020030936

Cover art: *Black Girl's Window*, 1969. Mixed media,
35¾ x 18 x 1½ inches. © Betye Saar. Digital image
© The Museum of Modern Art/Licensed by SCALA/
Art Resource, New York.

# Contents

# Acknowledgments

This book took a long time, so I have more than a decade of people and institutions to thank for their support. First, I'd like to thank my editor, Ken Wissoker, for his patience and faith in this project and the Duke University production team for their hard work. A big thank you to my anonymous readers. I appreciate your careful, thoughtful, and generous feedback, which was essential in this book's development.

I'd also like to thank the many friends and colleagues who were kind enough to read drafts of parts or all of this book: Bruce Dorsey, Macarena Gómez-Barris, Jack Halberstam, Saidiya Hartman, Lynn Hudson, Lisa Lowe, Fred Moten, Tavia Nyong'o, Ann Pellegrini, and Christina Sharpe. Your brilliance inspired me to think as widely as I could about blackness, queer worlding, feminism, music, narrative structure, relationality, and the spirit world—and to be vulnerable enough to try and write something alive. Thanks to Mel Y. Chen and Dana Luciano for guiding me as I was beginning to think about race and materialism, and for publishing what has become chapter 4 of this book. I thank José Muñoz in spirit for our discussions of Ernst Bloch and other things utopian. I wish we had had more time to work and think together.

I thank Robin Bernstein and my fellows at Harvard's Charles Warren Center for a wonderful fellowship year in 2012–13. Thanks to Bruce Dorsey and Ann Pellegrini for encouraging me not to be afraid to write about religion. Thanks to my writing partner, Lynn Hudson, for her enthusiasm. Thanks to Christina Sharpe and Lisa Lowe for hanging out with me that year, and to the women of the Dark Room Collective for an intellectually stimulating experience. Thanks to Tsitsi Jaji for being my brilliant friend and flatmate in

Somerville, Scott Poulson Bryant for being my bestie while at Harvard, and Emily Owens and Sandy Placido for hanging out with me. Thanks to Martin Summers and Karl Mundt for your unconditional support. You all kept me (reasonably) sane.

At UC Riverside, thanks to Dylan Rodriguez, for being a fearless comandante during rocky times, and to Dean Stephen Cullenberg, for having my back. Thanks to Aisha Finch for our Saturday movie nights. Thanks to Henri Lucas and the rest of the Downtown L.A. crew for morning and afternoon coffee hangouts.

I have many libraries and institutions to thank. In London, 2014-2015 I worked in the British Library's Rare Books and Manuscripts Room, and I thank the fine librarians there for helping me find those quirky odds and ends about utopian communities, colonialism, and eugenics, the latter of which I learned a great deal more about—in fact, more than I ever wanted to know—in the Eugenics Collection down the street at Wellcome House. Thanks always to Paul Gilroy, for your support and for my residence as a visiting fellow at King's College London. Back in the Los Angeles area, I thank the talented librarians at the Huntington Library in Pasadena, who helped me navigate through the voluminous Octavia E. Butler papers.

In 2017, I moved to Brooklyn and began teaching at Pratt Institute. Big thanks to Jon Beller, Ira Livingston, Mendi Obadike, Minh-Ha Pham, and Ethan Spigland for welcoming me to the Graduate Program in Media Studies and to Jennifer Miller for her playful approach to the very serious.

My heart is full as I thank my oldest and dearest friends. To my scar clan sister Catherine Fox, thank you for more than thirty years of friendship and for being a fabulous traveling companion. I thank my UK friends Loo How and Julie Stewart for decades of patience and humor. I will always have deep love for Macarena Gómez-Barris, who has shared her wisdom and strength with me for over a decade, and helped me navigate through choppy waters. I thank Tavia Nyong'o for his consistent friendship and intellectual generosity. You are all dear friends with whom I am proud to stay young, and I am looking forward to many more years of collaboration.

Thanks and big love to my bio family. Love to my mother for teaching me to wonder at the world. Thanks to my father for his sometimes-lucid dreaming. To my visionary artist sister, Geneva, and to my athletic and fiery niece Simone. And to my creative and brilliant niece Xandra, whom I thank for the gift of blue lipstick and for taking me to my first opera.

CODA: Since I began writing this book the world has become ever more apocalyptic as we face, among other conditions, a global pandemic; the climate crisis; a rampant, voracious, and brutal system of global capitalism; and authoritarianism and white supremacy. I dedicate this book to our collective endeavor as we try to imagine other possibilities after the final days to come.

# Introduction

I am black; I am in total fusion with the world, in sympathetic affinity with the earth, losing my id in the heart of the cosmos. . . . I am black, not because of a curse, but because my skin has been able to capture all the cosmic effluvia. I am truly a drop of sun under the earth.
—FRANTZ FANON, *Black Skin, White Masks* (1967)

## Prologue

This book is about the force of black speculative vision and practice. It is about the curious modes of being manifest in such visions and practices, modes that pay no mind to inclusion within the confines of the human. Dystopia, the horrific terms of being black in our earthly condition, is a starting point for critique; dystopia forms the terrain of our existence. But forms of black life and liveliness are claimed and created in the terror. These forms do not end with death, social or otherwise. What is on the other side of death, where we reside? What kinds of strange ways and worlds do we inhabit there? Looking past death, or considering it a limited construct, I am not arguing for life according to a model in which we have been restored to some original state, or for life in which we have been granted rights according to some social contract. I don't hope for that. In fact, I don't think utopia needs hope at all. Hope yearns for a future. Instead, we dream in place, in situ, in medias res, in layers, in dimensional frequencies. The quality of being I find in the speculations considered here is about existence beyond life or death, about the ways we reach into the unknowable, outside the bounds of past, present, and future, of selfhood and other. This is what I call utopia: the moments when those of us untethered from the hope of rights, recognition, or redress here on earth celebrate ourselves as elements in a cosmic effluvium.

I begin in the bleak and bloody dimension we are taught to call reality, with my father's story. Raised in rural Oklahoma, my father spent the first part of his adult life as a political activist and member of the Black Panther Party (BPP). But, after his exile and imprisonment, my father became a clairvoyant. In a series of self-published books he prophesied "the final days before the new days begin." My interest in dystopian narratives, utopian thought, and other science fictions is inspired by my father's speculative imaginings.

**My father has** a story like that of many other black radicals of his generation in the United States. He started out getting on the bus as a Freedom Rider and was arrested for the first time in Jackson, Mississippi, in 1961. He then spent his twenties and early thirties as a member of the BPP, living first in Oakland and then in Santa Cruz, California. Like many others who believed in revolution, he went underground as a result of COINTELPRO. In 1981 he was arrested for attempted murder, which was the result of a racist altercation. To avoid an all-white jury and what would surely have been a severe sentence, he jumped bail and went into exile. We thought he would be safe, but we underestimated the racist memory of the carceral state. Thirteen years later, when he was fifty-six, the FBI extradited him from the island in the Caribbean where he had been living, teaching high school and writing for the local newspaper. From a dank island jail he was brought back to the United States and placed in a medium-security unit, where he was the oldest inmate. After a few months he had a heart attack due to untreated high blood pressure. My sister and I visited him as he lay in a hospital bed, his wrists bound to the bedrail with heavy chains. These chains went with him everywhere; they bound him to his wheelchair on our subsequent visits to the jail and were wound around his waist and ankles as he stood in the courtroom.

My father was a writer and a poet, and gave quite a powerful speech before the judge. His sentence was fairly light—five years' probation and time served—as the judge took into consideration the racist nature of the initial confrontation and the character references sent in by his students and colleagues from the island. But after his trial my father's conversations and letters became increasingly epic and declarative in scope. With somber grandiosity, my father proclaimed himself a prophet. Born wrapped in his mother's caul, he told my sister and me, he was gifted with extreme sensitivity, premonitory powers, and the ability to speak with spirits. He announced that he was no longer African American but a Native of African descent, tracing his psychic and spiritual powers through our indigenous ancestors. After his days as a warrior, he explained, he would now spend the rest of his life as a seer, a truth-teller with direct access to the wisdom of our Creek and Cherokee ancestors from Alabama. He then migrated to Canada and began signing his letters first as Chief Two Eagles and then as Painted Wolf. (He addressed me as "Daughter of the Chief.")

Thus began my father's speculative visions of final days and the days to follow, which he collected in a number of volumes. He spent several years in trances and oracular states, channelling spirit beings, most often a nineteenth-century Creek chief named Oktaha and a spirit named Golden Ray. Through auditory visitations and dreams, and in the moments after waking, the chief or the spirit would speak to my father of disasters soon to come and of the new age to follow. First, there was to be a great reckoning; as the result of racism, capitalism, and other violent systems of oppression and exploitation, the world was to be destroyed through economic disaster, fire, flood, earthquakes, and disease. But a new age was to succeed this end of days. The human life that survived would be radically transformed. Capitalism would be dismantled. Forms of sociality were to shift; people would cohabit in collective units instead of families, sharing the responsibility for reproduction and child rearing. Adept spirits like Golden Ray, who already exist among us as vibration and frequency, would provide guidance. Humans would physically evolve; without the need for hierarchical power relations and systems of oppression, races and genders would cease to be relevant and disappear. All vocal speech would become redundant, replaced by extrasensory forms of communication. Finally, Golden Ray told my father, human beings would be biologically modified by astral beings from another dimension. These cosmic entities would alter human DNA, bringing in a new era of existence. Humans as such would die, as they evolved into new states of being.

"What will you do when the final days begin?" he asked me sternly. My first reaction was a deep compassion. As Frantz Fanon wrote, many of his generation suffered in the mind from the effects of direct combat in the wars against colonialism and the afterlives of slavery. But my sister made me think twice about my assumption that he was suffering from psychosis. "Who knows. Maybe he's right," she said. Soon after my father's admonishment came a terrifying series of disasters that disproportionately affected the poorest among us. There was disease: in 2003 an outbreak of SARS struck China. There were massive floods. In 2004 an underwater earthquake and subsequent tsunami devastated South Asia, killing more than 225,000 people and displac ing millions. That same year a flood killed in excess of 2,500 people in Haiti. In 2005 Hurricane Katrina struck the southern United States, and the levees breached in New Orleans; federal and state governments neglected those stranded in the city's Superdome and convention center, and white police officers refused to let black residents cross over a nearby bridge to safety. My father's prophetic visions of total planet-wide disaster actually seemed quite plausible.

But these events were not sudden or unforeseeable; they were horrific escalations of preexisting conditions. After all, people of the Global South (and black and brown people in the Global North) had been living in suspended apocalypse for some time. Certainly, my father's psychosis was a fair response to the apocalypse of the everyday, the fantastical obscenity of this world for black people, which, if looked at directly and/or experienced for too long, can easily appear as hallucination. Reality begins to lose its footing and becomes less and less meaningful. Had my father really been in danger of being caught or killed during his years in hiding, or was his belief grandiose paranoia? We asked ourselves these questions when he had insisted the phone was bugged and that we couldn't use names or refer to specific places while talking to him. Despite our derision, he had been right. Perhaps he was right about the rest.

My father's predictions of the mythical days to come began to appear to me as quite wonderful, and perhaps not improbable, considering the ongoing intimacy between fact and the fantastical and black lives' proximity to where they joined. Maybe my father *was* touched, gifted with mystical and mythological insight. After all, black people's existence is mythological in the first place. We don't really exist, according to the logic of the human. And what does this current plane of reality, also known as a mutually agreed-upon fiction, mean to us anyway? And who mutually agreed upon it? Since black people didn't seem to have been asked, it would make perfect sense that we would be more in touch with/at home in other realities. All of us very well might have extrasensory access to the spiritual afterlife, like my father, or be particularly open to other forms of material existence, other forms of energetics, sonic and haptic as well as visual.

I started this book without consciously making the connection between my father's prophecies and my own interest in utopian dissent—at least on a conscious level. I was and still am conflicted as I read my father's accounts of the end of days and times to follow and contemplate the connection between his visions and the speculative worlds I am drawn to write about. Where is the line between vision and madness? Does it matter? What does listening to other frequencies entail? Most of the artists and thinkers in this book are touched in some way; they are mad souls all. What does it mean to be open to these worlds? To a madness all my own? This project is a way of residing in spaces of ambiguity without trying to answer these questions. What I did do, in relation to my father's work, was resolve to write, in my own way, with the same dedication he had to seeing and feeling radically different worlds, practices, and modes of being.

**I did not** grow up with my father. He was a difficult man to be around. The last time we spoke he asked me what it was like working for The Man. "I have health benefits," I replied, spitefully, and refused to talk about my writing or its connection with his. I didn't want him to think that I was somehow carrying out his patriarchal legacy. He could be incredibly misogynistic and didn't treat women very well. In a softer moment I had promised him I would make sure his writings were left to an archive, but I grew so tired of his masculinist declarations that I haven't done so yet (Daughter of the Chief indeed). Still and all, I can see him as I did that day in the courtroom, a frail older man with a white halo of hair, wrapped in heavy metal chains but standing unflinchingly before the judge, still refusing to comply with a system designed to kill him or leave him in a state of permanent injury. This man I will continue to learn from, and with him I would go to the stars.

The day after I submitted this book to the press my father died. I hadn't had the chance to tell him how central his hallucinatory visions of the world to come were to this project. Or how important his previous political commitment was to my own process of intellectual inquiry. But I am glad to have remembered him here, and it pleases me to think of him now as free, as a "drop of sun under the earth."

Years ago I managed to rescue a box of his writings from the basement of one of his old acquaintances who had agreed years back to store them. Looking through these boxes I found files full of lesson plans for the Black Panther school where he taught. I found photos of all the Brothers and Sisters, young and full of swagger. There were pictures of him standing proudly with Huey Newton. And I found sheaves of poems and plays he had written over the years. I conclude with one of the poems he wrote in 1972:

*a war song: for sleeping giants*

so—
with tomorrow's frightful history
in my brain:

i prepared this song, (for those who would be slain),
and laughed a dirge for those: (our enemies),
in their <u>new</u> pain:

and with the sound of (chains) dancing
in my ears—
i wove a war of poetry,
(an attack on our fears),
and each morning that i
would poet/dream, I would dream an—
APOCALYPSE!

and launch legions against
these chains until they could no longer
rattle/sting,
and—at dawn: after our first bloody beginning:

something new was born—a new order!
a new civilization
quite complete where others—
(oppressed like me):
could also poet/dream—
with songs to launch
and rhymes to scheme!
    where we touched the sky and danced again
to the ANCESTORS daily rhythming!


Black Utopias

*Utopia* is often used as a pejorative to indicate the failure of a humanist project ("That's just utopian thinking!") or to acclaim the hope of its fulfillment, the achievement of the good life, in which all our earthly needs would be met by a given system. Neither applies here. Instead, I take the concept of utopia into a no-place, into an elsewhere. We are still made of matter, but we are rocketed into another dimension.

With black speculation as my methodology, I use the term *utopia* to signal the (im)possibilities for forms of subjectivity outside a recognizable ontological framework, and modes of existence conceived of in unfamiliar epistemes. These (im)possibilities open up where the human has abandoned us and onto a much bigger universe, when we jump into the unknowable. I say the unknowable, not the unknown, for the condition of utopia is to accept that we, in our present state, cannot fully know anything. Utopia is a state of being and doing. Sometimes we leave our bodies, and sometimes we don't; sometimes the flesh transmigrates, as utopia has materiality even as it materializes through strange frequencies. The versions of utopia I develop refer to forms of animation that are quite complex and that change the terms of engagement. These forms of what I call utopia—physical, visual, auditory, spatial, theoretical—supersede the juxtapositions of you and me, here and there, then and now.

Dominant social formations have denied African diasporans the rights and freedoms associated with being defined as human. My claim is that because black people have been excluded from the category *human*, we have a particular epistemic and ontological mobility. Unburdened by investments in belonging to a system created to exclude us in the first place, we develop marvelous modes of being in and perceiving the universe. I am claiming that there is real power to be found in such an untethered state—the power to destabilize the very idea of human supremacy and allow for entirely new ways to relate to each other and to the postapocalyptic ecologies, both organic and inorganic, in which we are enmeshed. I argue that those of us who are dislocated on the planet are perfectly positioned to break open the stubborn epistemological logics of human domination. To imagine as best we can outside these epistemological and ontological circumscriptions does not mean we save the human race, at least not that race as we know it. Salvage may not be possible at this point, although this is not necessarily a catastrophe. The untethered state does allow for the possibility of real change on a vast inhuman scale.

I am inspired by some new materialist thought, particularly its desire to challenge speciesism, decenter the human, and destabilize the category. But I balk at the all-too-familiar claims for the universalism of the Anthropocene. The catastrophe this new materialist thought seeks to avert has already happened, and continues to happen, for many beings. That we are in a crisis is not news for those already living amid the rubble, but my intervention challenges the bleak turn in black studies, which mourns our inhumanity, our "natal alienation."[1] I argue that because of such alienation we have the "freedom not to be," as the musician Sun Ra puts it. What I am claiming is that it is in precisely this shadow state that we have built, and continue to build, alternative worlds, in this dimension and in others, and practice alternative ways of being alive. Since fact and fiction are already indistinct, let us continue to live out our imaginations.

Dreaming in terms of utopia invokes an archive of black alternative worldmaking, to be found in the practices of black mystics and musicians and in the imaginative worlds of speculative fiction writers. The utopias I find in the speculative worlds of radical black visionaries bring into question definitions of well-being based in a liberal humanist model of the possessive individual, a model that directs us to limited notions of freedom. The art and practices I consider involve a *radical refusal* of the terms by which selfhood and subjectivity are widely lived and understood. Along the way arise questions of desire and fulfillment, seemingly key concepts at the heart of utopian thought. The texts I explore reach for ways desire and fulfillment can be imagined outside of the confines of individualist claims.

In re-visioning a self diffused within the elements of the universe, my utopian archive is part of a trajectory of black aesthetics and philosophy in which the metaphysical world is inseparable from material, elemental, and sometimes biological incarnation. Many of the radical black fictions I examine reach to the limits of our paradigms for life. Some speculation (like my father's), has the power to imagine humans out of existence. I am interested in what happens when we fully abandon the idea of the human or at least attempt to denaturalize the assumptions the term *human* carries regarding evolution, species, subjectivity, language, and sentience.

To talk about utopia requires that we think about time and how it folds. In the archives I explore, time has, as Sun Ra puts it, "officially ended."[2] Utopia requires a complete break with time as we know it—an entirely new paradigm. In his brilliant book *Cruising Utopia: The Then and There of Queer Futurity*, José Esteban Muñoz proposes that we "see and feel" our way "out of the quagmire of the present."[3] Rather than postponing to a "then and there," as Muñoz refers to his conceptualization of futurity, I argue for a spatial/temporal fold within the here and now. The versions of utopia I explore involve relationalities that radically disrupt the very idea of the future, as they tune into an alter-frequency. Utopia is a condition of being temporally estranged. I suggest that we see and feel our way not into a future but into an altogether different spatiotemporality that is not discoverable along a human timeline. Utopia is inaccessible because it requires a complete shift in how we understand time. It is not accessible in standard linear time or in normative spaces. As we open ourselves up to the possibility of new ways of being, we must be brave enough to accept the idea that there are temporalities and spatialities beyond human imagining. In this utopian dimension, "it's after the end of the world," as vocalist and Sun Ra collaborator June Tyson exclaims.[4]

As Sylvia Wynter elucidates, racialized and colonized subjects have been excluded from "the human," a category made ontological through the naturalization of Western imperial origin narratives. Wynter reaches for a new universalism as she posits the possibility for new genres of the human, for understandings of ourselves based in entirely different epistemes. Wynter writes, "In order to *speak* the conception of ontological sovereignty, we would have to move completely outside our present conception of what it is to be human and therefore outside the ground of the orthodox body of knowledge which institutes and reproduces this conception."[5] This provocation leads to a few questions for me: What does moving "completely outside our present conception" entail? What do we consider essential to the human, i.e., what do we assume is fundamental to the species? What is worth saving? What, exactly, do we want to preserve and retain about the human? And what if the answer to the entire question of being were not ontological sovereignty at all but a different ontology altogether, other forms of awareness beyond the self, beyond individuated autonomous will? What could individuation mean outside the model of possessive individualism? I explore this question of what happens when we let go of the idea of subjectivity as a stable and essential component of freedom and selfhood. We move from Wynter's call for a new genre of the human to new genres of *existence*, entirely different modes of material being and becoming. What if utopia had no humans at all, reenchanted or otherwise? To loosen anthropocentric notions of human sanctity is to imagine the possibility of a profound paradigm shift, a perspectival sea change to a view of ourselves as made of the same elements as the rest of the universe—and as enmeshed in a wider ecology.

I am thinking of practices, real and imagined, through which we access other realms—planes of material reality and consciousness that, as Henri Bergson writes in *The Creative Mind: An Introduction to Metaphysics*, are always with us and around us, like electricity or sound waves. "Nothing would prevent other worlds . . . from existing in the same place and the same time," he writes.[6] Bergson uses the metaphor of music to explain the nature of consciousness and time, matter, and memory: "In this way twenty different broadcasting stations throw out simultaneously twenty different concerts which coexist without any of them intermingling its sounds with the music of another, each one being heard, complete and alone, in the apparatus which has chosen for its reception the wave-length of that particular station."[7] Bergson writes, "Duration . . . is the uninterrupted humming of life's depths."[8] As G. William Barnard writes of Bergson's theory, "It is possible to hear a series of overlapping sounds in which each pulsation is qualitatively unique, and yet is intrinsically connected to the other pulsations of sound, sounds that have no definite and fixed spatial location, sounds that are both outside and inside us, simultaneously, sounds that have no clear cut boundaries—sounds that are a continuous, interconnected, yet ever changing whole."[9] We shut off access to these other worlds, but they can be tuned into. "If telepathy be real," Bergson states in his presidential acceptance speech to the Society for Psychical Research, "then it is possible that it is operating at every moment and everywhere."[10] We access these realms through states of ecstasy, the fulfillment of passions, the denial of passions; through sounds waves and vibration. The visions and practices I look into invite exploration of spatial and vibrational dimensions no less grounded in the material world. As Steve Goodman writes, "One way or another, it is vibration, after all, that connects every separate entity in the cosmos, organic or inorganic."[11] Vibrations/sound waves mark the porousness between this world and otherworldly states of being. For the musicians in my study, sound is not a metaphor but the pulse of other levels of consciousness. In Alice Coltrane/Turiyasangitananda's Hindu-based cosmology, sound vibration is the beginning of creation. Music is the vehicle through which to merge with a larger cosmic consciousness. Music, for Sun Ra, is a form of travel through which our material bodies transfigure past time and the human form into other worlds.

In *Creative Evolution*, Bergson is thinking biologically and embraces change as an overarching principle encompassing and linking the physical with the psychical. For a "conscious being," to exist is to change.[12] "I find first of all, that I pass from state to state. . . . I change without ceasing. . . . But this is not saying enough. Change is far more radical than we are at first inclined to suppose. . . . There is no feeling, no idea, no volition which is not undergoing change at every moment."[13] For Bergson, "We are creating ourselves continually."[14] Change is not a matter of will but of wonder. Everything is always in a state of Newness.

I am not interested in tracing utopian blueprints or totalizing remedies, but I am fascinated by how people have envisioned utopian worlds—in, through, and outside of the European tradition, which is long.[15] I therefore seek out black quotidian practices and visions of communality, sociality, and kinship already operating outside the bounds of normalizing imperatives. These practices are based in forms of relationality and reciprocity that bring into question marriage, heterosexualism, and capitalism. These existing practices and imagined worlds are important, considering the long history of black social and political conservatism that sees the repair of black life as possible only through the adoption of heteronormative models of gender, sexual reproduction, communal structures, and class aspiration. This book shows that intentional community building was, and is, not only the idealistic purview of a white privileged class. To miss the moments of intentional and improvised black collective-formation and kinship-making is to romanticize only certain black communities—those rooted in blood kinship, patriarchal institutions, or national affiliation—as authentic and natural.

In my research I found myself drawn to various black mystics and mad souls, from the Shaker Rebecca Cox Jackson to the musicians Alice Coltrane/ Turiyasangitananda and Sun Ra, who all claimed they had been chosen, like my father, not only to form alternative social structures but to lead us into alternative dimensions of existence. While all believed they were singularly chosen, the practices they used to travel to these alternative dimensions— ecstatic worship, music, dance, and vocalization—were always collective. These mystics consistently practiced multiple and relational formations. To this end, I begin the book with black women mystics, both historical and fictional. I begin with them because their beliefs and practices reflect a utopian response to living as subjects removed in multiple ways from the center of the human fold—black and female, aliens amid the alienated. The women mystics were among those least served by such liberalist notions of self and community and were therefore free to envision new worlds and forms of subjectivity. Chapter 1, "Along the Psychic Highway: Black Women Mystics and Utopias of the Ecstatic," follows Sojourner Truth, Zilpha Elaw, Jarena Lee, and Rebecca Cox Jackson as they preach to mixed crowds under the bowers of trees, at prayer camps, and in schoolhouses and living rooms: provisional utopian enclaves, forming non- and, often, anti-institutional, publics. I explore the ways their "spiritual theater" demonstrated alternative forms of subjectivity as they and their women's prayer bands practiced the "nonunitary vision of the subject."[16] I argue for the sensual nature of the ecstatic, looking to the ways Jackson and Truth were drawn to spaces—women's holy bands and intentional communities—where emotional, spiritual, and physical intensities often melted into each other.

The politics of touch reaches under the skin. As Gregg and Seigworth say, touch brings us "both into and out of . . . the intracellular divulgences of sinew, tissue, and gut economies, and the vaporous evanescences of the incorporeal (events, atmospheres, feeling-tones)."[17] I refer here to flesh rather than bodies— fleshliness as well as embodiment—because to surrender to touch, to our sensations, is to loosen the bounds of individualism, to mingle with other flesh and with the elements. Hortense Spillers delineates sternly and mournfully between flesh and the body. While Spillers asserts our "New World diasporic flight . . . sever[s] the captive body from its motive will, its active desire," I am not sure that desire is exclusively the property of individual will.[18] Flesh can be ripped apart but has the ability to reinvigorate itself, to reach for a con dition of liveliness. Flesh is not synonymous with a "captive . . . subject position"; rather it is free of the need for subjectivity.[19] I contend there is freedom in flesh, in the moments when it is excluded from being marked, as it feels, and responds to, touch.

In her reflections on her life, black mystic and preacher Jarena Lee fondly recalled times with her women's prayer bands. These were times of enacted intimacies, about being touched, often in a literal sense. Lee describes moments of communal strength as "melting time[s]," a dissolve into the ineffable.[20] This state was not a loss of self; Lee, like other radical women mystics I write about, practiced and performed "non-linearity, non-fixity and non-unitary subjectivity" in her ecstatic modes of being.[21]

I follow the first chapter with another mystic, the musician Alice Coltrane, who in 1976 became a swamini and founded an ashram in the Agoura Hills of Southern California. Chapter 2, "Lovely Sky Boat: Alice Coltrane and the Metaphysics of Sound," follows Alice/Turiyasangitananda's musico-devotional practice, musical sessions that were "melting times" when the self was "saturated in god consciousness," diffused into elements within a wide expanse of immaterial and material forces.[22] Through her devotion, Alice/Turiya gained the ability to achieve other states of beingness beyond the boundaries of space or time. Like Rebecca Cox Jackson, she traveled from astral plane to astral plane. Alice/Turiya's devotional practice, music, and syncretic cosmology were part of a long history of black alter-world-making and refusal to participate in the perceived reality of dominant consensus, with its assumed parameters and priorities. To change reality was not to retreat from the world but to redefine (or indefine) it, to be released into absolute consciousness.

This diffusion, or letting go of the individual, also affects how we think of the biological, of life itself. I became obsessed with science fiction that imagines the reconfiguration or disappearance of humans. I am interested especially in how black science fictions imagine processes of biological transformation, with or without extraterrestrials. My third chapter reads the visions of the black mystic Lauren Olamina, the protagonist in Octavia E. Butler's *Parable* series, for the ways her visions meld the mystical with the material, and I focus on how the author, in her texts, thinks through the biological, particularly by exploring ideas of evolution. In chapter 3, "Our Place Is among the Stars: Octavia E. Butler and the Preservation of Species," I take the series' protagonist as an echo of the nineteenth-century visionaries from chapter 1 as I follow her across a dystopian landscape, with her own vision of God and band of fellow travelers, to the utopian community—dedicated to taking the human species to extrasolar worlds—that her group establishes. This chapter's central exploration is the ways in which, for Butler, particular formulations of the human, biology, nature, and evolution shape utopian possibility. I argue that the texts' biological determinism and investment in the idea of human species exceptionalism limit the *Parable* series' central tenet of change. What is it that Olamina wants to preserve through bringing humans into space? Here I have my father's visions in mind: If God is change itself, as Olamina believes, what is to say the human species will not, through a process of continual becoming, turn into something unrecognizable?

In chapter 4, "Speculative Life: Utopia Without the Human," I marvel at the organic and biological. I explore the strange and miraculous lability of living matter for the ways such exploration can release us from accepted ideas of the human. I continue exploring the idea of infinite changeability of biological matter as I am profoundly interested in the possibilities, real and imagined, for "utterly new mode(s) of existence for human matter"—as in the potential for alternative versions of life and liveliness.[23]

When imaginings of biological lability retain notions of human superiority, and racial, gendered, and ablest hierarchies, when they harbor transhumanist dream of species perfectibility, they breed eugenical fantasies. If we estrange our perceptions of life itself, however, we can think expansively about what it means to be biological entities. What happens if we expand our thinking spatially, at the level of cells and molecules, and temporally, across greater expanses of time than we can see?

I am purposefully not using the term *posthuman* as this term actually stabilizes the idea of the human, universalizes it, and retains it as the determining center of analysis. Inherent in the term is the white man's burden to carry history forward, to continue shaping the world and determining its course. In contrast, I pursue perspectives, either embodied or envisioned, in which all notions of the human are denaturalized and the elements of the universe, of which we are made, are sources of marvel. To see what this estrangement can produce is a productive utopian thought experiment.

But what of pleasure, desire, and the fulfillment of our needs? These would seem the bedrock of any materialist exploration of utopia. Chapter 5, "In the Realm of the Senses: Heterotopias of Subjectivity, Desire, and Discourse," is about queer utopias of gender, sexuality, and sociality in Samuel R. Delany's novel *Triton,* and in the outlandish vision of nineteenth-century socialist utopian Charles Fourier. Both envision utopian worlds based in the total fulfillment of human desires and passions. Delany's utopian satellite, Triton, and Fourier's Harmony appear to be worlds of infinite freedom. But Delany's text holds an implicit critique of the ordering of this kind of utopia. The core of its critique is of Triton's liberal humanist model of the subject: whole, stable, autonomous. In order to be inviolable, the subject must be fixed in place, with firm boundaries around itself. Both Triton society and Fourier's world are built around classification, on the hardening of predilection into fixed identities. Such fixation, the problem of language itself, and Triton's underpinning philosophy that the "subjective reality" of all individuals is "politically inviolable" occlude the mutability of human passions and their tendency to be fluid and protean.[24] There is crisis between such protean surfaces and the need for fixation. Does the self need a bounded wholeness in order to feel? Or can it thrive in the effluent?

Surely our desires have some bearing on what individualizes us—shapes us as discrete bodies as opposed to fairy dust. But does desire need a stable subject? If we decenter, or abandon, the liberal notion of the human, how do we account for pleasure and joy? At their basic level, needs and desires are corporeal and sensual, and they shape us. An individual's desires, their favored sensations, are fundamental to the formation of selfhood. As Sara Ahmed argues, the senses individuate us, demarcate our boundaries. "It is through the recognition or interpretation of sensations, which are responses to the impressions of objects and others, that bodily surfaces take shape," she writes.[25] But sensations also mark the ways our bodies are open. The body, the self, is porous, receptive, impressionable, and not so easily individuated. We are flesh that both gives and receives chemical and electrical signals from other sensate and insensate worlds. The senses therefore make the self both coherent and porous, both unitary and multiple. Moments of utopia happen through the gratification of sensual desires; we open up and let ourselves go.

Perhaps we can think of desire differently: not as consumption but as relational and charged with the potential to explode all attempts to order and contain it. Critical social and fictional utopias and social arrangements based in utopian ideals commit to seeing and feeling our needs and desires past the aim of personal and private gratification to a politics of fulfillment. Herbert Marcuse figures utopia as a "qualitative change in the character of wants and needs."[26] The education of desire is to "teach desire to desire, to desire better, to desire more, and above all to desire in a different way."[27] We can think of desire, and especially its fulfillment, as deeply political in the context of black life.

The Future, or, Time and Time Again

Ideas of the future, and concepts of futurity, are intimately bound up with the way utopia has been defined. My use of the term *utopia* involves time but does not rely on the idea of a future. I resist the deferment of fulfillment to a then and there, and I disengage temporality from a narrative of past-present-future. I dream instead of the possibilities for coeval otherworlds that instead require a complete break with time as we know it. Utopia refers to a quality of the unknown, or of the unknowable, and of the unexpected—the leaps in all directions that are an element of change in the universe. We must jump into the break, the cut, into an entirely different paradigm.

The future appears, implicitly and explicitly, across fields, courses, and disciplines. Concepts of the future have been crucial in the development of politics of liberation. Different ideas of what a future means cluster around emancipatory agendas. My conversation is with Afrofuturism, queer theory, and utopian studies as I respond to concepts of the future and futurity in those fields. I suggest we open up the possibility for radical temporalities: those not governed by earth time and that are intertwined with equally radical notions of spatiality.

Futurity as it is embedded in the creative field of Afrofuturism is generative of all kinds of temporal distortions that refuse a Western chronology of civilization. In John Akomfrah's film, *The Last Angel of History*, a key text in the identification and definition of the concept of Afrofuturism, the data thief, a "hoodlum, bad boy," shuttles back and forth in time, disrupting linear notions of progress.[28] Queer theories of futurity, particularly as formulated by José Esteban Muñoz in *Cruising Utopia*, also break with dominant ordering regimes. They refuse heteronormative time at the same time as they complicate and challenge a strain of queer theory, à la Leo Bersani and Lee Edelman, around the concept of antirelationality and particular models of negativity.[29] Commonsense understandings see the future as a state of being subsequent to the present, as the contiguous culmination of preceding actions. In this sense, the future is situated in normative linear chronologies of time, which implies the notion of some kind of continuous progress or, in dystopian imaginings, degradation. But this model of the future is limited as it can only lead to compensatory utopian dreams or dystopian nightmares that project the outcome of current conditions.

Ideas of the future are key within utopian thought, particularly in interpretations of the work of Ernst Bloch. As utopian studies scholars have elucidated, for utopia to avoid the dangers of totality we must remember that utopia remains always unfinished and never fully attainable. We cannot fully know the details of what a state of Newness would be like because utopian realization remains just beyond the horizon. We can't realize utopian totalities, for they will be the consequence of historically situated processes and we are unable to imagine past our current paradigm. This is to understand utopia as a continual reaching forward. My own use of the term does not have in mind realizability or totality but, instead, ongoing processes that we can never bring to a completion as they exceed our own limited terms.

Bloch's concept of the "Not Yet" inspires many utopian thinkers in their models of the future.[30] For Bloch, utopia resides in the state of "anticipatory illumination," a utopian propensity or proclivity that infuses cultural practices, a thread of consciousness that manifests in daily forms of life and with particular force in artistic forms including literature, music, and dance.[31] What animates collective and communal artistic creation, to use Fredric Jameson's term (à la Aristotle), is a utopian "energeia."[32] Instead of totalities, we look for currents, processes, and practices rooted in a creative urge, or pulse, particularly present in music and art. This pulse would be incorrectly interpreted as an essential human quality, an ontological a priori. Such an interpretation does not fit with Bloch's Marxist understanding of historical materialism. Bloch states that "there is no fixed generic essence of man. . . . Rather the entire course of human history is evidence of a progressive transformation of human nature."[33] Jameson interprets Bloch's concept of a utopian pulse as inherently political, a "political unconscious" that spans historical moments and movements and "produces in any instance a space, a stance, a possibility that is necessarily suspicious and unwilling to locate its own achievement in terms of any present alternative."[34] As such, the utopian pulse comes through as "recoverable traces of radical longing in various cultural forms," utopian theorist Tom Moylan writes.[35]

Radical longing, or as Sun Ra puts it, the "burning need for something else," is a key element in the creative movement called Afrofuturism.[36] Sun Ra's mixing of science and the fantastical make him an (retroactively enlisted) elder statesman of this movement. Afrofuturism "uses extraterrestriality as a hyperbolic trope" standing in for a sense of black alienation and the possibility of other worlds.[37] I do not lean on the term *Afrofuturism*, for the concept is often masculinist: Afrofuturism, and studies done under its aegis, have given us a host of beloved brothers and patriarchs. From Sun Ra to George Clinton, the Mothership is manned, so to speak. The (feminized) ship is the ultimate symbol of the diaspora and of Michel Foucault's heterotopias, of the mode of transcendence into the galaxy, away from the limited human idea of

Earth—but it is men who direct the ship. We have Lee Scratch Perry's Black Ark (where it all went down), Sun Ra's famous breast-like vessel, and the great Pfunk Mothership, now at the Smithsonian National Museum for African American History and Culture.

Afrofuturism takes as its main force a temporal propulsion. The term recognizes the ways African diasporans have long understood the sense of fracturing, disorientation, and alienation associated with modernity and holds an epistemology of the future that challenges a linear Western model of progress. Improvised uses of science and technology, coupled with references to arcane and ancient African and Asian forms of knowledge and culture, refuse Western historical time, based in Greco-Roman origins and the idea that the most advanced civilizations are European. I am interested in this disruption, for instance, in the way Sun Ra's music troubles time. As Kodwo Eshun puts it, Afrofuturism is a "program for recovering the histories of counter-futures."[38] Afrofuturism's evocation of the future is a powerful way to estrange us from the present and trouble linearity. The concept of Afrofuturism is most notable for resisting disciplinary boundaries and remaining an amorphous category that refers to a wide and eclectic range of collective black artistic practices. It can, however, in some cases, desiccate into a shallow term of surface and style rather than remaining an inquiring concept.

Like Afrofuturism, the concept of futurity in queer theory troubles normative, and normalizing, temporalities as it affirms a forward-leaning desire for life lived otherwise. Here I am very much in conversation with José Esteban Muñoz, who powerfully responds, in *Cruising Utopia*, to the antirelational approach in queer theory, such as that articulated by Leo Bersani. Lee Edelman continues this antirelational argument in *No Future: Queer Theory and the Death Drive*, in which he argues against what he calls "reproductive futurity."[39] Edelman conflates any desire for a future with an attachment to biological reproduction, marking any such desire as heteronormative. Muñoz recuperates what is useful about negativity, namely its critique of essentialized notions of queer communality. But Muñoz refuses to give up a future on these terms. The future, Muñoz argues, is a forward moving and collective "doing," a reaching for a potentiality always on the horizon. Muñoz writes, "Queerness is a structuring and educated mode of desiring that allows us to see and feel beyond the quagmire of the present. . . . Queerness is also a performative because it is not simply a being but a doing for and toward the future."[40] While I like the idea that queer utopia is a "doing," I think that the present is actually dimensional and the place of great improvisations. I suggest we descend into the quagmire, for it holds great depth.

I am deeply grateful for Muñoz's careful readings of Ernst Bloch, which situates the potential for queer theory to contain concrete utopian possibility. Muñoz's reading and my reading of Ernst Bloch's *The Principle of Hope* are slightly different, which bears witness to the rich complexity of Bloch's three volumes. While Muñoz's engagement is with the future as a recuperable concept in the face of queer anti-utopianism, I am interested in the synchronic layering of Bloch's spatial terminology and metaphor rather than in diachronic interpretation of his theories of hope. My observation is that Bloch writes in spatial and geographical terms more often than with a language of temporality. I pick up the full version of his phrase, which is the "Not-Yet-*Conscious* [my italics]," as the utopian exists as a state of consciousness.[41] The Not-Yet-Conscious is not the same as a preconscious state or a Freudian repressed consciousness, which are of the past. It refers to another state of consciousness altogether—a utopian consciousness. There is not a future here but an entirely different dimension; Bloch writes in spatial terms, as the Not-Yet-Conscious bends "towards its other side, forwards rather than backwards. Towards the side of something new that is dawning up, that has never been conscious before."[42] I am interested in Bloch's concept of this third kind of consciousness, capable of conjuring otherworldly forms of existence. Bloch's concept of *Not-Yet*, of anticipating that which is always on the horizon, is a more architectural idea than wishing into a future.

As Henri Bergson writes, everything is constantly changing. So, as I ask in chapter 4, what is this process of change? While we may need to reconfigure what we mean by "the future," any change requires movement. What kind of movement brings about a radical transformation? While Bloch's concept of the Not-Yet-Conscious is anticipatory, a state of newness is only achievable through a dialectical process. He writes, "Real venturing beyond never goes into the mere vacuum of an In-Front-of-Us, merely fanatically, merely visualizing abstractions. Instead, it grasps the New as something that is mediated in what exists and is in motion, although to be revealed the New demands the most extreme effort of will. Real venturing beyond knows and activates the tendency which is inherent in history and which proceeds dialectically."[43] For Bloch, radical change is the result of a Hegelian dialectic, the interplay of oppositional forces with a material basis. Bloch's stance is quite muscular, requiring individual endurance; utopian change is only possible through the "goal determination of the human will."[44] Bloch refers to the quality of the "New" as the "Novum," the results of struggle and stamina.

I am inspired by Bloch's theories of utopia, but throughout this book I question the Hegelian/Marxian dialectical model for understanding historical change. I argue that instead of thinking of processes of change as necessarily based in a binary of opposition and antagonism, we can consider the possibility for processes of becoming that involve multiple forms of relations—cooperative, desirous, sometimes conflictual—between multiple elements. In this I am drawn to Bergson's theories of change. In Bergson's temporal theory of *durée*, life is constant change, a continual becoming. Durée was Bergson's complex understanding of the "temporal flux of our consciousness" in the context of a vast vibratory fluidity we call the universe.[45] We do not experience existence as a succession of static states, in linear progression. Instead, conscious experience of time is as a constant swirl, with no linear coordinates, no beginning, middle, or end. Our conscious perception is a filter, electing what it wants to perceive out of the swirling potential, creating as it does so the illusion of past, present, and future.

In *The Principle of Hope* Ernst Bloch reserves his most biting criticism for Bergson. "There is absolutely no genuine Novum in Bergson," Bloch writes. "He has in fact only developed his concept from sheer excess into capitalistic fashion-novelty and thus stabilized it; élan vital and nothing more is and remains itself a Fixum of contemplation. The social reason for Bergson's pseudo-Novum lies in the late-bourgeoisie, which has within it absolutely nothing new in terms of content."[46] Bergson, Bloch says, speaks only of unceasing repetition.

Bloch had an aversion to Bergson's idea of a continuum, but I adopt a Bergsonian approach for its simultaneity and multiple forms of recognition. With Bergson there is no need for a phallic Novum; instead, there are multitudinous waves and crests, or nodes—convergences in space and time. I argue that a Marxian orthodoxy misses what is so powerful about Bergson's philosophy. For him, change is not dependent on dialectical conflict; instead, change is organic, indeterminate, unpredictable. Change is the unforeseeable materialization of multiple relationalities, ecologies of interchange and interdependence. It may be the uncontrollability of life and its ineffable qualities, as postulated by Bergson, that we can look to for profound epistemological shifts in how we think about life itself. Life and the forms it takes are "indeterminate, i.e. unforeseeable," Bergson writes. "More and more indeterminate also, more and more free, is the activity to which these forms serve as the vehicle."[47] Bergson looks to neurons, "at the extremity of each [of which] manifold ways open in which manifold questions present themselves, [a]s a veritable *reservoir of indetermination*" (my italics).[48] By thinking on a different scale, we must be willing to accept a process of change that sends us into the unknown and the unknowable.

As in the utopian practices of Sojourner Truth, Jarena Lee, and Rebecca Cox Jackson, Sun Ra reaches through his music and performance for a radical utopianism that helps us recalibrate, or expand, what we mean by *radical* and *political*. In chapter 6, "The Freedom Not to Be: Sun Ra's Alternative Ontology," I consider Sun Ra's conceptualizations of the human and his larger idea of beingness in a universe that is not human centered. Unlike Sylvia Wynter, Sun Ra does not wish for a new genre of the human but, rather, calls for alternative modes of existence itself. He calls for us to embrace our inhumanness, to "transmolecularize," to join in the material phenomena of the universe.[49] As I continue my exploration of radical worlds and subjectivities. I am interested in how Sun Ra's philosophies of time, space, and existence reach beyond a politics of black nationalism or struggle for inclusion in a US or global body politic. Sun Ra's music and philosophy cast out into the galaxies, away from the "earthman" and into an expansive kind of existence.

With this book I hope to kick up some dust, to leave loose ends, to raise more questions than answers. I hope I am able to make it all seem even more impossible, unrealistic, and escapist.

# PART I
# ECSTASY

# ALONG THE PSYCHIC HIGHWAY

Black Women Mystics and Utopias of the Ecstatic

1

On June 1, 1843, radical mystic Isabella Van Wagenen packed a change of clothes and left the home of her employers in New York City. She told the Whitings that God had urged her to "go east," so she headed toward Long Island to preach her faith (ST, 148). "I just put a change of clothes in a pillowcase and started," a reporter recounted her as saying. "All the money I had with me was twenty-five cents given to me by a good man at a prayer meeting."[1] To mark this moment of change Isabella chose a new name, leaving behind all the names of the men who had bought and sold her during her time as a slave. She chose the name Sojourner, and as she began her journey she prayed for God to send her a surname. He answered, and Truth became her patronymic.

Truth was not just wandering but heading for a region in northeastern New England where many of her spiritual and activist friends and associates were living. She was far from alone in her travels. Truth was participating in a heavily trafficked culture of the road, as spiritual visionaries and radical preachers had been trekking the "psychic highway" for years.[2] It was the Second Great Awakening, and this was so well-worn a region for religious seekers and seers that it became known as the Burned-Over District.

Truth's belief in her spiritual calling and commitment to the hard life of itinerancy echoed the choices of three other early-nineteenth-century black women preachers: Jarena Lee, Zilpha Elaw, and Rebecca Cox Jackson.[3] All three women were born into what was called freedom; Jarena Lee was born in New Jersey in 1783, and like most black women, worked as a servant. She was the first—and one of the only—women granted permission to preach in the African Methodist Episcopal Church and, in 1836 was the first black woman in the United States to write and publish an autobiography. Zilpha Elaw was born in Pennsylvania in 1790. She received angelic visitation in 1825 and went first to preach among enslaved people in the southern states before emigrating to Britain in 1840. Rebecca Cox Jackson was born in 1795, also in Pennsylvania. Her spiritual calling came during a thunderstorm in 1830. In 1858, Jackson and her lifelong partner, Rebecca Perot, founded a Shaker community in Philadelphia. In the 1830s all of them were touring the same region where Truth was headed. The women walked the roads of the Northeastern states, preaching to black, white, and mixed congregations at camp meetings, private houses, rented halls, and sometimes church halls. "In these days I felt it my duty to travel up and down the world, and promulgate the gospel of Christ, especially among my own people," Lee wrote of her activities in 1823 (JL, 30).

All four women had experiences of being touched by the Creator. They had been chosen, and in direct communion with God they created spaces of freedom and power much broader than those they were expected to occupy as black women, slave or free, in antebellum America. These spaces were also of great comfort and succor, sanctuaries from the cruelty of the slaveholding nation. Being touched, they would in turn touch others in shared moments of communality and rituals of ecstatic worship.

The affective preaching practices of Truth, Lee, Elaw, and Jackson open my exploration of black radical otherworlds and forms of subjectivity. I consider the worlds created by these women, in communion and in their dreams and visions, as utopian practice, profoundly of other temporal dimensions and ethereal cartographies. The women's rituals of "spiritual theater" insisted on radical forms of conjoining. Their enactments of joy and insistence on being heard were not appeals nor supplications on bended knee. The women were not concerned with inclusion in, or recognition from, any institution—nation-state, organized church, or any other. Sites and means were improvised as these women walked mile upon mile, stopping to gather with others under the bower of a tree, in a woman's front room, in the basement of a public hall.

I try to get at something embedded within, but in excess of, their religiosity. Religion was the condition of communication, the language of change and mode of possibility for many activists and spiritual innovators. In a black episteme, radical spiritual practices gave release to alternate forms of being and selfhood. Ecstatic enactments of communion, often practiced in all-women prayer bands, produced realms generated in what we could call ecstatic time. Ecstasy, a state of intensely heightened sensual feeling, creates a space of timelessness, of suspension in the space where the material and immaterial comingle, both in the body and out of the body. The experience of conversion and sanctification was intensely powerful for these women. "I think some people would understand the quintessence of sanctifying grace if they could be black about twenty-four hours," wrote later religious leader Amanda Smith.[4] Each of the women's experiences of saving grace was an exceptionally private and internal event, one in which deep powers could both rise and enter. But they were also fiercely communal.

Lee often describes moments of communal strength as "melting time[s]," the dissolve between the I and the We (JL, 24). As it was with the Quakers, contact with the divine light within "dissolve[ed] . . . the boundaries that separated individuals from one another. This dissolution . . . that Friends perceived as a sensation of melting, was expressed through the loosening of all bodily inhibition into tears, groans and shaking."[5] Such a state is a "radical disengagement" from self.[6] The feeling self is not a stable, unified self but an unstoppable flow of becoming. Moments of melting are not about permanent states but about the utopian urge of felt experience, which allows for touching of a collective sense of self.

Such alternative senses of self are radical and political in that they refuse to attach themselves to the liberal humanist definitions of freedom and equality. These forms of selfhood eschew the idea that natural rights are dependent on human systems of governance. These radical forms of selfhood are beyond human, produced in worlds of dream states, spirit, and temporal impulses not fettered by the cycle of life and death. Thus, Truth, Lee, Elaw, and Jackson were mystics able to reside between life and death, the real and the surreal, the phantasmagoric and the visceral.

States of ecstasy and the restoration of individual and social health were understood in the nineteenth century as the result of being touched: spiritu ally, physically, and sexually. The spiritual enactments the four women participated in were intensely intimate. As we shall see, throughout her life Truth could be found at sites of such intensities, and the communities that Truth, Lee, Elaw, and Jackson were a part of were often places where the lines between forms of feeling grew thin, sites where the boundaries between intimacy, love, eroticism, and sexual and spiritual ecstasy were porous.

My exploration of otherworldly realms, temporalities, and modes of being is grounded in the material. For these women mystics, as for later mystics both real and imagined, the lines between the physical and the metaphysical were often irrelevant. Throughout the book I prioritize the haptic and the aural, and I do so in the context of an expansive anthropo*de*centric elemental sphere. As Alice Coltrane stated more than a hundred years later, the spirit is molecular, and electricity can be understood as the linking elemental. As many theorists of affect have shown, feeling is intensely personal but is also about contact: intimate experiences of an intensity that flow like electricity between people. As Olive Gilbert describes it, Sojourner Truth's "powerful and sonorous voice ran through the multitude, like an electric shock" (NST, 81). In the nineteenth century electricity often refers to the force that disrupts the boundaries between you, me, and we, and between modes of being, at the same time as it conducts connective forces. The shock is about being touched, or "touched," as many visionaries could be classified.

Rebecca Cox Jackson's conversion was carried to her in bolts of lightning. The moment of conversion occurred during a thunder-and-lightning storm, of which she had a mortal fear. As she describes the event, in the midst of her prayers "The lightning, which was a moment ago the messenger of death, became the messenger of peace, joy and consolation. . . . I opened the door to let the lightning in the house for it was like sheets of glory to my soul" (GP, 72). Her fear lifted, Jackson was subsequently filled with strict devotion, spiritual vision, and supernatural abilities, including the gift of prophecy and the ability to heal others.

One of my investments in this chapter is to show that a historical and theoretical focus on early female radical visionaries makes us redefine what the very term *radical* means. Such focus requires us to rethink prominent histories of black political radicalism and their (re)enlistment in contemporary theories of blackness. Select histories of black militancy and nationalism have come to shape commonsense notions of black radical resistance. Many genealogies of black radicalism choose as a flashpoint the Colonization and Back-to-Africa movements following the enactment of the Fugitive Slave Act of 1850, when many black activists fled to England and Canada. Disillusioned with the hopes for emancipation in the United States and angered by the concessions Northern white liberals had made to the Southern slave states, some activists began organizing for black migration, an exodus, away from the United States. Martin R. Delany and others advocated for migration to South America and the Caribbean.

Based on models of the national citizen and the settler colonial, these movements were inherently masculinist. "That country is the best in which our manhood—morally, mentally, physically—can be best developed—in which we have an untrammeled right to the enjoyment of civil and religious liberty; and the West Indies, Central and South America, present now such advantages, superiorly preferable to all other countries," said Delany in a speech at the National Emigration Convention of Colored People, held in Ohio in July 1854.[7] Delany declared that colored people must "strike out for ourselves a bold and manly course."[8] A militant agenda was needed for such a striking out, and rebellion, once taking formal shape as militant, most often reconstructs conventional social structures and male hierarchy.

Delany and other migrationists' resettlement and settler colonial projects were cartographies grounded in the very principles of the nation, and nation-building, that they were seeking to leave and were equally fused to the sovereignty of the male individual landowner, granted by God. "That the right to breathe the Air and use the soil on which the Creator has placed us, is co-inherent with the birth of man, and coeval with his existence. . . . Hence, man cannot be independent without possessing the land on which he resides," states the 1854 National Emigration Convention of Colored People's "Declaration of Sentiments."[9] Nationalist movements embraced a capitalist, possessive, individualist model for freedom. An ample amount of scholarship has gone into this period of black nationalism, and later periods of black radicalism have taken the activities of Henry Bibb, Delany, and other migrationists as their prehistory. I argue that these histories of militancy have obscured practices of black social radicalism.

The utopian urge within militant forms of resistance is ultimately of a type shaped by the same liberal politics these seek to challenge, as the aim of such movements is forms of freedom and equality defined by patriarchal nationalist belonging and political recognition. In contrast, the radical utopian practices of the preaching women included challenges to state and capitalist control, alternatives to heterosexual marriage and motherhood, feminisms, experimental health and religious practices, and the wild worlds of dreams and visions. These alternative practices did not preclude reform or revolution at the level of nation-state politics, but these were not the central aim. Their radical utopian animus was the elsewhere, the (im)possible, the altruistic, and the otherworldly.

Truth, Lee, and Elaw practiced what Phyllis Mack calls "spiritual theatre."[10] Because they were public performers, we can never be sure of their embodied practices: the strategies of self-representation and engagement they employed in their gestural language and their preaching styles and singing, and speaking voices. "The impressions made by Isabella [Truth] on her auditors, when moved by lofty or deep feeling, can never be transmitted to paper (to use the words of another)," writes Olive Gilbert, "till by some Daguerrian art, we are enabled to transfer the look, the gesture, the tones of voice, in connection with the quaint, yet fit expressions used, and the spirit stirring animation that, at such a time, pervades all that she says" (NST 30–31). In Truth's case we can consider this description an attempt to trace the untraceable, the way she was an "embodiment of an asignifying intensity," caught in the timbre and vibration of her voice and in the sweep of her movements.[11] I doubt the ability of the visual, the shadow of any Daguerrian art, to actually transfer the substance of what was so powerful about witnessing her, which I am arguing was profoundly physical and participatory.

The concept of "feeling" is freighted, and was especially so in the nineteenth century, as it was associated with sentimentalism. Much abolitionist strategy employed a kind of empathy based in imagined access to the suffering of the slave. The concept of metempsychosis, in accordance with the spiritualist beliefs of the era, saw the lines between the dead and the living as porous and a departed spirit's feelings from their time on earth as available to the sensitive and receptive among the living. These "touching modalities," it can be argued, were therapeutic rather than political, based in whites' sense of absolution, and a form of "emotional tourism."[12] My focus on feeling in this chapter is not aimed at rescuing sentimentalism. Feeling together does not secure a place free of hierarchical relationships nor affirm a universalism based in the notion of oceanic unification. I am not invested in conciliatory politics, in some notion of symmetrical reciprocity. Rather, I want to get at something that sentimentality attempts to but can never fully harness , for feeling, as we explore it here, is anarchistic, a modality that cannot be controlled or always directed.

Critical attention to the senses most often gives primacy to the visual. This prevents us from understanding the importance of the other senses in the experience of ecstasy, spiritual or otherwise. Challenging the primacy of the visual as a semiotic field, this project is most interested in the "other" senses ranked below vision on the hierarchical scale, as Gregory J. Seigworth and

Melissa Gregg write: "the 'lower' or proximal senses (such as touch, taste, smell, rhythm and motion-sense, or, alternately/ultimately, the autonomic nervous system)."[13] While many visionaries were ascetics, eschewing physical expression and desires as carnal sin, often spiritual practice was also very much about spiritual expression through and inside the body, about moments when the physical and the insubstantial merged. Filled with the spirit, practitioners of ecstatic religion shook, quaked, shivered, trembled, and sometimes danced. Worship was about an excess of emotion, which overflowed and loosened the body's inhibitions. In the eighteenth century, the senses were the way believers could access the spiritual contact they sought. "Life gives [the soul] a feeling, a sight, a tasting, a hearing, a smelling, of the heavenly things," writes the Quaker Isaac Penington, "and from this measure of life . . . the senses grow stronger; it sees more, feels more, tastes more, hears more, smells more."[14] Rebecca Cox Jackson, as we shall see, uses quite graphic bodily imagery and metaphor, much like earlier Quakers and other radical religious sects. These often involved the parts of the body associated with bodily functions. "My bowels do yearn toward thee," writes one Quaker to another.[15] Jackson's descriptions of her visions and dreams, as well as of her encounters with other female Shakers, are also highly erotic.

There are connections between the extrasensory and the deeply sensorial, the weaving motion between the fleshly and the flow of feeling. As Elaw explains her conversion experience, she was both 'in the body and out of the body,' referencing the Apostle Paul from Corinthians 12:3. Rebecca Jackson, when at death's door, repeatedly leaves and reenters her body. Yet there is profound ambivalence about physicality and sexuality among visionaries, from Truth and Jackson to Alice Coltrane and Sun Ra. Many reach for their contact and communication with God and the other spirits through severe ascetic practices, from fasting to self-immolation. Intense discipline is key for Jackson, Alice Coltrane, and Sun Ra, as is celibacy. Acts of self-discipline are both a claiming and a distancing from the physical form—experiments in the body's capacities but also flight from them. For practitioners, the extreme control of the body somehow leads to forms of surrender and release into an uncontrollable state of spiritual elevation.

Feelings are not cleanly separable into those that are pleasurable, painful, coercive, oppressive, or liberating. Jackson, in particular, practiced extreme forms of painful and debilitating asceticism, following what she called the "self-denying path" to achieve an intense state of holiness. "No soul can be saved without walking in it," Jackson states (GP, 131). Traveling long distances along this path—often on foot, often in the cold—women demonstrated de votion and commitment. Jarena Lee marked her journal with regular yearly assessments of the length of her travels and the number of sermons she preached. "[In 1827] I traveled two thousand three hundred and twenty-five miles, and preached one hundred and seventy eight sermons," she writes (JL, 51). Such travel took endurance and stamina, the willingness to suffer for God.

Practices of deep discipline, asceticism, and celibacy are common features of devotional lives, and much work has been done on the practices of white religious women.[16] Two such women with radical religious beliefs preceded Truth in the geographic region she was called to. The visionaries and sect leaders Mother Ann Lee and Jemima Wilkinson helped lay the ground for the Burned-Over District, which had its epicenter in upstate New York.[17] Directed by a vision, religious leader Mother Ann—or "Ann the Word," as she often called herself—left Manchester, England, bound for New York State with a band of followers. Officially the band was called the United Society of Believers in the Second Coming of Christ, but because of their demonstrative forms of worship they became known as the Shakers. In 1776 the Shakers built a colony in Niskayuna, a town in Northern New York later renamed Watervliet. Mother Ann was believed to be the twin spirit mate of Jesus and to have powerful spiritual gifts, including the gift of healing hands—the ability to clear out disease from the body by touch. Rebecca Cox Jackson joined the community in 1840.

Also in 1776, a charismatic young woman named Jemima Wilkinson was expelled from the Rhode Island Quaker community she had grown up in for worshipping at a Baptist church. Soon after her expulsion, Wilkinson developed a fever. Awakening from the fever, she announced that Jemima Wilkinson had died and that the genderless spirit now inhabiting her body was to be referred to thereafter as the "Publick Universal Friend." After she "appear'd to meet the Shock of Death,"[18] the Publick Universal Friend explains, "the Spirit took full possession off [sic] the Body it now animates."[19] The phenomenon in this period of young religious women coming back from death laden with messages from the other side was not uncommon—and was how, I argue, women traveled and occupied multiple spatial and temporal dimensions. But not all such travelers came back as spirits or guided entire sects, as Wilkinson did.

Accompanied by her brothers, sister, and father (whom she no longer recognized as close relations) and other influential and wealthy people, the Publick Universal Friend and her followers originally leased land from the Seneca Indians in upstate New York and established the town of Jerusalem in 1787. The Publick Universal Friend wore long, flowing robes and big-brimmed hats, and her gender-nonconforming appearance, riding into a village with her entourage, presented quite a sight. Several African Americans lived as part of the Society of Universal Friends. Chloe Towerhill, a former slave, was in charge of the kitchen.[20] "William Potters, Negro Boy, Cuff" and "Jacob Weaver, an Ethiopian" are listed in the Friends' Death Book, a record kept of all members who had "left time."[21] Both societies—the Shakers and the followers of the Publick Universal Friend—were organized around their spiritual leader's power, but they were also communities built on principles of collectivity.

By claiming to be a genderless spirit and dressing in manly fashion, Wilkinson refused the constraints of her sex. Practicing celibacy, Mother Ann did the same. Catherine Brekus argues that both women denied their gender and "regarded their sex as a problem that had to be overcome."[22] Brekus argues that Wilkinson, by denying her gender, actually reinforced patriarchal structures. I disagree; it was not necessarily their gender from which these women sought distance but the ideas of womanhood and sexuality under patriarchy. And, perhaps, they sought to find selves free of the very idea of gender altogether.

## "I Am a Woman's Rights"

Rather than the young Isabella Van Wagenen, history most readily recalls the abolitionist and feminist Sojourner Truth of the 1850s and 1860s who succeeded her (Isabella disappears from the historical record for nine years, between 1834 and 1843). As with most waves of social activism, there were a range of agendas and motivations during the nineteenth century, a century of plentiful causes. More-conservative activists aimed for moral reforms, while the more radical activists Truth chose to associate with sought broader and deeper kinds of change. However, Truth is most often remembered through the lens of liberal feminism, associated with an appeal for black women's inclusion in the gendered fold. Truth, called a foremother in black history, is often mistakenly associated with the slavery of the South and affiliation with the black church. Isabella was in fact owned by Dutch masters and decidedly anticlerical. Remembering as best we can an earlier Truth, in the specific context of anticlerical Christian revivalism and utopian experimentation, challenges these forms of reclamation and opens up on alternative forms of radicalism. My argument is a feminist intervention, allowing for utopian forms of thought and activism to emerge.

A lot of work has gone into producing Truth as a symbol for moderate versions of feminist and abolitionist emancipation.[23] The familiar abolitionist image of a supplicating slave woman, titled "Am I Not a Sister?," profoundly shaped the titling of the fictional speech "Aren't I a Woman?" attributed to Truth by the reformer-activist-abolitionist Frances Gage in 1863. Phrased as a question, the speech's title leaves the enslaved woman's status in relation to the human up for white approval, for the appeal is directed toward them. The editor of the Ohio *Anti-Slavery Bugle*, Marius Robinson, in the audience during Truth's speech, recorded her words as "I Am a Woman's Rights" (ST, 229). Robinson's version refuses to perform the function of entreaty. Truth's travels, her participation in three utopian communities, and her later tours with radical abolitionist agents, including her close friend, the activist-feminist Abby Kelley Foster, allow us to think differently about Truth as a committed activist. Truth did not conform to the persona of the long-suffering black female slave, or to the proprieties of the middle-class race woman, although she probably could perform these positionalities when necessary or useful.

As Truth's biographers Nell Painter and Margaret Washington have argued, the Sojourner Truth of popular memory is a severely edited version, a palimpsest of projections and distortions passed down over the hundred-plus years since she emerged into the public eye. I am not attempting to assess the use of Olive Gilbert's *Narrative of Sojourner Truth*, or any of the other biographical accounts through which we trace Truth, but I am attracted to the places in them that are muddy, contradictory, confusing, and particularly freighted as sites to further explore.

Despite the difficulties of archival evidence, and the remaining silences and ambiguities, the careful recuperative work of Painter and Washington has made it possible for us to engage in critical reconsiderations of Truth—not in search of the "real" person nor to try and pick free her true voice from the web of ventriloquisms, but to pay renewed attention to what we know about her particular involvements and political choices. Much is at stake in doing so. Truth was full of contradictions and what we know of her choices and attachments is often problematic. Considering her life demands that we reexamine the accepted definitions and histories of black activism, which allows us to trace alternative genealogies of black radical thought and practice.

For most of her life Truth was happiest traveling and living among white fanatics—Perfectionists, ultraists, anticlerics, antiauthoritarian come-outers, spiritualists, Garrisonian abolitionists and feminists, health reformers, and communitarians. Unlike in the official black churches, Truth could preach and speak among these groups. Radical reformers saw true social and political change as necessarily holistic, to be fought for on all fronts, and Truth was a wholesale radical of her times. The religious, social, and political movements she was a part of overlapped, but as in all later liberation movements, including those today, the originating spark was a fight for black people's rights. We can think of Truth's visionary mysticism as a reach for the New, the desire to create something that had never been before. This was part of her commitment to her people and to the principles of freedom; there was a radical utopian space she sought to access.

Truth had places to stay as she walked east, as she knew people from various religious and radical reform movement circles, and there were a number of welcoming utopian communities and religious enclaves in the region. Truth preached in black settlements, although not in the African Methodist Episcopal churches, for most denominations forbade women from preaching (although they could exhort). On the road Truth was at liberty to speak at various other churches, halls, and private homes; among the Quakers and the Shakers; and at camp revival meetings. Truth gathered crowds with her deep, resonant voice, her singing, and her spiritual intensity.

Truth also preferred communal living. When she "sought an abiding place" after a cold winter traveling and preaching throughout northern New England, she turned down several offers in private homes (ST, 154). Instead, she considered the agrarian Fruitlands community in Harvard, Massachusetts, set up by Garrisonian abolitionist friends and fellow Perfectionists Amos Bronson Alcott and Charles Lane. She also considered the Shaker village in Enfield, Connecticut. Ultimately, Truth decided to reside with the Northampton Association of Education and Industry in Massachusetts, after spending a night there.

Radical activists formed the Northampton Association in 1842; William Lloyd Garrison's brother-in-law, the abolitionist George Benson, was one of the founders, and most of the residents were Garrisonians. Like most radical activists, residents supported many causes, including pacifism, women's rights, and vegetarianism. Economically, the association functioned primarily on the running of a silk mill, whose stock investors shared in its income, and although the community used money, most services were free. Most members lived in a large communally organized house and shared all domestic duties. Truth became an important figure in this community.

There were not many black people living at Northampton, although fugitive slaves on the Underground Railroad often came through.[24] Frederick Douglass was also a frequent visitor. At Northampton Truth met and worked with resident David Ruggles, the black abolitionist from New York whose work as a founder of the Underground Railroad and journalist was well known. Ruggles had come to Northampton in 1841, exhausted and in poor health, after years of dangerous and stressful antislavery activism. After being severely ill, Ruggles went blind. Undergoing hydropathy treatments with the therapy's innovator, Dr. William Wesselhöft, he regained some of his sight and, most importantly, developed a heightened sensitivity in his perception. Ruggles set up his own clinic as a hydropathic practitioner in Northampton.[25] Ruggles's clinic was the first devoted to hydrotherapy in the nation.[26]

Truth, coming out of the winter cold, was also severely ill and became Ruggles's patient. When Ruggles began treating Truth, her treatment initially was quite painful; such regimens, while they drew out the poisonous toxins from the body, were often grueling, but Truth became a devout follower of the water cure for the rest of her life. It was in Northampton, wrapped in the wet sheets of Ruggles's cure, that Truth began to recount her life story to fellow resident Olive Gilbert.

Lords and Masters

Direct connection with a higher authority gave the mystic women of this chapter autonomy from dominant sociopolitical regimes. They were also part of a tradition of radical religious sects whose members directly challenged political and church authority. Truth publicly separated her spiritual practices from the Christian church. She was known to go to churches with activists called 'come-outers,'—people who purposefully disrupted the services. As a Shaker, Jackson's principal guide was a female spirit, Mother Ann Lee, and she lived all of her life in predominantly female communities.

At the same time as they were decidedly antiauthoritarian, several of the women I write about in this book were also devoutly supplicant to Lord and Master, sometimes in very strict ways. All call God their Master, expressing a true faith based in total devotion. In the case of Sojourner Truth, her devotion to God often blurred into her devotion to dominant men: first to her master John Dumont, who she was with throughout her teenage years, and later to the Prophet Matthias (Robert Matthews), a religious leader who was a severe patriarch and for whom she gave up preaching. None of the women explicitly challenged notions of women's subordinate position. But, as many feminist religious scholars have shown, the relationship between patriarchy and Christianity is quite complex, and Truth had a complicated relationship to male dominance. God was a liberating Master, and Truth took her devotion to her owners as a demonstration of her faith. Olive Gilbert quotes Truth as she explains how she was given her last name: "Thou art my last master and thy name is Truth, and Truth shall be my abiding name until I die. I had before five other masters; and at the age of over forty, and the mother of five children, I was liberated" (NST, 239). Truth maintained a decades-long relationship with her former master, Dumont, most likely the father of her second child, Elizabeth (ST, 52). "He sometimes whipped me soundly, though never cruelly," Truth said, according to Gilbert (NST, 22). "She glories in the fact that she was true to her master," writes Gilbert, quoting Truth as saying, "It made me true to my God" (NST, 22). Truth's relationship with Dumont is a site of anxiety throughout *Narrative*, which the text attempts to resolve by its last words, in which Truth forgives her former master his sins.

There is a quality of the relationship between Truth and Dumont that is hard to translate from this earlier historical period. Truth's bond with Dumont seems as difficult to explain as the power struggle between Harriet Jacobs, her master, and her lover (as recounted in her autobiography, *Incidents in the Life of a Slave Girl*). Perhaps in accepting this intimate blur between oppressive, coercive, and pleasurable relationships we can begin to understand the intensity of Truth's devotional enthrallment.

Dumont was not the last patriarch Truth served. After she attained freedom Isabella committed herself to the Prophet Matthias. No women were allowed to preach or lead prayer in his sect, and so Isabella stopped preaching. Accounts of Truth's time in the sect are quick to dismiss her three years or more of profound loyalty to Matthias, describing it as a brief period of aberration from her feminist and abolitionist convictions. Yet, as with Dumont, Truth never fully renounced Matthias and continued to maintain that he was the voice of God. We cannot ignore that throughout her life Truth "retained the old patriarchal bond" (ST, 113). Our investments in remembering her as a feminist may obscure the more difficult contradictions of her life and commitments.

Truth's relationship with her children was also complicated. Truth left her owner, Dumont, in 1826. Walking away from his farm, she "took her freedom openly and in broad daylight" (ST, 58). She also left behind three of her five children, all of whom still belonged to Dumont. These children stayed with Dumont for many years. Because ideals of true womanhood and the innocence of the child were just emerging at that time, it is not accurate to judge these relationships anachronistically. Truth's story cannot be told as one of the sacrificial mother, but neither was she completely out of touch with her children. She fought publicly for the freedom of her son, Peter, before finding him a position as an apprentice. Later in life, in the periods when she was sedentary, she lived with three daughters, first in Northampton and then in Harmonia Village, an abolitionist, spiritualist, and racially mixed commune in

Michigan. She then lived with her daughters in a home of their own in Michigan (ST, 279).

Truth does not fit into any one narrative of either womanhood or activism. Her claims to humanity were not based in normative models of femininity. To let their performances of womanhood plead for inclusion in the polity of women—that is, to be seen as capable of piety—chastity centered in (one's own) home was often the tactic of women activists with more conservative agendas, as well as of black women suffragists after emancipation. This anxiety over a politics of respectability still haunts black sexual politics today. Truth and the other women preachers in this book violated the normative strictures black women both adopted and worked around as strategies for reform. After achieving her freedom, Truth chose an itinerant life, rejected economic individualism, and chose communal living over the life of wife and mother in a nuclear family. While living as a member of various communities she was in charge of domestic duties. There are important differences between these forms of domestic work. While in the communities, Truth was part of a work cooperative and so operated with a certain amount of autonomy. She was also an active member of these spiritual communities.

Familial relationships were also complicated for Jarena Lee and Zilpha Elaw. Married with a child, Lee expressed ambivalence about the choice between what she refers to as "housekeeping" and the call to travel and preach. Explaining one of her longer journeys, Lee writes, "I remained one week and during the whole time not a thought of my little son came into my mind; it was hid from me, lest I should have been diverted from the work I had to [do], to look after my son," she recalls (JL, 45). Lee returns from her tour to find him well, "though I had left it very sick," she remembers. "Friends had taken care of it. . . . I now began thinking seriously of breaking up housekeeping, and forsaking all to preach the everlasting Gospel" (JL, 46). Whatever arrangements Lee made, she speaks only infrequently about her child throughout her narrative. Also married, Elaw too speaks ambivalently about leaving her daughter.[27] None of the three—Truth, Lee, or Elaw—mentions missing her husband at all.

Truth's biographer Margaret Washington argues that history has suppressed Truth as a sexual being. The most common image of Truth we have, captured in the photographs she sold toward the end of her life, is as an older woman. In fact, she seems always to have been old; a young Truth seems scarcely to have entered the public imagination. Truth's depiction as a wise crone, with knitting in her lap, perhaps eases public anxiety about her freedom of movement, her disengagement from conventional family formation, and her involvement in radical politics. Truth's sexuality, as in many but not all black women's narratives from the nineteenth century, is referred to only obliquely. Most familiar to readers is Olive Gilbert's often-cited reference to the "hard things that crosses Isabella's life during slavery," unspeakable things "not for the public ear" because they were "so unreasonable, and what is usually called so unnatural (though it may be questioned whether people do not always act naturally) they would not easily believe it" (NST, 56). Washington adds to this assessment of Truth's early sexual experiences the assertion that Truth's second child, Elizabeth, was most likely Dumont's. But Washington also points us to a much more complex sexual world Truth was a part of. Without making claims for Truth's sexuality, we do know that the communities where she chose to live, particularly in her early years in the Kingdom of Matthias, were places where intense, erotic, and unconventional forms of intimacy were practiced. While Truth was with the Kingdom of Matthias, Truth participated in the ritual of same-sex communal bathing, practiced regularly and frequently in the sect. Opening up discussion of Truth's involvement in other forms of erotically charged intimacies leads us to question the surety of the category "sexual" and to examine the sites where boundaries between friendship, fellowship, religious passion, and the politics of touching blur.

Many religious women, including Lee, Elaw, and Jackson, embraced deep emotionalism and demonstrative practices of faith and worship such as the "groans and shedding of tears" evoked by the touch of the Spirit (JL, 37). The Love of God is physical, sensorial, a matter of direct contact with God and not dry textual understanding. This understanding of worship, Elaw writes, resisted the regimented discipline of more conventional churches. "The life and power of religion is not identified with, not in proportion to, the polish of the minister, the respectability of the congregation, or the regularity and method of its services," Elaw explains (ML, 107). Worship is about intense intimacy and collective feeling: "The most abrupt and extraordinary vicissitudes of weather are frequently productive of more benefit than the nicest graduated scale of temperature; and had it not been for some of these instances, in which the Almighty displayed the wonders of his victorious grace. . . . there are many churches lively and flourishing, which . . . would now be but little more than so much religious automata" (ML, 107). The difference in the quality of connection between God and other beings is explained in physical terms. Elaw's use of temperature and climate as metaphors for the qualities of communal service evokes the senses as a barometer for an ephemeral state. Access to other realms can be felt as rising heat in a body.

In the Kingdom of Matthias

Sojourner Truth was drawn to a climate of intense religiosity in the 1830s, while working as a domestic in the circle of Perfectionists gathered around New York City's Bower Hill. Truth, still known as Isabella at this stage, was introduced to this religious circle when she began working for James La Tourette, a prominent figure in the Perfectionist movement. Perfectionists believed in "miracles, spirit possession, [and] the gift of prophecy," all beliefs the moderate Methodists found too extreme (ST, 85). Truth's attraction to the band of extreme Perfectionists may have been to the emotional fervency accompanying the strictness of their beliefs and practices. They also held a commitment to temperance, a simple, clean life of plain food, and an environment and a self free of adornment. Any extravagance was sublimated into passionate worship. But in this climate of restriction there was also spiritual ecstasy.

Truth began preaching while she was with La Tourette. Perfectionist women were forming "holy bands," and the movement supported women's leadership. La Tourette introduced Truth to another Perfectionist, Elijah Pierson, known for his particularly extreme beliefs. While working for Pierson, Truth had the freedom to practice her religious beliefs autonomously and had a certain type of freedom in the household that she may not have found in others. Part of the reason may have been her belief in communal living. Although her place remained in the kitchen, Truth had autonomous control of it. At least in some ways or moments she lived with Pierson's group as equal beings in God. But when Pierson eventually let a man called Matthias (Robert Matthews) into his house and surrendered leadership to him, women were no longer allowed to lead, preach, or speak. Matthias was a cruel patriarch. "The spirit of Truth, Matthias explained, was the spirit of male government."[28] Yet Isabella stayed devoted to Matthias, moving with him even after the scandalous dissolution of the sect. The end came after Pierson died suddenly, and Matthias and Isabella were accused of poisoning him.

One way we can understand Truth differently, as Margaret Washington stresses, is to understand her as a sexual being. I would amend and broaden this to think of her in a deeper sense as a passional being, a quality that may have drawn her in and kept her with the Kingdom of Matthias for the full three years of its existence. Intensities melted into each other in the community. Both physical and spiritual intimacies were ecstatically shared. All members participated in forms of physical intimacy that we cannot assume were sexual but were also not free of eroticism. These included the acts of frequent same-sex bathing as well as sleeping arrangements in the Pierson house.

At the center of the poisoning scandal were the sexual arrangements between the sect's core members: Matthias, Elijah Pierson, Ann and Benjamin Folger, Catherine Galloway, and Isabella. As with many religious communities, vows of marriage made outside the Kingdom of Matthias were rendered void of meaning. Instead, Matthias announced what he called "match spirits."[29] Eventually, Ann Folger became Matthias's match spirit and the house mother. Matthias granted Benjamin Folger a match spirit in the house servant Catherine Galloway. Isabella, apparently, did not have a match spirit. Just how to interpret this is ambiguous. "She might have joined the coupling, she said, but no match spirit could be found for her," writes Washington (ST, 111). In the section of Narrative titled "The Matthias Delusion," Gilbert writes that Isabella "happily escaped the contamination that surrounded her" (NST, 64). In truth, we cannot know this from the record.

Following the scandal, a lawyer named Gilbert Vale wrote a pamphlet in defense of Truth's innocence when the accusations eventually blew up the Matthias community. In Fanaticism: Its Source, Vale blamed an excess of feeling and emotion for the religious fanaticisms of the age. "Like Matthias, Pierson, B. Folger and a whole host of females, [Truth] mistook her feelings for divine impressions, and this mistake, common to so many, we may take as the great source of fanaticism," Vale asserts.[30] Vale was critical of the Perfectionists, who, he argued, "mistook their feelings for the effects of the Spirit, and their transient thoughts for emanations from the Spirit; and being thus enlightened according to their leisure and to the encouragement they gave to their thoughts and fancies, they could frequently see farther than other people into the Scriptures and the will of God, or fancied they could; and Mr. Pierson possessed these qualities in a superlative degree, and was hence highly respected by the party, while the world thought him a little deranged."[31] Vale's argument was that the impressionable "coloured, unlettered woman" Isabella had been caught up in the Perfectionist misconception.[32]

Vale writes, "Isabella . . . is candid enough to say, that if she escaped the peculiar pollution which threatened to affect the whole community at Sing Sing, that she believes she owes it to circumstances, as much as anything (she is near forty, not handsome, and coloured) for this spirit which affected the head, was infectious, and threatened the whole body. She said it pleased God to preserve her, as no match spirit was found in the establishment for her."[33] What, or who, Isabella wanted will never be known. Others—like Vale, with his dismissive description—must have been unable to imagine Isabella as sexual, for while accused of poisoning Pierson and of excess loyalty to Matthias, she was never implicated in the sexual goings-on in the Kingdom.

That Isabella was not implicated is, in a sense, odd and sits in juxtaposition to one particular detail Vale recorded involving sleeping arrangements in the Kingdom. After many back-and-forths, Ann Folger settled on maintaining sexual relationships with both Benjamin Folger and Matthias. But in between nights with each man Ann would share a bed with Isabella. Vale records what happened in the bed with a curious amount of frankness. "When Mrs. B. Folger was in bed with Isabella, and when Matthias was spoken of, Mrs. Folger actually showed Isabella how Matthias kissed or embraced her."[34] What form of intimacy was this moment? Did Isabella kiss back? Was she embracing her fantasy of Matthias, of Ann, or of both? Was Ann a type of medium, channeling for Isabella the intimacy she craved with Matthias, or was the touch between all three? Was this experience one of touching God?

It is quite interesting that reportage of the intimacy between Isabella and Ann gets translated in various ways. In Vale's account Ann "actually showed Isabella how Matthias kissed and embraced her." For the historians of Matthias, "Ann gave Isabella detailed descriptions of how Matthias kissed and embraced her."[35] These accounts of what occurred between Ann and Isabella deserve pause, but not so we can try and parse out the truth of what "really" happened. In fact, this is a moment to acknowledge that, considering the intensity of feeling created in the community, how Ann's embrace of Isabella should be classified today seems irrelevant. What matters more than finding out the truth is what this moment tells us about the ways in which, in such nineteenth-century communities, the lines between the physical and the spiritual blurred and became indistinct. It also reveals the ways in which others cannot read Isabella as agential in this situation. Isabella is represented as nonsexual—a passive recipient—as opposed to the ways racialized discourse usually hypersexualizes black women. In all of the accounts, Isabella can't be read as reciprocating a white woman's touch. She seems to disappear in Ann's embrace, leaving only her own outline, the impress of her body on the sheets.

Isabella did, in fact, clear her name of association with the murder of Elijah Pierson. Her biographers are quick to whisk her away from the Kingdom: Olive Gilbert gives this section of her autobiography the title "The Matthias Delusion"; Washington writes that, after a hiatus, Isabella "returned to her previous lifestyle" (ST, 129). But, troublingly, for the rest of her life she refused to condemn Matthias. Compartmentalizing this period of Truth's life as somehow an aberration from her "normal" way of living reveals the presence of anxiety around black sexuality still prevalent in black public discourse. We can instead acknowledge this period of Truth's life as part of her openness to experiment with alternate, often extreme communal arrangements and modes of being.

## The Work of the Flesh

Not all touch involves the flesh in the same way, and for some mystics devout asceticism meant renouncing the needs and wants of the body. After divorcing her husband, Rebecca Cox Jackson swore to strict celibacy; like the Shakers, she believed avoiding the "work of the flesh" was the only way to achieve true holiness (GP, 80). Of her conversion and sanctification Jackson writes, "The first had removed my fear of thunder and lightning, the other had destroyed the lust of my flesh and made me to utterly hate it. And of all things it seemed the most filthy in the sight of God—both in the married and unmarried" (GP, 88). Jackson engaged in deep and intense forms of intimacy in her holy bands and in her personal life. Around 1850, Rebecca Cox Jackson met Rebecca Perot. The "two Rebeccas," as they were called, lived together as close companions until Jackson's death in 1871.[36]

After achieving literacy, which she attributes to a divine power answering her earnest prayer, Jackson began recording her spiritual life: her dreams, visions, premonitions, and other examples of the divine working through her. She wrote copiously, and her writings were carefully preserved after her death by Perot. In her record of her waking states, we learn of Jackson's supernatural powers to heal and see the future. But Jackson's autobiographical writings, particularly her dreams, are often indistinguishable from her visions; whether or not she was sleeping seems immaterial.

Despite her renouncing of the flesh, Jackson's dreams could turn surprisingly erotic. Her most sensual and sweet dreams, visions, and memories are of her communal prayers with other Shaker women. Many are visions that show her as particularly close to the Shakers' Mother Ann, also bride to the Savior. In 1843, Jackson has a "Vision of the Bride and Groom," in which she sees Mother Ann. "Her presence brought me to the floor," she writes. "Them eyes! Them heavenly eyes! Her lips were like a thread of scarlet" (GP, 169). Other dreams show Jackson's closeness to the Shaker eldresses at Watervliet. She dreams of Shaker eldress Paulina: "I kissed and embraced her and loved her as I did my own soul. You may whip me and do anything you want to do

**Figure 1.1**
Rebecca Perot.

with me, in love . . . and I loved her as I love myself. I thought she looked so beautiful I could not take my eyes *off* from her" (GP, 270).

Jackson's most intensely sensual dreams are of her long-term partner, Rebecca Perot. In 1850, after meeting Perot, Jackson had a particularly erotic dream. "I dreamt that Rebecca and me lived together," she writes. A river of "a beautiful white water" runs past their house:

> I stood . . . looking westward on the beautiful river. I saw Rebecca Perot coming in the river, her face to the east, and she aplunging in the water every few steps, head foremost, abathing herself. She only had on her undergarment. She was pure and clean, even as the water in which she abathing. She came facing me out of the water. I wondered she was not afraid. Sometimes she would be hid, for a moment, and then she would rise again. She looked like an Angel, oh, how bright! (GP, 225).

Such erotic language was not uncommon among eighteenth- and nineteenth-century religious believers. According to Phyllis Mack, the early Quakers "not only bathed in a sea of polymorphous spiritual nurture and eroticism; they occasionally wrote as if they had succeeded in floating above gender altogether."[37] A language of same-sex intimacy in the nineteenth century should not be read in relation to contemporary usage. But the level of intensity with which Jackson consistently depicts the women she loves deepens our understanding of the passional. It calls into question whether or not we need to assess such erotic intimacy as sexual; in fact, celibacy in Jackson's case forms a radical set of intimacies, both collective and non-normative. Drawing boundaries between the physical, the mystical, and the incorporeal seems irrelevant.

## Ruggles's Water Cure

After the Matthias scandal, Truth disappears from the historical record. But she did find her way in 1843 to Northampton and the purifying touch of David Ruggles's water cure. Like other forms of health care advocated in the nineteenth century, the water cure was an alternative to allopathic medicine, which relied on invasive treatments, medication, and the authority of doctors. Ruggles describes his experience with allopathic medicine in the pages of Frederick Douglass's periodical, the *North Star*:

> After six years of suffering, and in the care of the most eminent physicians in the country, during which time I was repeatedly bled, leeched, cupped, plastered, blistered, salivated, dosed with arsenic, nuxvonica, iodine, strychnine, and a variety of other poisonous drugs, which contracted the enlargement of the liver, the worst kind of dyspepsia, irritation of the lungs, chronic inflammation of the bowels, costiveness, piles, nervous and mental debility, and a numb or palsied state of the skin, which rendered me insensible to the prick of a pin or extreme heat; and, after blindness has shut me out from the light of day, in the opinion of gentlemen standing high in the profession, my life was limited to a few weeks.[38]

In contrast, the water cure, along with other treatments advocated at the time, was part of a movement based in the philosophy of holistic health. The water cure involved a series of different regimens. Ruggles writes of his recovery, "My health finally [became] established, with an equilibrium of circulation" after undergoing the water cure, which "comprised the daily course" of "packing in a wet sheet once and twice a day, the lunge or shallow wash bath, the douche five minutes, three hip baths, from 15–60 minutes each, two eye baths, and a foot bath."[39] An essential part of the water cure was that the role of the practitioner was temporary. The emphasis was on training patients to care for themselves through home water treatments in combination with nutrition, exercise, and adequate sleep.[40]

David Ruggles attributed his success as a hydropathic practitioner to his supernatural ability to feel, through touch, the fluxes and flows of electricity through the body. Ruggles believed a person's health was detectable through these electrical fluxes and flows, and developed the theory of what he called "cutaneous electricity."[41] His practice treating patients with the water cure "*strengthened* this acute sense of touch, until the conviction was *irresistible*, that the *skin* is the *organ* through which the *symptoms* and *character* of the disease are indicated. . . . I can feel beneath the surface of the skin of a healthy person, a regular and forcible *action*, or *emission*, indicating vitality, or power. This, I think, is electricity."[42] Through his "acute sense of touch," he could interpret the level of a patient's well-being and develop the appropriate water cure regimen.[43]

If we follow the senses inward and under the skin, we encounter the electrical activity of the flesh. Currents of electricity animate flesh, as "everything is underpinned by ionic channel activity."[44] Electricity is the ultimate balance between receptivity and response; it conducts a delicate and enduring liveliness. To accept Ruggles's biological assertion is not to deny the world of the spirit; with Jackson we can welcome the lightning in, let it run through us.

In the Body and Under the Bower

Forms of ecstasy are intensely in the physical realm in ways that refuse language: weeping, shaking, swooning, fainting, screaming, singing. Ecstasy is a state felt in the body—and also expressed by it. A visitor to Rebecca Cox Jackson's Shaker community in Philadelphia reported of its services that the "exercises were beautiful and zealous. . . . When they attempt a shake, they get right down, almost to the floor, and bow, bend, and strip off pride and bondage."[45] Dancing and song—and sex—were contentious in many religious communities. Although they practiced the physicalization of ecstatic states, the Shakers kept the sexes strictly separated. There was a central tension around controlling the nature of proximity between bodies as well as regulating the sensorial experiences of the body. Such regulation—the discipline or mortification of the body—however, also leads to states of psychic and physical sensations and, ironically, full circle back to often uncontrollable pleasure.

Emotionalism was highly feminized and, as such, could be considered confining, but our four women, particularly Jarena Lee, write of the evocation of deep feeling as key to their powers and gifts. Feeling and touching were particularly potent forms of disarming the unbelieving as well as those men resistant to allowing a woman to preach. As women preachers, all four repeatedly met harsh opposition. Like Truth, Lee was accused of being a man. Preaching to a black congregation in New Jersey in the 1820s, Lee met "some ill-behaved persons, who talked roughly, and said, among other things, 'I was not a woman, but a man dressed in female clothes'" (JL, 23). Like Elaw and Truth, Lee refused to stop speaking in public. "May the lord pardon them, and make them be careful how they handle edged tools," Lee writes (JL, 77).

Even black ministers could be turned into admirers before the performative manifestation of Lee's spiritual power. In the fall of 1822, while in Woodstown, New Jersey, Lee spoke first to a "respectable congregation of mix of white and colored in a school house" but then wanted to speak at a "colored meeting house." The black Methodist minister refused to even shake her hand. Yet, while listening to her speak, "the minister got happy, and often shouted 'Amen, sister,'" Lee writes (JL, 24). Even slave owners could be turned, and Lee makes a point of noting the instances when slave owners were part of her congregation. In one instance she encounters the intimidating stares of a "Deist" and "great slave holder . . . who was very cruel; thinking nothing of knocking down a slave with a fence stake," but Lee's channeling of spiritual force is strong enough to convince him that she had "the worth of souls at heart." After her service he "became greatly altered in his ways for the better" (JL, 19). Lee's point is that her spiritual prowess, gifts of clairvoyance, and healing abilities allowed her to channel the power of God.

Feeling was communally generated and reliant on forms of contact. Lee recounts a trip to Philadelphia, where she had a particularly trying time. "The oppositions I met with were numerous, so much so, that I was tempted to withdraw from the Methodist Church, lest some might go into ruin by their persecution of me," Lee writes, ending with a threat (JL, 24). After "relating the feelings of her mind" to her sister, Lee "embraced the sister in my arms, and we had a melting time together" (JL, 24). It is a moment of intimacy with a woman of the congregation that comforts her.

All of the four women loved camp meetings, where, as Zilpha Elaw explains, "many thousands assemble in the open air, and beneath the overspreading bowers, to own and worship our common Lord, the Proprietor of the Universe" (ML, 64). These multidenominational, often week-long events were known for being raucous, as people were overcome with a religious zeal that often bled over into other forms of intense communion among the rabble of black, white, and sometimes Indian believers. As Washington writes, "Isabella's attraction to camp meetings put her on the fringe of religious respectability," as most organized denominations disapproved of them (ST, 72). Elaw fondly describes "an American camp meeting" to her British friends. "The grove is teeming with life and activity," she writes. "The numberless private conferences, the earnest inquiries of sinners, the pressing exhortations of anxious saints, the concourse of pedestrians, the arrival of horses and carriages of all descriptions render the scene portentously interesting and intensely surprising" (ML, 65). Truth was attracted to the populist quality of these gatherings; she had loved Pinkster celebrations, which were also boisterous events. What such festivals and meetings had in common was the element of surprise, the unexpected, the uncontrollable, which may have led states of spiritual ecstasy to blur into moments of bacchanalia.

Lee and Elaw share an investment in the leveling force of worship. Lee describes God's unifying power, especially in moments of collective song. In Delaware, at a camp meeting of the African Methodist Episcopal faith, Lee writes, "There was immense large congregations. . . . The people came from all parts, without distinction of sex, size, or color, and the display of God's power commenced from singing. . . . There appeared to be a great union with the white friends" (JL, 45). The women's accounts of conviviality in the worship of a common Lord indicate their belief as preachers in the power of communal worship to create a space that transcended race, gender, hierarchical relationships, or worldly politics. Such a belief can be critiqued as a misguided notion of both humanist universalism and religious subservience.

Criticisms of maintaining an apolitical stance could hold true, but only alongside the women's commitments to antislavery and to their own black congregations. Both Lee and Elaw traveled to the slave states, risking capture, and Jackson, in response to the racism at the Shaker village in Watervliet, began her own Shaker community of mostly Black women in Philadelphia. The Shakers have been criticized for their insularity, their establishment of a utopia sealed off from the rest of the world. Even Jackson critiqued the Shakers for this insularity. In a journal entry dated March 1850, Jackson criticizes the Believers for how they "gathered to themselves, in praying for themselves and not for the world. . . . I wondered how the world was to be saved, if Shakers were the only people of God on earth, and they seemed to be busy with their own concerns" (GP, 220). Jackson found, and expresses through a recorded dream, that black congregants were mistreated, and this was her motivation in establishing the Philadelphia community. The four women's spiritual practices must also be remembered in the long tradition of radical religious sects' direct challenges to both political and organized church authority.

Utopian dreaming makes us think more seriously about the import of escapist fantasy and messianic wish. Escapism is a powerful form of refusal. Outlandish fancies articulate with historical and material practices, from slave rebellions and social justice movements to expressive cultures and daily improvisations of black life.

Most abolitionist and other reform movements of the time were based in a kind of universalism. But despite universalist convictions or intentions, consideration of the four women's practices and states of feeling are crucial if we are to understand their commitment to forms of collectivity. In feeling together, people experienced themselves outside of a binary relation to official, legal, juridical powers and instead as part of an alternative sociality. This is not an ahistorical claim for the transcendent power of religion, but it is a reminder of the ways in which political radicalism was coupled with forms of populist religiosity.

Rosi Braidotti argues for the ethical importance of a "non-unitary vision of the subject."[46] Elaw recounts her own experience of sanctification at a camp meeting during communal prayer:

> Whether I was in the body, or out of the body, on that auspicious day I cannot say. . . . I became so overpowered with the presence of God that I sank down upon the ground, and laid there for a considerable time; and while I was thus prostrate on the earth, my spirit seemed to ascend up into the clear circle of the Sun's disc. . . . When I recovered from that trance or ecstasy into which I had fallen . . . hundreds of persons were standing around me weeping. (ML, 66–67)

In describing the ecstasy of her sanctification, Elaw paraphrases a section from 2 Corinthians 12:3, in which Paul describes a man "caught up in the third heaven . . . whether in the body or out of the body, I do not knoweth."[47] Elaw is not sure whether she is in or out of her body—she may be both—in a state brought on by sensorial stimulation and its evanescence. Traveling out of her body, she ascends not into the personified arms of God, but into the galaxy, the clear circle of earth's star, to a third heaven. Elaw's experience points to a form of communalism that does not reach for the universal but brings into question a humanist investment in a stable, rational, unified self

To achieve the state of ecstasy is described as self-annihilation, a condition when a centered sense of subjectivity explodes or melts away. Of her baptism Elaw writes, "I was so overwhelmed with the love of God that self seemed annihilated: I was completely lost and absorbed in the divine fascinations" (ML, 61). The state of being lost, of being absorbed, refuses the rational order of things. Such states, in which the self is dissolved, show the instability of reality itself. Individual perception of both temporality and immediate place disappear, as does the need to know the coordinates of the actual. The senses do not tell the facts; they seem to respond to another dimension entirely. Although Elaw describes her experience as ascendance, it is more accurately described as transformative rather than transcendent. Elaw returns to the circle of weeping witnesses strengthened and fortified. She does not rise above the human condition; rather, such extraterrestrial experience is folded into that very condition.

## Death and Life After

The precarity of life for black people showed the boundaries between the living and the dead as porous. People in the nineteenth century generally had a much more intimate relationship with mortality; death was always close and often long and painful. In Jackson's account, instances of death are rarely accompanied by mourning or grief; they are met with grim, unceremonious acceptance, in contrast to the sentimental and ornate mourning practices and funereal rites common among the white middle classes of the later 1800s.[48] These four black women's visions, particularly those of Jackson, who writes most often of her experiences in conversation with the other side, are not always benevolent; often they are messages laden with accusatory demands for atonement and signs of a cruel and arbitrary God.

Lee, Elaw, and Jackson all speak often of sickness and death, and of their experiences of being brought close to death. They write of being sick frequently themselves, often for long periods of time. As with radical religious women of an earlier era, the sickbed was often a powerful site for contact with spirits on the other side, and many awoke with messages to the living. Violent ailments, associated with great feeling, are common in both Lee's and Jackson's narratives. Recovery is often miraculous, rarely the result of allopathic remedies, and frequently connected to religious rites of passage. In a section of her collected writings titled "Afflicted for Instruction," Jackson relates one period of illness in which she experiences dying six times, leaving her body and flying over the Mediterranean (GP, 110). "I went three times to . . . Jordan, three times into the air with . . . angels. This made six times I left the body," she relates (GP, 112). Another six-month bout of illness in 1857 leaves Jackson almost blinded. She is "brought near to the spiritual world" (GP, 274) but is told to remain on the earthly plane and establishes her black Shaker community in Philadelphia the next year. Frequently sick, experiencing death, and attending to others in their illness, Jackson regularly receives direct messages from spirits and feels an ability to reside "between the living and the dead" (GP, 84). Jackson's strict obedience to her guides from the spirit world gives her powers beyond the human. She is able to read people's thoughts, predict the weather, and heal ailments with a single touch. Her abilities also speak to a time when the lines between the physical and the metaphysical were not as clearly drawn.

Lee describes life itself as a general sickness, a daily unwellness (JL, 5), and a language of violence permeates the women's narratives. Lee graphically relates her recurring attempts to commit suicide. Twice she is tempted by an inner urge to drown herself, even after her conversion. Pursued by the temptation, she writes, "I was then beset to hang myself with a cord suspended from the wall enclosing the secluded spot" (JL, 6). After being touched by God, she still struggles and suffers. Lee describes being "then again sunk back into sorrow. . . . For four years I continued in this way, laboring under the awful apprehension, that I could never be happy in this life" (JL, 3). For a third time Lee contemplates suicide. "When about to end my life," she writes, "the awful gulf of hell seemed to be open beneath me" (JL, 6). Although her daily life as a black woman is never specifically referenced, we do know that life for slave and free was hard and cruel enough to constitute a dimension of feeling of its own, an indescribable condition beyond words, as unbounded by space and time as the spiritual ecstasy the women found as their cure. The hellish conditions of black people's lives were a constant apparition; death and great suffering hovered, even when not spoken of directly. Such conditions are coded into the account of the despondent Lee, whose chronic illness is her desperately sad state of mind. Lee's mental condition is lifted only by following her calling and by continual participation in spiritual community.

Jackson's visions are epic in scope, and they are not comforting. Many are bloody, violent, and persecutory. They often combine great physical disturbance and sickness with religious exultation. Her visions incorporate a logically understandable sense of dread and terror, as black people were (are) hunted and tortured with legal impunity. God possesses Jackson in violent fits. "My eyes snapped like one in a fit, swift as lightning," she writes after a visitation from the Bride and Groom. "The operation ran from my head to my foot. And on my left side below my breast there was a motion which caused a white foam to rise up and work out of the left corner of my mouth, while the right corner was as if clenched in death. . . . When Eldress Rebecca took my hand it caused the operation to stop. And then I was filled with weeping, rejoicing and thanksgiving, and singing and praising of God" (GP, 170). For Jackson, the place where the physical meets the spiritual is not always one of peace. The body becomes a fraught site of possession as it is seized by the spirit.

Jackson's visions are often not only turbulent and terrifying; they are also murderous. In a trance Jackson sees "two infants playing in the gutter. One was trying to destroy the other, by holding it under the mud and water. I stood and hallooed, and then ran and took up the child that was under. And it was lifeless." In this case she "restore[s] it to life," although in other cases of such fatal violence any attempt to intervene is hopeless (GP, 209). Her visions are grounded in a very real dystopia of racial terror.

In one of Jackson's dreams (recorded as occurring in 1850, the year of the Fugitive Slave Act), she and Rebecca Perot are walking in a garden, when she senses that there are people in the garden "designed to kill us" (GP, 223). Jackson sees that "the men had killed all the women and children, and were dragging them like dogs through the streets" (GP, 223). She and Perot must then "fly to Philadelphia" (GP, 223). Jackson's fear of the threat and the very real presence of male violence is obvious, and although she does not note the race of the murderers, she is most likely referencing the horrible racial violence that accompanied implementation of the Fugitive Slave Act. In other dreams, the murderers are explicitly white. In the dream she titles "Dream from Ten Years of Age," Jackson combs the hair of a white woman, who, turning out to be a witch, murders Jackson's brother, sister, and mother. An unspecified "they" murder the rest of her family (GP, 235–36).

Jackson's "Dream of Slaughter" is her most violent and surreal vision. In this dream she is eviscerated and disemboweled by an unknown murderer:

> He took a lance and laid my nose open and then he cut my head on the right side, from the back to the front above my nose, and pulled the skin down over that side. Then he cut the left, did the same way, and pulled the skin down. The skin and blood covered me like a veil from my head to my lap. . . . Then he took a long knife and cut my chest open in the form of the cross and took all by [sic] bowels out and laid them on the floor by my right side, and then went in search of all the rest of the family. (GP, 94–95)

Jean Humez interprets this dream as reflecting the climate of white violence in Philadelphia at the time. Jackson makes little direct reference to political circumstance, but it is not a leap to consider that the extreme violence of her dreams graphically references the violent persecution and suffering of black people, both slave and free.

In all of her writings Jackson expresses her sense of the condition of life as particularly adversarial, cruel, and torturous. She has a vigilant awareness of her "persecutors"—those who do not believe in her powers—who are often male representatives of the Christian church. Her intense aversion to patriarchal dominance is evident in her dreams. Immediately following her "Dream of Slaughter," Jackson relates the violent flaying of her body to her perceived persecution at the hands of a Methodist preacher. "He persecuted me in as cruel a manner as he treated my body in the dream as he tried to . . . stop my spiritual useful influence among the people and destroy my spirit life" (GP, 95). In an act of righteousness God strikes the preacher dead. "He troubled me no more . . . and so he was not allowed to take out my heart," she writes (GP, 96). Jackson accords her spiritual body—her spiritual life—as much legitimacy as her existence on the physical plane.

Looking to life after death is often referred to in studies of black resistance as the way religion deluded black people and kept them from organizing in revolutionary struggle. But one has only to think of such figures as Nat Turner to remember that rebellions and slave revolts were often led by spiritual convictions unbounded by the organized church. The claim to life after death, while coded in the language of Christian belief, is a profoundly political claim by the living that they cannot ever truly be killed, enabling them to claim the space between life and death as another dimension of consciousness.

Lee, Elaw, Jackson, and Truth all held beliefs about contact with the spiritual world and in their own abilities to communicate between worlds. Their spiritualist beliefs predate the famous Rochester rappings of 1848. Spiritualism, the form of belief in psychic phenomena, developed using the Fox sisters' revelations as its firm date of birth, has been well studied as a movement among middle-class white people, primarily white women.[49] The gift of mediumship was most often granted young white girls, and visitations were associated with the domestic sphere, primarily conducted around the séance table, which most often was located in the parlors of its practitioners' privately owned houses. Trance speaking and performances of contact with spirits of the dead were forums for women to have a voice of authority.

Spiritualism accompanied various intertwined reform movements. Molly McGarry quotes a naysayer writing in the *Herald of Progress* in 1864: "How is it when we meet a vegetarian, he is almost sure to be a phrenologist, a free lover, a root doctor, a woman's rights [*sic*], a mesmerist, a Spiritualist, a socialist, a cold waterist, a ranting abolitionist, and abnegator of the Bible, the Sabbath day, and the religion of his father?"[50] Spiritualists were "wild-eyed, long-haired reformers," which could also describe Truth's compatriots. Many mediums channeled great political and religious reformers as well as family members. Even William Lloyd Garrison availed himself of the spiritual world, contacting past reformers for inspiration and confirmation. After a night at a séance, Jackson's companion, Rebecca Perot, is visited in a dream by the spirits that had been in the room, including Lord Bacon and Emmanuel Swedenborg (GP, 242).

Later rituals of visitation took on a scientific pretense as the craze was caught up in excitement about emergent technologies of communication: the telegraph, telephone, and photograph. Men of science took up the possibilities of contact outside common material reality, including mediumship, mesmerism, and telepathy. Science, not faith nor divine gift, would legitimate such phenomena. The religious scholar William James was a founding member of the American Society for Psychical Research (ASPR), established in 1885. James was very clear that psychic phenomena must not be confused with the ecstasies and excesses of religion. James's (and his colleague Henri Bergson's) belief in the mind's potential abilities for telepathic communication and hypnotism follows the line of inquiry that had found new, scientifically based articulation following the Spiritualist movement of the late 1800s. Mystical phenomena passed from being the province of a gaggle of women to the object of measured study by "learned men."[51] James and Bergson theorized about the potential of human consciousness to realize its wider capacities. Both participated in a wider community of investigators: James served as president of the ASPR IN 1896, and Bergson headed the identically named British organization, known as the SPR, in 1913. In his presidential address before the ASPR, James stressed the "immense importance of the new method which we have introduced" and encouraged the society to continue its work with the "impartiality and completeness of record . . . even more rigorously in the future."[52] He argues, "The excesses to which the romantic and personal view of Nature may lead, if wholly unchecked by impersonal rationalism, are direful."[53] He associates such excesses with non-European cosmologies, which he derogates. "Central African Mumbo-jumboism is one of unchecked romanticism's fruits," he writes.[54] According to him, European rationalism, reason, and science, rather than "primitive" superstition or ritual, are superior ways to explain the unknown spiritual realm. As James argues, we must take heed of *"facts of experience."*[55] Henri Bergson was open to a wider definition of consciousness. In his presidential address to the SPR, Bergson suggests gently that the current scientific methods, based in mathematics, may not be applicable in the study of the mind. "The essence of mental things . . . do not lend themselves to measurement," he states.[56]

The term *spiritualism* in the nineteenth century acted as an umbrella for many practices and beliefs predating the Fox sisters and antedating their direct influence. Spiritual abilities were not limited to conversations with dead relatives or dependent on the will of individual spirits. Tapping into an abstract spiritual energy granted practitioners powers beyond human capacity. The gifted had various psychic abilities: they could cure the sick, see the future, and communicate telepathically not only with spirits but with entities residing in other dominions and galaxies. Certain people were more sensitive to messages from the other side. Many spiritualists rejected Christianity while embracing the immanence of God in man and nature. Others were proponents of free love and believed in the concept of "spiritual affinities": that lovers should be spiritually matched.[57]

Spiritualism migrated from being the domain of young women and girls to the province of objective men. In order to legitimate this shift, scientific, medical, and technological explanations proliferated. The "scientific" manipulation of forces of nature such as magnetism and electricity was a way to access or call forth spiritual realms. For instance, in describing the power of John Spear—a former minister, ardent temperance reformer, and abolitionist-turned-prolific-trance-writer—clairvoyant and historian of American Spiritualism Emma Hardinge states that Spear was "gifted with strong psychometric power. . . . Among the other revelations which this gentleman alleged to have received from 'on high' was that of the existence of divers societies on the upper spheres, whose names and functions he was especially instructed to make known to mankind."[58] Spear claimed to have been told by a "general assembly" of great spirits (including Socrates, Rousseau, and Swedenborg) to establish a new order. This was to consist of seven associations: "Electrilizers, Healthfulizers, Educationalizers, Agriculturalizers, Elementizers, Governmentizers, and the association of Benificents."[59] In 1853, Spear and a group of spiritualists established the Kiantone community around what they called a "magnetic spring" in upstate New York. Spear and his utopian community then announced that they had discovered an entirely new source of energy, which they called the New Motive Power. Together, the community began to construct a machine, to be run on this spiritual potency. Andrew Jackson Davis writes, "They invest the very materialism of the mechanism with principles of interpretation which give out an emanation of religious feeling altogether new, in the development of scientific truth. Each wire is precious, sacred, as a spiritual verse."[60] Before it could be fully proven to work, the people of the town where Spear's group had built the machine destroyed it.

What led the townspeople to destroy the Kiantone experiment was the philosophy behind this new source of power: Spear's belief that sexual energy flows were the underlying fundament of the entire universe. A polarization between male and female, and their union, were key to producing this energy. In order for the machine to run, it needed to be impregnated, creating what was called the "electric child."[61] After the failure of this machine, Spear's next plan was to engineer and power a "magical sewing machine."[62]

Another radical Spiritualist that Truth and Jackson most likely knew of (although likely did not associate with) was a black man by the name of Paschal Beverly Randolph. Born in New York, after a life at sea Randolph settled in Utica in 1852. He advertised himself as "Dr. Paschal Beverly Randolph, clairvoyant physician and psycho-phrenologist."[63] Randolph was a trance speaker who began his career as an advocate of free-love Spiritualism and was associated with the Modern Times utopian community.

Randolph's specialty was sex and curing sexual ailments. "True Sex-power is God-power," he wrote.[64] Medical disorders had to do with imbalances of energy in the body. In his "medical views, human vital energy and happiness could be increased by mutual sexual fulfillment."[65] Randolph also marketed special elixirs to enhance sexual energy. All of these potions contained hashish as their main ingredient, and his skills in concocting these elixirs gained from his travels in Asia while a seaman. Randolph would sell these potions for the rest of his life.[66] Emma Hardinge denounced Randolph, calling him one of "a class of fungi" made up of "spiritual mountebanks and dishonest mediums."[67] Hardinge writes, "They consist for the most part of persons endowed with genuine mediumistic gifts . . . who use these gifts as a means of pandering either to the marvel seeker or the opposition, whichever chances . . . to pay the best."[68] When Randolph recanted his spiritual beliefs, Hardinge thought perhaps he was "just that destitute of a sensation, and was glad to accept of anything short of negro minstrelsy."[69] Randolph preceded the renowned Russian spiritualist Madame Helena Petrovna Blavatsky, cofounder of the Theosophical Society, in her travels to Asia and Northern Africa in 1861. Turning to what would be referred to later as "occultism," Randolph credited the "Ansaireh or Nusa'iri of Syria" as his source for knowledge of sexual magic.[70]

For both Blavatsky and Randolph visitations were from spirits of humans and nonhumans alike. Both believed in a universal spiritualism, one that held the Supreme Creator as above and beyond a Christian God. In his "spiritualist utopia," written in 1868 and titled *After Death, the Disembodiment of Man: The World of Spirits, Its Location, Extent, Appearance*, Randolph writes, "One life, one origin, one God, one destiny, one religion, one humanity, is the universal (coming) creed."[71] A few years previously Randolph had shocked and alienated a Christian audience in Chicago by proclaiming "the great fact that God is electricity, is motion and light."[72] We find this belief in God as material phenomena later in the philosophies of mystic Alice Coltrane, as well as imagined by Octavia E. Butler in her *Parable* series as part of the belief system of her character Lauren Olamina.

Certain unverifiable lore links Randolph and Blavatsky in antagonistic relationship to each other. According to a third party, Madame Blavatsky would be suddenly visited by Randolph telepathically. On one occasion, she cried, "Now the Nigger is shooting at me! . . . So now the Devil has him." According to this third party, Blavatsky claimed that "Randolph just then wanted to murder her in a magical way."[73]

Belief in after- and otherworlds was not limited to chatting with relatives or channeling reformers and famous people. Spiritual contact was in the service of greater human knowledge of the secrets of the universe, which could be achieved through study and exploration rather than passive reception, and through intellectual pursuit, self-discipline, will, and intuition rather than ecstatic worship.

Rebecca Cox Jackson's spiritual abilities preceded and exceeded those of the mediums who sprang up after the Fox sisters. Jackson dated the beginning of her "tuition of invisible spirits" from 1830 (GP, 222). When Jackson participated in the ritual of the séance, it was not to contact dead relatives but to commune with "higher spirits" (GP, 241). During these communions, the spirits granted her extrasensory abilities. "By this means I have been able to tell people's thoughts, and to tell them words they have spoken many miles distant from me. And also to tell them things they would do a year beforehand. . . . I had a gift when the day was clear, to tell when it was agoing to thunder," she explains (GP, 222). Visions and auditory communications, signs and wonders came through from alternate temporalities and spatialities—from the other side of time. Marvelous fascinations came through from other worlds and not always from spirits of the dead.

Jackson's visions were singularly strange in relation to the wider culture of visions and dreams practiced by religious sects, including the Quakers and the Shakers. Jackson's visions came to her alone, as a chosen visionary; she was a part of the Shakers' community of belief, but she also held herself at a distance as a singular recipient of spiritual communication whose visionary maps tell a different geography. Spiritualism, for Jackson, meant the ability to travel to and in mythical cosmological realms.

In her journal, Jackson tracks her ecstatic contact with God, but surprisingly, her visions are not often part of a Christian, or even a religious, lexicon. Instead, they describe her journeys through multidimensional realms and otherworldly states of being. She is visited by angels and saints, but more often she records being in the presence of powerful archetypal figures and manifestations of abstract forces. Jackson is frequently visited by magical entities representing the elemental forces of the universe. Her "Vision of Singular Movements Among the Stars" is particularly surrealist:

> I saw a large body of stars in the heavens above my head. They were brilliant, and some were larger in size than any I had ever seen. I looked east, and saw a train coming from that direction to meet them. I looked north, and saw a body of them coming from the north, in the form of a diamond. They were large and bright. A company of horsemen moved before them, bearing their course south. On the southwest corner of the first rank rode a Great One on a large white horse, waving a banner or a sword. When these met the other two bodies of stars that were over the house where I was, they began to shower down sparks of light upon the house and upon me. These sparks were like silver, when it reflects the sun from its surface. (GP, 209–210)

A train and a trail of bright diamonds chart this vision's geography, led by a powerful figure of strength and righteousness. There is a clash, an eruption, the climax of a collision between celestial powers, and Jackson is showered with the resulting sparks. The source of her powers is not located in a personified God nor in a supreme Father or Lord but in the all-powerful elemental energies of the universe.

With her celestial visions Jackson creates an alternate, often astral cartography. In describing her visions, Jackson is careful to always chart the directions of the compass, including both her own position and the direction and placement of her visions in most of her entries. The celestial is an open space of possibility, and access to the stars cannot be policed. As well as being over Jackson's head, the stars form a diamond coming from the north. This may be informed by the importance of the north to black geographies of freedom. It is the North Star that leads Harriet Tubman and others on the Underground Railroad, an alternative set of coordinates and timetable for a stolen earthly geography.

As Carla Gerona writes of early Quaker beliefs in the power of dreaming and trance states, dreams were like maps.[74] Gerona argues that, for Quakers, their dreams not only were part of their awakening to a political commitment to antislavery but also the way they naturalized their participation in US settler colonialism.[75] That Jackson's visions and dreams are maps is clear; she consistently refers to the points of the compass in her descriptions. But Jackson's geographies are black geographies; her dreams map a very different terrain of dystopian terror and utopian cartography.

Jackson's residence in the surreal, often dystopian landscapes of her dreams charts with precision the cruel touch of black existence and the phenomenon of black survival. Jackson chose to exist in her surreal interior world. But this claim to interiority is political, as any kind of complex sense of self is not granted black people by the dominant racialized regime. Jackson grounded her sense of self and subjectivity in her power and ability to move and to act, between worlds, with her spiritual self as real and effective as her bodily one.

# LOVELY SKY BOAT

Alice Coltrane and the Metaphysics of Sound

**2**

Turning to the musician and mystic Alice Coltrane, I trace an important genealogy that places her in communion with the visionary black women explored
in the last chapter. I am thinking further about forms of radical worldmaking
and modes of being: In what ways did black women continue to claim the ability to see and feel, with others, beyond the self, beyond the constrictions of
life and death, past, present and future? Like Sojourner Truth, Alice Coltrane
believed she was chosen by God to be in direct connection with the greater
forces of the universe. Like Truth, Alice took on a new title; after years of devotion, she became Swamini, the title given to a profound spiritual teacher.
She was also given the name Turiyasangitananda. Like Rebecca Cox Jackson,
Alice was gifted with supraterrestrial powers and heightened abilities. In a
black episteme, spiritual calling is a route to the stars. Alice's travels between

galaxies, dimensions, and time frames are part of black speculative practice. Turning to Alice allows us to further explore realms of consciousness beyond self-awareness and a search for sovereignty, to dwell in a sense of diffusion—in the body and out of the body, material and immaterial.

Alice was raised in the Christian faith and trained on the piano and organ, playing for Baptist churches in and around Detroit in the 1950s. As a "devotional musician," music for Alice was an essential part of collective ecstatic worship as she and her bands and congregations created sound environments inseparable from spiritual expression (FB, 3). But Alice was more than Christian; over her lifetime she observed an alternative cosmology. Like other jazz musicians of her time, her spiritual belief system was capacious and universalist, with her musical practices and forms of worship framed by Hindu philosophy. Many of her devotees were also musicians, and with Alice would develop a "new devotional genre," a mix of praise singing from the black Christian church, jazz, and Hindu worship songs (FB, 85). Their practice drew on the Hindu belief that sound is the fundamental generative force of the universe, its mode of creation. To chant OM was to breathe the breath of life, or *pneuma*, into matter. The music of Alice and her congregation was a utopian practice of attunement with an infinite universe of aural vibratory phenomena.

Radha Botofasina-Reyes, a member of Alice's congregation, relates the experience of "going all over the universe" with Coltrane in their music:

> *Bhajan*, it's a Sanskrit word. It means "soul chant." You're chanting the names of the Lord. It's just keeping you always saturated in God consciousness. Oh my God, they could go on for two or three hours, and she would go all over the universe. Sometimes you might have a spiritual heart attack where you would just cry and cry and cry. Sometimes you couldn't sing anymore; all you could do is just *say*, and then Swamini would explain, "The end of all bhajan is mantra. Even if you don't believe it's gonna help, just by saying it, it will help."[1]

These periods of worship with Alice were melting times, where language ceased and the metaphysics of sound began.

Alice's concept of God was based in the idea that all religions sought out and worshipped what was ultimately the same force, or source of power. As she writes in her book *Monument Eternal*, this power held "myriad attributes, such as an infinite variety of names, forms, formless manifestations, and innumerable expansions" (ME, 12). Through their musical devotion she and her congregation were dedicated to the unification, or rejoining, of self with "Absolute Consciousness" (ME, 9). The Absolute was the infinite universe, manifesting materially, from the atoms to the stars, and spiritually, as gods. To consider the self as made of the same elements as the rest of the cosmos changed the very notion of self and subjectivity; to awaken into Absolute Consciousness was to transfigure into a different mode of being not governed by human-centered understandings of the universe.

Absolute Consciousness was made up of forces and vibrations that could be expressed scientifically and materially, for the spirit was molecular. "In reality, the proton, electron and neutron are none other than the Father, Son, and the Holy Ghost in minute form—the Holy Trinity hidden behind the veil of human awareness. This holy triune universal support is also known as the Supreme Lord in three persons: Brahma, Vishnu, Siva; and in mundane terminology Power, Light, Energy," Alice writes (ME, 10). The phenomenon of electricity embodies this triune of forces; it runs through the body as it does the skies. Like Rebecca Cox Jackson, Alice was touched by lightning. Alice describes an incident in which she is entered by "sugary fire." She writes, "A lightning bolt coming from the ceiling struck my physical body. This silvery flash of light lit up the room, yet it was so subtle that it barely could be felt" (ME, 29). Electricity is the element that conjoins the worlds of spirit, body, and matter, its current running through the ethereal, the living, and the inanimate.

Musical sessions were "melting times" when the self was diffused into Absolute Consciousness, as elements within a wide expanse of material forces. "There . . . exists within each particle of atomic energy a supreme and irrefutable universal order of Absolute Consciousness," Alice writes. "This clarifies to my being the reason that even the smallest atoms in existence can never be destroyed—when bombarded, or cut by force, they only transform themselves" (ME, 9–10). All entities were part of the phenomena of existence that also bring into question, or a state of estrangement, normative temporal regimes. Life and death no longer refer to the human lifespan. They are no longer beginning and end but part of an endless process of change.

For Alice the experience of contact, through worship and making music, was filled with the absolute joy of the spirit, but it was also fraught with sufferings and painful physical manifestations. Alice, like Jackson, is often both in conflict with the body and in its embrace. As shown through her writings, earthly physical manifestation was a site of ambivalence for Alice, the needs and desires of the flesh a bondage to be transcended. The music she and her congregation created may have been driven by a Vedantic understanding of alter planes of existence and the bliss of Absolute Consciousness, but Alice's philosophy was far from peaceful. There was a great contrast between the gods and belief systems in Alice's pantheon, with the Hindu gods not always meshing with the Christian God. There were contrasts and dissonances in Alice's music, as the gods are both fearsome and loving, multiple and singular. The Hindu concepts of consciousness and the promise of enlightenment often sat uneasily with the Christian concept of sin and the vengeful, punishing servitude demanded by the Old Testament–style God found in her verses. This jealous God is most evident in the first volume of *Endless Wisdom*, the book of commandments dictated to her by the Lord. The conflict between gods and systems of thought converged in her extreme ascetic practices. The body was a burden and the result of true devotion was the ability to escape the flesh, to be transmuted into formless matter latticed with thought and thought's manifestation as various selves in different dimensions.

Alice's practices of devotional endurance were part of her larger musical and spiritual belief system, as through her devotion she gained the ability to achieve other states of beingness. Traveling from astral plane to astral plane, Alice's being "transcend[ed] the limitations of time and space" (ME, 27). Alongside her personal supraterrestrial experiences, collective devotional worship was a key mode of travel between dimensions. The music she made with her congregation at the ashram invoked modes of existence outside the realm of earthly life.

Alice/Turiyasangitananda is part of a black radical tradition. Remembering her helps us reroute what we think of as radical, a term that cannot be confined to a humanism based in individualist notions of freedom or justice within the system that excludes black people. Considering her work invites exploration of other ways—delinked from earthly precepts and preconditions—to conceive of freedom. To insist on the possibility of peace, joy, pleasure, and serenity is a defiantly political act.

Whither Alice?

Alice Coltrane is relatively absent from scholarship, with the notable exception of Franya Berkman's excellent biography. There are many reasons why Alice Coltrane has not received the kind of scholarly attention her music and life merit. Musically, her greatness is overshadowed by her role as John Coltrane's wife. Alice wholeheartedly embraced this role and kept the structure and intention of John's music and work as the core of her own. She called John her mentor and "Father," and "made little attempt to distinguish her music and her spiritual mission from those of her husband" (FB, 64). Because of this her first albums as bandleader, *A Monastic Trio* (1967), *Huntington Ash-ram Monastery* (1969), and *Ptah the El Daoud* (1970), were criticized as "too derivative of John's musical concepts" (FB, 64). This criticism is tone deaf to the true meaning of Alice's devotion to John's philosophy and musical theories. With the music she produced in the first years after his death, Alice was consciously continuing on the musico-spiritual path she and John had traveled together.

Alice's harp and piano playing on these recordings demonstrates her principles of devotion and collectivity; Alice's harp runs behind and around the other instruments, which included Pharaoh Sanders's saxophone, Vishnu Woods's oud, and Rashied Ali's drums. All three of these musicians shared in her Eastern-influenced spiritual vision. The movement of her music on these albums is filled with quiet sadness, in homage to John Coltrane. These albums were criticized by reviewers as lacking originality and "reminiscent of her collaborations with her late husband." It was when Alice produced the album *Universal Consciousness* in 1971, after her return from India, that reviewers began recognizing the power of her music.

Alice's artistic and spiritual expansion is often credited to John's influence over their five-year association and marriage, and Alice herself, in her devotion to John, gives us no reason to think otherwise. But, as Berkman argues, John's biographers no doubt underestimate Alice's influence on John, or at least the ways that each contributed to the other's spiritual experience. It was during their marriage that John produced *A Love Supreme* (1965), *Ascension* (1966), and *Meditations* (1966), his most radical and explicitly spiritual music. Alice saw the universe and the music that was a part of it as grounded in a sense of self that was larger than the individual. This made the music a flow between herself, John, and myriad other manifestations of the cosmos.

Key to Alice's musical direction on these albums, and her continuing reverence for John, is an expression of the spiritual principle of devotion. Devotion is what she was practicing through her music as she paid open tribute to John's influence. The principle of devotion is grounded in a deeper philosophy of selflessness, a decentered sense of selfhood, that does not jive with the tenets of jazz scholarship, which organizes itself around individual genius. Celebrated geniuses are almost always male. Alice's innovative work on the piano, and her place as one of very few jazz harpists, are not taken seriously by mainstream jazz scholarship, which feminizes these instruments, relegating them to supporting positions and evaluating their players as less capable of innovation. Jazz scholarship focuses instead on instruments characterized as masculine, above all the saxophone, trumpet, and trombone, with their muscular tones. When Alice replaced McCoy Tyner on piano in John Coltrane's final quartet, she was deeply resented and marginalized by John's fans and music critics, who held her responsible for breaking up an "iconic homosocial band," as jazz scholar Sherrie Tucker calls it.[2]

Feminist jazz studies has also found it difficult to account for Alice. "I think the ambivalence of jazz scholars in general toward the change in the quartet made Alice Coltrane a risky subject for feminist jazz scholars," says Tucker.[3] Feminists are uncomfortable with her open devotion to John Coltrane. In addition, in posing a challenge to masculinized music scholarship, feminist jazz scholars feel that strategically they have to focus on women who master the horn or the drums. "Feminist jazz scholars (like me) [looked to] women who played instruments that had been thought of as masculine," says Sherrie Tucker, at least in terms of insisting on women's musical visibility within jazz studies. "We wanted DRUMMERS. TRUMPET PLAYERS. Like that. Or we wanted vocalists with explicitly critical lyrics."[4] Tucker's explanation here must be understood in the context of her long-term scholarly dedication to female jazz musicians, including Alice Coltrane, and her continuous fight to have them remembered. But Alice Coltrane's quietness—her work's lack of explicit political content and the mellifluousness of Alice's harp and piano—confounded familiar categorization with which to challenge masculinist mainstream jazz scholarship.

Similarly, African American studies most often looks to hard politics as an indicator of achievement. Secular intellectual inquiry may be uncomfortable with Alice Coltrane's fervent spiritual commitment as she did not ground her concepts of freedom or justice on an earthly plane. In addition, studies of African American religious practices may be uncomfortable with her religious eclecticism and approach to worship. African American religious studies tends to center on the organized Christian church. Alice Coltrane drew on her training in Christian church music and integrated church music into her own style, particularly in the later work with her Ashram choir. But her alternative cosmology and musical philosophy, which situates Egyptian and Hindu gods and sages alongside the Father, Son, and Holy Ghost, go against the monotheist core of the Christian fellowship.

Like jazz studies, African American studies also prioritizes individual distinction. Alice, however, was deeply reticent about performing a public persona. Her reclusiveness, combined with a lack of critical attention, make her a difficult figure to recover with these approaches. I will not attempt to uncover the "true" Alice Coltrane, nor do I want to replicate Franya Berkman's thoroughly researched and thoughtfully written biography. I am more interested

**Figure 2.1** Alice Coltrane and her harp.

in Alice's later life and her spiritual devotion as part of a history of African American refusal to exist according to the normative terms that excluded them in the first place. As were Sojourner Truth and Rebecca Cox Jackson, Alice was dedicated to developing deeper senses of the self and subjectivity in ways that challenge liberal notions of the possessive individual and open up on infinite otherworlds.

## Absolute Consciousness

The concept of consciousness is commonly used to refer to a state of awareness of the self and is associated with the equally elusive idea of sentience. Science often centers consciousness in the mind and counts it as a mental state explainable as the result of purely mechanical functions of the brain. Consciousness is used to demarcate humans as the pinnacle of evolution, to indicate humans as the most evolved species. Yet the concept refuses to be fully accounted for.[5] Daniel Dennett argues, in *Consciousness Explained,* that "the various phenomena that compose what we call consciousness . . . are all physical effects of the brain's activities."[6] David Chalmers coined the term Hard Problem to describe the core difficulty in studying consciousness. He does not agree that consciousness can be explained with our current scientific abilities.

nor does he attempt to "solve the problem of consciousness," but he does try to "rein it in."[7] His argument is that consciousness is an irreducible element, and that studying it will lead to a new scientific method.[8] Both scholars are invested in the notion that through science man can explain everything—and in the utility of doing so. But consciousness still defies control and classification. Despite scientific claims, it remains elusive, an unknown and perhaps unknowable quality. With the concept of Ernst Bloch's utopian consciousness in mind, I am interested in the concept of Absolute Consciousness as a great abyss of elemental forces.

The field of consciousness is much broader than the human mind can perceive. The physical universe is an immense "vibratory field."[9] Telepathy, then, is a tuning-in to a larger frequency. Using the metaphor of electricity, Henri Bergson explains that telepathy could be in the same way "natural" and, "whenever the day comes that we know its conditions, it will no more be necessary to wait for a 'phantasm of the living' in order to obtain telepathic effect."[10] After all, he argues, we don't have to wait for lightning to see an electric spark.

The mind, or our consciousness, is not contained within nor produced by the brain.[11] Bergson explains "our mental life to be much more vast than the cerebral life."[12] Instead, the brain is an "organ of pantomime" or operates like a symphony conductor, "marking out motor articulations."[13] Its job is to "contract the field of consciousness," so as to "keep [our] attention fixed on life. . . . Once we become accustomed to this idea of a consciousness overflowing the organism, the more natural we find it to suppose that the soul survives the body."[14] I adopt a Blochian sense of the *Not-Yet Conscious* to extrapolate the possibility of a third kind of consciousness, a utopian consciousness, tapped into through rituals of worship and musical vibration.

In the context of the Western adoption of South Asian spiritual philosophies in the 1960s and 1970s, Western spiritual tourism often turned the idea of consciousness into a narcissistic practice of self-exploration and improvement. I argue that Alice's practice, based in reclusive devotion, was not based in a model of consumption. Consciousness, for her, meant not just awareness of the self but an awareness of the self as part of infinite temporal and spatial dimensions. Consciousness was not just the brain-centric mental capacity of humans but an ineffable, expansive rhythm, of which the material world and human existence were only part.

Thinking of consciousness as the encompassing phenomena of existence blurs the lines between religious and secular, spiritual and scientific. Henri Bergson knew this and believed our individual internal lives to be part of a continuous flow of energy. Psychic phenomena, or other states of conscious-ness, as Bergson posits, is when some of what swirls around us enters our consciousness unfiltered. Bergson uses music, rather than the visual, as a way to explain consciousness: "To ourselves, there is neither a rigid, immovable substratum nor distinct states passing over it like actors on a stage. There is simply the continuous melody of inner life—a melody which is going on and will go on, indivisible, from the beginning to the end of our conscious exis-tence."[15] Our internal consciousness is a "melody where the past enters into the present and forms with it an undivided whole which remains undivided and even indivisible in spite of what is added at every instant."[16] The running of sound through our bodies was for Alice the spiritual flow of consciousness.

## Swamini Turiyasangitananda

As for Truth, Jackson, Elaw, and Lee, Alice's spiritual journey had several stages. Following John Coltrane's death in 1967, she underwent a period of deep sorrow and spiritual renewal marked by extreme forms of fleshly morti-fication, called *tapas*, which Alice describes as spiritual "examinations" (ME, 17). Her music reflected her transformative spiritual experience as she began to incorporate Indian *bhajan*s into her compositions and Indian instruments, such as the oud, into her arrangements.

In 1969 Alice met Swami Satchidananda around the time he opened for the Woodstock Festival, and by 1970 she had recorded her album *Journey in Satchidananda*. That December Alice Coltrane traveled to India with the swami. She wrote of her upcoming trip in the liner notes to *Journey*. "Bombay will be the first stop in my five-week stay in India," she writes, anticipating her next stops to be "New Delhi, Rishikesh, Madras . . . Ceylon."[17] As her biogra-pher, Berkman, relates, Alice's itinerary included attending the World Sci-entific Yoga Conference and visiting the Ganges and the Divine Life Society, founded by the renowned Swami Sivananda, whose teachings Alice had read before meeting Satchidananda. She brought her harp (FB, 78).

As a result of her devotional endurance through the tapas, Alice developed supra-terrestrial abilities and a deep and direct connection with the Supreme Lord, or Lord of Lords, the source for the title of the album she released in 1973. In 1976 she had a particularly powerful spiritual communication. She was directed to become Swamini and to found a spiritual community. In *Monument Eternal*, Alice describes her calling. "It started with taking sanyas," she writes, accepting the life stage, or *ashrama*, which requires renouncing attachments to the material world and committing to an ascetic life.

**Figure 2.2** Alice Coltrane with Swami Satchidananda. Photo courtesy Satchidananda Ashram–Yogaville, Inc./Integral Yoga Archives.

**Figure 2.3** Alice Coltrane and Swami Satchidananda laughing together. Photo courtesy Satchidananda Ashram–Yogaville, Inc./Integral Yoga Archives.

**Figure 2.4** Alice Coltrane and Swami Satchidananda in India. Photo courtesy Satchidananda Ashram–Yogaville, Inc./Integral Yoga Archives.

> That was a total mystical experience. . . . I was told the night and time, and to be prepared, so I got ready and put on a white dress and all, and I noticed when the time came, the colors of orange were poured into the cloth of the dress I was wearing. . . . My name was given, of course, and the whole outline of the duty, the work and mission were also revealed. One of the directives given to me was to start the Ashram.[18]

Donning orange robes, Alice Coltrane took the name Turiyasangitananda and, with the mostly black spiritual community that had gathered around her since the early 1970s, established a vedantic center in Woodland Hills, north of Los Angeles. In 1983 Alice/Turiyasangitananda would relocate her community a few miles west to the Agoura Hills and found the Sai Anantam Ashram.

Alice produced six albums between 1971 and 1976, the year of her calling: *Universal Consciousness* (1971), *World Galaxy* (1972), *Lord of Lords* (1973), *Illuminations* (1974), *Eternity* (1975), and *Radha-Krsna Nama Sankirtana* (1976). The music grew close to her spiritual practice. *Eternity*, recorded in 1975, distinctly marked her relocation to California and featured Alice's followers and spiritual fellows. The music quietens, becomes less frenetic and conflictual, than it is on her critically celebrated *Universal Consciousness.* We begin to hear the sound of congregational chanting. As Suriya Botofasina, who grew up in Alice/Turiyasangitananda's Ashram, remembers, "time would stand still" during their devotional sessions:

> The chanting, the music. When she would turn that organ into a whole different thing. That room would go into . . . a room of very intense passionate chanting. . . . Since we did have so many people that were raised in different areas of music, whether it be avant garde, whether it be from the church, all of that would be mixed into one room, singing in Sanskrit, with inflections of singers that had obviously sung a lot of hymns in their lives with one organ, and a lot of drums, tambourines, shakers, all of this going on with her leading us. And that is where time would stand still. People would pass out, people would burst into tears of joy. This music completely went directly through the souls of every-one. The place she would take one song, on this journey, it would feel endless. There was times when she would just seem to hold one chord out for ever but it would be changing, it would be moving.[19]

To practice sound was to exist in a sense of time without normative breaks. Existence is not the result of an antagonistic dialectic, but of flows and vibrations. It is continuous and ceaseless change.

Alice's spiritual journey can be read as part of the cultural climate of the late 1960s, which saw a resurgence of Eastern spiritual philosophies being adopted, and adapted, in the West, primarily by anti-establishment first-worlders as part of their search for alternative ways of life. This adoption was sometimes idealist and harkened back to the use of Eastern religious principles in Western alternative belief systems, such as those of the Transcendentalists. Sometimes this adoption was based in dissent, tied to the antiwar movement among young middle-class white Americans, exposed to the ideas coming from Southeast Asia during the Cold War in the 1950s, 1960s, and 1970s. It also meant, at other times and/or at the same time, shopping the third world in accordance with a capitalist consumerist ethos and with the long-standing precedent of colonialist entitlement.

There are important parallels between the 1960s–1970s era and earlier periods. In the early 1800s white radicals, sparked by their involvement in abolitionism, became all-around activists and utopians, which included practicing forms of holistic social experimentation. Waves of Western interest in South Asian mysticism followed as later nineteenth- and twentieth-century spiritualists, such as George Gurdjieff, incorporated (or misused) Hindu religious lore into their belief systems and practices.

The 1960s and 1970s were a time in which, with the example of revolutions in Africa and Asia, the idea of deep change became a real possibility. This, of course, did not develop evenly as active or continued support for black freedom, but the continued struggle for black freedom laid a template for critiques of all kinds.

The 1960s ushered in a spiritual radicalism, similar to the utopian and activist movements of the early 1800s, in which religious idealism spurred practices of social change and preexisting forms of radicalism and social experimentation took on new life. Such idealism found its way into the fervid anti-establishment culture. So-called Jesus freaks were young people who followed what they considered the more liberating aspects of Jesus's message. Religious philosopher Alan Watts articulated the spirit of the age in his writings and teachings. "Jesus was one, of many, who had an intense experience of cosmic consciousness—of the vivid realization that oneself is a manifestation of the eternal energy of the universe," he writes in his guiding words to the young Jesus freaks.[20] "Christianity has universality . . . only in recognizing that Jesus is realized in the Buddha, in Lao-Tzu, and in such modern avatars as Ramana Maharishi, Ramakrishna, Aurobindo and Inayat Khan."[21] Alice and John Coltrane shared this syncretic idea, but it resonates differently in the context of black culture: it frees subjects from the organized Christian church and its religious narrative and allows for a sense of self in which slavery does not function as our origin tale. As Alice explains in her writings, her existence spanned thousands of years, even millennia, as did her intimate relationship with God.

As in the 1800s, this era was remarkable for its ethos of social experimentation. A number of utopian communities were founded in the 1960s and 1970s, and existing communities re-enlivened. The Koinonia community was one such commune. Established in 1942 on a Georgia farm by Clarence Jordan, a white Baptist minister, it was intentionally interracial. As a result, being called a "menace to capitalism and white supremacy," Koinonia was targeted for violence by the Ku Klux Klan and the farm's produce boycotted by white residents of neighboring towns.[22] "Dynamited by the Klan in 1957," the community nonetheless survived and was reinvigorated in 1968.[23] A number of 1960s-era spiritual utopian enclaves still exist. The cooperative Ananda Community (now called Ananda Village) was established in 1969 to follow the teachings of the Indian Yogi Paramhansa Yogananda. Yogananda had come to the United States in 1920 and established the Self-Realization Fellowship that year. In 1925, he established a center for the Fellowship in Los Angeles, California. In 1957, the center hosted the first US appearance of musician Ravi Shankar, a sitar player who greatly inspired both Alice and John Coltrane; they named their son after him. In the 1960s, Westerners began to follow yoga precepts with varying levels of commitment. The Self-Realization Fellowship is still thriving. With the exception of Yogananda, most Gurus, like the founder of Transcendental Meditation Maharishi Mahesh Yogi, came to the West in the 1960s.

Many black artists, activists, and musicians looked to Eastern spiritual philosophies and practices. Black people's adoption of Eastern religion, music, and philosophy had a genealogy and resonance that both converged and diverged from first-world motivations. As with the work of W. E. B. Du Bois, there is a black radical tradition of identifying with the anticolonial struggle in India. In the 1930s, such religious figures as Howard Thurman brought Eastern principles to black cultural attention, partly supplementing and partly replacing a deep Christian tradition. In the 1950s and 1960s, the pacifist-activist Bayard Rustin brought the principles of nonviolent confrontation practiced by Mahatma Gandhi to the attention of rights activists. Reverend Martin Luther King Jr. based his call for nonviolent direct action on Gandhi's teachings. Conscious connections made along political lines led to broader cultural forms of identification. For black Americans, anticolonial struggles and independence movements across Africa and Asia led to a more radical awareness of a history that extended before and beyond the history of black enslavement and cultural deracination.

John and Alice Coltrane were not the only jazz musicians to find spiritual and musical inspiration in Indian and other non-Christian and Eastern religious beliefs. Eastern religion allowed for forms of spiritual syncretism that superseded the dominating force of the Christian church. Black consciousness no longer had to be understood as limited to a history of slavery and European indoctrination; a collective sense of self was no longer lost in the irrevocable break of the Middle Passage. The black self was freed to explore and ally with established sets of beliefs and traditions outside a Western episteme. Alice's adoption of Eastern ideas, while not explicitly political, was therefore radical in its politics. Hindu religion furnished the backbone of Alice's syncretic musical and spiritual practice, but she supplemented it with African American musical and spiritual culture. Her approach invokes a kind of universalism that allows for particularity.

Austerities

Alice's devotion was more than a passing fashion, shallow gesture, or form of therapy. Alice's commitment was whole-hearted and encompassing, and at the center of her belief was the principle of devotion. Devotion required a complete surrender of the self to the will of the Divine Spirit. As with Rebecca Cox Jackson, this surrender was not always a peaceful process. The acts required to prove devotion were often physically debilitating.

In her writings Alice takes care to explain that her call to spiritual duty began with exercises of devotional endurance that involved extreme forms of physical pain, torture, and suffering, and she wrote about them with emphasis. The often bloody "austerities" she was called to perform feature prominently in *Monument Eternal*, published in 1977, a short autobiographical account of her spiritual revelations and experiences in this lifetime as a being with extraordinary powers (written at the Lord's request). "For more than 600 million years of human life the Supreme Lord has gently instructed me on the ways of tapas," Alice writes. But these instructions are anything but gentle. Her trials of suffering also appear in the first volume of *Endless Wisdom*, written in 1979, scriptural verses communicated directly to her by the Lord.

In the context of the ascetic traditions of both Hinduism and Christianity, Alice's tests functioned in three primary ways: as proof of love of God, as acts of purification, and ultimately as processes facilitating complete spiritual transformation. In *Endless Wisdom* Alice relays the Lord's instructions. "Forasmuch as you have underwent ages of tapasya with devotion, resolution, and austere fortitude," Alice records, "I have assayed the capacity of your tapasya by subjecting you to all manner of sufferings, torturement, self effacement, rejection, and opposition. . . . Your tapasya was then in the ancient days and is now, a living testament to your steadfast faith and trust in Me, and your willingness to serve others" (EW 1, 43). Alice's God demands her blood and flesh, a vicious process of separation from her earthly manifestation. Perhaps this reflects her ambivalence about being caught in a human body, a belief in the body as the lower region driven by desires and needs, distracting from the higher possibilities of the spirit. For Alice, freedom meant to be loosed from the human body, and converted back into a material world of elements. Passing through the stages of deepening awareness, a state of "absolute formlessness" was the ultimate destination. "When engaged in devotional service," Alice writes, the being exists in "an indescribable state of manifest formlessness which can function in and beyond the smallest atom" (ME, 37– 38). This state of formlessness is a refuge for Alice, a liberation not from materiality but from the confines of human existence.

Like Rebecca Cox Jackson's, Alice's spiritual world is quite bloody. The tests of endurance are particularly severe forms of preparatory training, followed by an elevated state of consciousness and the ability to move between various cosmic dimensions. The series of tests following John's death began with tests of deprivation, in which Alice was called to stop sleeping or eating. These were followed by tests of fleshly mortification. Often Alice describes these sufferings as if they were absent of any personal agency, as if they happened of their own accord. She describes a particularly gruesome experience. "During an excruciating test to withstand heat, my right hand succumbed to a third-degree burn. After watching the flesh fall away and the nails turn black from the intense heat, it was all I could do to wrap the remaining flesh in a linen cloth to keep it in place" (ME, 18). In some instances, the forms of self-sacrifice have a distinctly Christian reference. "Whenever metals were introduced into a test, more often than not they entered my body," she writes. "Marked from head to toe, the greater part of my body resembled the stigmata of a crucified person—blood issued from almost every part of it" (ME, 19). Alice reports becoming severely emaciated and remembers her family's concern for her "mental and physical health" (ME, 24). Alice was hospitalized for ten days; she refused to take medication and instead received the "healing life breath of the Lord" (ME, 30).

Tapas were processes of purification and transformation. "The mental and physical territories had to undergo a purificatory spiritualization to bring about the expansion and heightening of my consciousness-awareness level," she writes in *Monument Eternal*. "A human who is going through the austerity aspects of the spiritual revelation must be able to withstand the effects of purification, which is analogous to the processes and the results of empirical chemistry performed by the alchemist who transmutes base metal in to gold" (ME, 13). The body is base but transmutable through processes of deep separation from its demands and limitations.

Most of the tests that Alice describes in *Monument* are like medieval tortures, and the psychic phenomena she experiences as part of her tests read like nineteenth-century Spiritualist accounts of life in the netherworlds. She writes, "The physical tests continued for several weeks, finally yielding to the mental ones . . . which began with radiations directed upon the mind: Such things as electronic elementals, cosmic sounds, astral explosions, intrafractory rays, oceanic and abyssal waves, astral earthquakes, subterranean shocks, and etheric sirens were brought to bear upon it. There were meetings and confrontations with both disembodied souls and phantasmagoric entities with astral deformations" (ME, 20). Alice enters a hallucinatory state that opens up on planes of perception and existence beyond the human realm. While uncomfortable with the biological body, there is freedom when loosed into the cosmic and elemental worlds; there is still an association with the materiality of the universe. Alice relates that her sufferings led to a profound freedom. "The results of this practice promotes one to a high level of mental preparedness," she writes. "For example, you become readily adaptable to all types of change, or conditions, ready to chart a new or alternate course; altered to encoding and decoding techniques; ready to abandon traditions, prepared to sever any attachments, prepared to discard, or renounce everything" (ME, 25). Like Jackson, following her extensive sufferings Alice is gifted with a suppleness of spirit and is ready to "chart an alternate course." Now proven in her devotion, Alice has a direct line of communication with God. She has earned a unique and exalted relationship with the Supreme Lord.

Alice's God is a vengeful God, and the version of austerities in *Endless Wisdom* read with Old Testament fire and fury. Rather than purification, the "torturements" are a bloody purging of sin. Rather than endurance, the model here is sacrifice, and the body is fundamentally sinful and weak. "By virtue of sacrifice, and through my mercy, the fetters of [one's] sins will be cut, and the evil that binds one to the ways of the world shall be rent asunder" (EW, 111). All manner of sin needs to be burned out of the flesh. "Sacrifice is the divine conflagration that shall burn all manner of treachery, wickedness and sloth in one's life to a cinder," God dictates (EW, 113). God, in *Endless Wisdom*, calls for chastity and moral discipline. The long list of commandments Alice relates in *Endless Wisdom* echoes Leviticus. One must avoid "evil engagements in lewd revelment," for if not restrained, the senses will "cast him down into the ire of moral decay and ruin" (EW, 52, 54). Surprisingly, Alice draws a moral division between sacred and profane forms of music, a distinction traditionally made within African American Christian culture. Music, she proclaims, must be sacred, for "the vibrational force that unsacred music sets forth troubles the minds of children insomuch that it causes them to behave in divers, unspiritual, disorderly ways. Albeit, the vibrational force that sacred, devotional music sends forth, can unto one bestow, equipoise, quietude, and peace of mind" (EW, 67). This is a strange differentiation and commandment for God to give to a musician of such breadth of talent and skill.

The God in *Endless* is a cruel and punishing God. The punishments for transgressions include "the hundreds of thousands of purgatorial regions" described in graphic detail in a chapter titled "Divine Law." Those who have brought "grievous suffering" to another "shall be cast down in a vermin-ridden gutter" (EW, 94). Those that "disfigure or mutilate the limbs of another . . . shall see their parts and members divided limb from limb" without relief (EW, 94). "They that rob the righteous, the blind or the poor man . . . shall be scorched within the pressure of burning tongs" (EW, 95). Those that lie will be "cast down from a mountain peak onto . . . a sea of glass that shall rent them asunder" and "those that . . . torment refugees . . . cinctured in chains and placed upon a gridiron" (EW, 95). Alice channels instructions for a horrific list of tortures: "Those that shall foolishly think themselves gods . . . shall . . . be . . . cast into a river of fire and brimstone" (EW, 96). This vengeful God is no less scolding in the second volume of *Endless Wisdom*.

Alice's spiritual world was one of conflict and turmoil. We can experience this intensity and violence in Alice's cosmology on her album *Universal Consciousness*, released in 1971 after she returned from her first visit to India. Alice switched from harp and piano to a much more commanding Wurlitzer electric organ, which replicated the drone sound of the Indian oud. This album was welcomed by establishment jazz critics. It is muscular, strident, and focused on the solo performer. *Universal Consciousness* is epic in its musical breadth; it is orchestral. But it is full of dissonance. Using free form, Alice produced an album that is improvisational, experimental, and marked by clashing symbols and shattering strings. Universal consciousness is not reached peacefully nor maintained easily. Alice's play on the Wurlitzer, especially on the tracks "Universal Consciousness" and "Battle at Armageddon," is fierce, often dissonant and unrelenting: "The Great spiritual battle takes place within the nethermost regions of the human soul, literally, every day. The conflagrations of the satanic forces of evil wax strong until the day when the God-spirit within one's heart deals the final death blow which annihilates his enemy (ego), burns the raging flames of sins to ashes, and purifies one's lower nature" (FB, 81). The music on *Universal* evokes an epic internal conflict between higher and lower self, God and Satan, good and evil.

Alice/Turiya's second volume of *Endless Wisdom*, not published until 1998, does offer bloom-filled passages of blessed peace and sacredness in which "fountains of heavenly elixir and the coffers of divine opulences shall be accessible to all."[24] The worlds that open up for the spiritually devoted and disciplined are ultimately full of beauty and peace. Yet this peace is never described as a Christian heaven. Like Rebecca Cox Jackson's, instead of angels Alice's visions are full of entities and abstract phenomena.

Astral Travel and Other Powers

For her travels, the Supreme Lord provides Alice with a map of the universe. The Lord shows her paths of light—"Aeroastropaths"—on which she could travel to "all *lokas* in the universe" (EW, 44). Untethered from epistemic obligations, Alice is able to travel astrally to and from alternate realities. With her powers, Alice encounters astral beings and other nonhuman entities and travels to eras before life emerged on Earth. Life and death become immaterial as her spiritual devotion and abilities extend beyond her one lifetime. Alice is able to travel through time and space into other dimensions. "When looking through the spiritual eye, or the third eye encased in the human mind," she explains, "one can see vividly beyond the ken of human eyesight, beyond the material atom, and into the future, thereby transcending the limitations of time and space" (ME, 27). Alice is able to completely disengage from the idea of perceived reality and its priorities and assumed parameters.

Although the spiritually chosen and enlightened can see beyond the atom, there is a material substrate in Alice's belief system, a curious mixture of the elements and psychic activity. Mind-substance is the basis for the organization of self, but Alice conceives of selfhood as porous, responsive to the infinite absolute in which all matter and energy swirl. Selfhood forms, through the mind and through thought, in temporary moments. She writes, "There is an infinite storehouse of mind-substance, where atoms of thought-materials exist in a fragmentary form. . . . When you are inspired with a thought, the particles of mind-cells formulate, and conception—the basis for all thoughts—begins" (ME, 45–46). The dynamic strength of thought formation can take on a materiality. Modes of being form where the material and the immaterial mix. In an enlightened state, Alice transits into what she calls an astral body. In this porous body, Alice travels the waves of thought particles across dimensions. Thought, the activity of molecules and atoms, is the basis for the ability to travel rapidly across great distances. "If an astral body thinks of traveling to a city in the East, or elsewhere, the astral body can reach the destination as fast as it takes to think the thought" (ME, 46). Alice's means of travel are "spirit levitation, or invisible transfer" (ME, 45). She writes, "I was astrally projected from the physical body very frequently, practically every day, and permitted to travel from plane to plane." She does so in different bodily emanations. She describes passing through several stages of psychophysical manifestation. "I was . . . projected into a subtler third-stage etheric body, which is [a] bluish-white or silvery ectoplasmic apparition," she writes. She then enters "into a fourth stage causal body, transparent and circular in form" (ME, 20). The last stage is "Absolute Manifest Formlessness," one of "pure consciousness" (ME, 20). In her conception of this phase, Alice draws on Hindu beliefs but mixes them with her particularly severe version of the Christian God. This stage of consciousness is one of access to the "Absolute Sovereignty of the Lord" (ME, 20). The contrasts here are stark—between a subtle, gentle state of commune with the elements of the universe and a demand for strict obedience to an authoritarian God.

Even as she wrote of fire and brimstone, Alice's music became increasingly peace-filled and serene. Her album *Rhada-Krsna Nama Sankirtana* was released in 1977, the year after she was called to become Turiyasangitananda. Alice returns to the harp and piano and plays the organ as well, and the album is filled with the distinct voices of the members of her congregation, singing the gospel in Sanskrit; it is the first album to feature their chants. "Rhada Krsna" is notable for its simplicity of melody and its joyousness where gospel and bhajan meet. The track "Govinda Jai" has a simple melody with no vocal harmonies. This song, or chant, is kept to rhythm by hand clapping on the second beat. A polyrhythmic element gives the track a distinct danceability. But what is particularly notable is the lack of vocal virtuosity. Alice's voice is forefronted only slightly. The aim was to focus on the humility of devotion and the collective nature of worship rather than individual greatness. On "Ganesha," Alice's harp introduces a quiet coolness as she improvises on top of a gentle four-note melody played on a tamboura by her sixteen-year-old daughter, Sita (Michelle) Coltrane, who was born in Paris in 1960 to Alice and her first husband, scat singer Kenny "Pancho" Hagood. "Prema Muditha" features Alice on her new Fender Rhodes, again repeating a deceptively simple melody. The voices of the congregation enter with a tambourine and simple harmonies. On the track "Om Nama Sivaya," Alice plays her Wurlitzer, while her twelve-year-old son Arjun John Coltrane Jr., born in 1964, plays drums. Here she is using the Wurlitzer to create an environment for participation, engaging with the instrument in an entirely different way than she did on *Universal Consciousness*.

Her next albums, *Transcendence* and *Transfiguration*, are even more committed to the sound of spiritual serenity. Alice's voice continues to refuse virtuosity, stressing sound as coming from a communal source. The music seems turned inward, tuned into a spiritual world rather than an audience. As we hear on *Transfiguration*, Alice remains a jazz musician. But after the founding of her ashram, Alice turned to music solely as part of worship. She produced three cassettes, *Divine Songs* (1987), *Infinite Chants* (1990), and *Glorious Chants* (1995), released by the ashram's publishing unit, Avatar Book

Institute. In 2018, selections from these cassettes were remastered and issued by Luaka Bop as *The Ecstatic Music of Alice Coltrane/Turiyasangitananda*.

Although she turned to her harp, the piano, and a Fender Rhodes, Alice kept a relationship with her Wurlitzer. While her son, Ravi Coltrane, and daughter, Michelle Coltrane, followed in her footsteps as jazz musicians, her great-nephew Steven Ellison continues her legacy in a post-Wurlitzer spirit, making computer-generated music. "I'm of the Nintendo generation. . . . I'm used to hearing bleeps. It's a comforting sound to some people," he says.[25] Under the name Flying Lotus, he creates a music that is generous in its warmth and breadth, referencing jazz, funk, hip-hop, and dance music in his compositions. Ellison makes direct reference to his aunt on a number of tracks. "More than a musical mentor she was my spiritual advisor," he says.[26] On his first album, *Los Angeles* (2008), his track "Auntie's Harp" layers multiple sounds including bells, drums, birdcalls, and chimes on the top of the strings of a harp. A 2010 remix makes a much more explicit reference to her music, as it mixes the sounds of sitar, harp, *oud*, and a soft drone, loosely incorporating the original melody. "Auntie's Lock/Infinitum" weaves serene women's voices chanting OM with electronic bass tones and a blurry, soft static mixed with the sound of rainfall. Flying Lotus continually references his aunt's astral travels on his albums. On *Cosmogramma* (2010) his tracks include "Zodiac Sh***t" and "Do the Astral Plane." While ultimately private and solitary in its making, Flying Lotus's music is deeply dialogic and intertextual, weaving multiple sources and voices together.

Flying Lotus remembers growing up visiting the ashram. "Alice Coltrane was my aunt. To me she was Auntie," he says:

> I remember the ashram as kind of a journey. You were going to a magical place. It had that feel to it. You were going there on a magical Sunday. As soon as you arrive it's just so quiet. There's all these people dressed up in white, there's a little [recording inaudible] that everyone would go into, and all be seated there on these little pillows, all these little instruments everywhere, all different races; I really liked seeing that as a kid. I was, "Oh, wow, there's just everyone getting down, everyone would come in with such a positive energy. It had that feel to it: this is the real-deal spiritual place. Auntie would come out, say some really inspiring words, and then she would start playing music. Everyone else would join in. They might go two, three, four hours of doing that, then everyone would leave. Wow. As a child going to the ashram was deep. The music was always crazy. Being encouraged to join in the circle of music

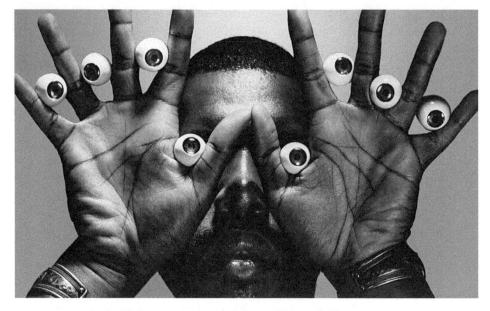

**Figure 2.5** Alice Coltrane's grand-nephew Steven Ellison, aka Flying Lotus.

happening—that was a very cool experience to have. Be surrounded by all these people who were supporting you, picking up some instruments, singing some stuff. All these people you'd be around so long. *Oh man, he's funky. . . . You didn't see it coming she can sing like that, wow.* She'd always say that the voice is the most powerful instrument. And the importance of playing every note. Using the whole instrument for everything that it has. Which can be applied to everything creative. Use everything. Have an understanding of the tools and when to use them.[27]

The phenomenon of the universe is material in Alice Coltrane's worship and music; sound is the energy of creation. Yet Alice resisted manifestation in biological earthly existence; that existence, for her, may have been partly a tool, but it was limiting and to be transcended. Alice's universal God Consciousness challenges Western notions of consciousness as simply confined to the mechanics of the brain. Consciousness becomes an infinity, an ineffable dimension or level of existence beyond what is considered human. But Alice Coltrane's contribution also includes the concrete: the creation of community. Like Rebecca Cox Jackson's Shaker community, Alice's model could be considered escapist. But escape is an important trope in African American culture, one that insists on an interiority, an inward and infinite expanse of potentiality.

# PART II
# EVOLUTION

# OUR PLACE IS AMONG THE STARS

## 3

Octavia E. Butler and the Preservation of Species

Using black speculation as method allows us to roam a landscape of black creativity. According to this method, a genealogy of black women mystics could include not only historical but fictional figures. Lauren Olamina, the protagonist of Octavia E. Butler's novels *Parable of the Sower* and *Parable of the Talents*, is a literary evocation of the itinerant black women preachers as well as of musician Alice Coltrane. Alice's astral travel and Olamina's exodus North with her community and her dream of the stars allow us to think further about utopian possibilities for black existence. But considering these women's alternate worlds advances questions of what we mean when we talk of being human—and of just what discomfort and anxiety such a perceived condition holds for black beings. Alice/Turiyasangitananda and Rebecca Cox

Jackson felt a profound ambivalence about being in human form. Olamina has a fear of letting that form go.

Behind Olamina is her author, Octavia E. Butler, and this chapter is also concerned with her complex author's vision as explored through the *Parable* novels and related files in her archive at the Huntington Library in Pasadena, California. A black woman in the white male world of science fiction, Butler has been enthusiastically embraced by a popular audience as well as by specialized academics. Her work has inspired conversations about gender, feminism, nonnormative sexuality, and biological phenomena. My turn to Butler, particularly after the opening of her archival collection at the Huntington Library in Pasadena, California, is part of a move to recognize the author in the world of arts and letters. But one of my aims is to avoid the hagiographic tendencies of such celebration. I think it is an act of respect to acknowledge the complexities and contradictions in her work.

Butler's fiction moves the conversation into the realm of the biological. The biological exists as the medium through which Butler explores complex relationships of power and ethical ambiguity. Biology is the mechanism by which she troubles the lines between love and hate, rape and ecstasy, freedom and bondage. Butler's works are dominated by a particularly grim version of Darwinism at the same time as they consider biological forms of cooperation, symbiosis, and commensality. Butler's narrative signature is the way her texts force these divergent forms of survival together. The result is an unrelenting tension between consent and coercion, compulsion, and repulsion.

In Butler's novels we are forced to ask questions about which behaviors we assume are inherent to the human species and what the species would do in conditions of crisis and devastation. In the *Parable* novels, utopia lives in the glimmers of hope that humans could foster ways of living together based in cooperative, nonhierarchical forms of community. But these are only glimmers.

Apocalypse Now

One morning in 2027, eighteen-year-old Lauren Olamina sets out along a Southern California highway. She leaves behind a destroyed community, once a carefully gated neighborhood in a suburb of Los Angeles, decimated the night before, her neighbors and family raped and murdered and their houses burned to the ground. Olamina had long anticipated the destruction of her community, as hers is an apocalyptic era: privatization, a crumbling economy, and manmade climatic disaster have led to widespread scarcity, disease, and starvation. Olamina is not alone as she hits the road; she is traveling with two other survivors of her community. Olamina and her fellow survivors "join a broad river of people walking west on the freeway" to reach Highway 101 and head north, in hope of jobs, water, food, and safe places to live (PS, 176).

Olamina is guided by spiritual conviction. She is the daughter of a pastor, but she comes to discover a sense of God very different than her father's. Rather than belief in a supreme being, to be worshipped through rapture, Olamina's conception of God is based in a cool intellectual awareness that there is no larger presence outside of material phenomena, that the basic principle of the universe is change, and that God is nothing more and nothing less than the processes of change itself. According to Olamina's vision, the ultimate aim of human existence is not to leave the body and reach a heaven or join an absolute consciousness but to achieve species immortality by taking biological life from Earth into extrasolar space. The goal of Olamina's religious dedication is to "pry [people] loose from a rotting world" and replant them on other planets (PS, 79). She calls this belief system Earthseed.

People join Olamina and her companions as they walk along Highway 101, mostly for protection. Olamina only gradually introduces them to Earthseed, first through her collection of verses and then in conversation. Some stay with the group purely for survival. Others begin to believe. By the time they reach their destination, a small plot of land in Northern California, Olamina has gathered thirteen people in all: five women, four men, and four children—mostly people of color. Once the group arrives, the travelers give their utopian community the name Acorn. In *Parable of the Talents*, Acorn blossoms into a community of more than sixty people who more or less follow Olamina's creed. To stay alive, the people of Acorn learn to work together cooperatively. They learn which plants are edible, how to dig wells and build houses, and how to match individual abilities to suitable tasks. They learn to use what they have: for a protective fence, they construct a border of spiked aloe vera and agave plants.

A utopian community seems for a moment to have been realized. But Acorn's walls of spiked succulents prove no defense against encroaching armies of enslavers and violent Christian fundamentalists, and the community is destroyed. Olamina's grim determination remains one of fulfilling a (manifest) Destiny of human extraterrestrial colonization.

The *Parable* novels have also struck a chord as the narrative's descriptions of a near future (the narrative opens in 2024) have proven ominously prescient. The United States they envision is eerily close in its particulars to the

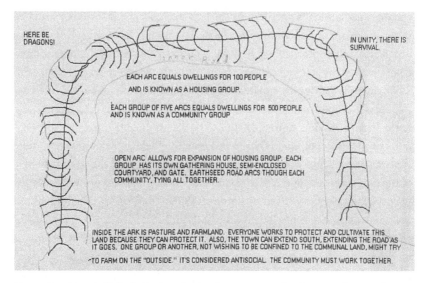

The figure contains the following labels:

HERE BE DRAGONS!

IN UNITY, THERE IS SURVIVAL.

EACH ARC EQUALS DWELLINGS FOR 100 PEOPLE AND IS KNOWN AS A HOUSING GROUP.

EACH GROUP OF FIVE ARCS EQUALS DWELLINGS FOR 500 PEOPLE AND IS KNOWN AS A COMMUNITY GROUP

OPEN ARC ALLOWS FOR EXPANSION OF HOUSING GROUP. EACH GROUP HAS ITS OWN GATHERING HOUSE, SEMI-ENCLOSED COURTYARD, AND GATE. EARTHSEED ROAD ARCS THOUGH EACH COMMUNITY, TYING ALL TOGETHER.

INSIDE THE ARK IS PASTURE AND FARMLAND. EVERYONE WORKS TO PROTECT AND CULTIVATE THIS LAND BECAUSE THEY CAN PROTECT IT. ALSO, THE TOWN CAN EXTEND SOUTH, EXTENDING THE ROAD AS IT GOES. ONE GROUP OR ANOTHER, NOT WISHING TO BE CONFINED TO THE COMMUNAL LAND, MIGHT TRY TO FARM ON THE "OUTSIDE." IT'S CONSIDERED ANTISOCIAL. THE COMMUNITY MUST WORK TOGETHER.

**Figure 3.1** Octavia E. Butler's plans for the Acorn community. Courtesy Octavia E. Butler Collection, Huntington Library, Pasadena, CA.

United States around the projected timeline in which the novels take place. Andrew Steele Jarrett, an authoritarian, populist president elected in the narrative, mirrors Donald J. Trump, an equally populist aspiring autocrat elected in the United States in 2016 by appealing to an extreme right wing comprised of armed white supremacists and fundamentalist Christians. In fact, Jarrett and Trump share the same election slogan, "Make America Great Again!" The incarceration of migrant children from Central and South America, separated from their parents and placed in caged facilities at the US border with Mexico, echoes the establishment of "reeducation camps" in *Parable of the Talents*. The parallels abound.

Butler opens *Talents* with an all-too-believable context:

> The period of upheaval the journalists have begun to refer to as "The Apocalypse" or more commonly . . . "the Pox" lasted from 2015 through 2030. . . . This is untrue. The Pox has been a much longer torment. It began well before 2015, perhaps even before the turn of the millennium. It has not ended. I have . . . read that the Pox was caused by accidentally coinciding climatic, economic, and sociological crises. . . . I have watched as convenience, profit, and inertia excused greater and more dangerous environmental degradation. I have watched poverty, hunger, and disease become inevitable for more and more people. (PT, 14)

What is described in the *Parable* series captures our current moment of apocalypse almost exactly, as ours is an era of rising authoritarianism, pandemic disease, a new period of mass extinction, and massive socioeconomic suffering.

But apocalypse holds awful promise; times of crisis open up possibility. A crisis could mean a total paradigmatic break, and imagining such a break is an opportunity for expansive speculation. What kinds of change does this apocalyptic moment harbinger? What could happen if we were loosed from structurally and institutionally enforced forms of relation? Which ways of living, now subordinated and suppressed, would we be able to develop? What could we create in the time of the New?

Artists and musicians have crafted works that respond to Butler's novels. In 2017 the musician Toshi Reagon developed a beautifully choreographed and scored musical theatre piece, "Octavia E. Butler's *Parable of the Sower*," that emphasized the criticality of collectivity and cooperation. In 2019, performance artists Alexandro Segade and Malik Gaines produced an opera that imagined possible developments following the settlement of the *Parable* novels' astral travelers on the extrasolar planet. I end this chapter with their opera, "Star Choir: Founding, Dissolution and Reconstitution of the Colonies on planet 85K: Aurora," because of its alternative vision of astral migration and species interrelations. My agenda for reading Butler in this way is to continue to speculate on how black people have envisioned alternate forms of beingness and how far we have been able to go in doing so.

What Is Change?

Olamina's signature verse reads:

All that you touch
You Change.
All that you Change
Changes you.
The only lasting truth
Is Change.
God is Change. (PS, 3)

This verse has inspired readers as particularly profound and liberating, as an affirmation of some kind of agency, some form of action to take outside of the frustrating constraints of state power, capitalist exploitation, and structural racism and sexism. The verse naturalizes the act of change as inevitable and driven by larger processes than we can control but that we must interact with. But what, exactly, does Olamina mean by change? What kind of change is God in the *Parable* novels? What kind of movement, and in what kind of time?

The concept of change evokes a range of possible processes and temporal schemas. We know in the *Parable* novels that although we are in some kind of more-than-scientific realm, we are not in an ecstatic temporal dimension, as we were with the black women mystics, who left the chrononormative world and tuned into an alternate frequency. Considering the centrality of the biological in Butler's fiction, the temporal propulsion would seem to be some version of evolution.

We could imagine one such model of evolution as a Bergsonian state of continual becoming. In *Creative Evolution*, Bergson embraces change as an overarching principle encompassing and linking the physical and psychical. In Bergson's temporal theory of durée, life is constant change. For a "conscious being," to exist is to change.[1] "I find first of all, that I pass from state to state. . . . I change without ceasing. . . . But this is not saying enough. Change is far more radical than we are at first inclined to suppose. . . . There is no feeling, no idea, no volition which is not undergoing change at every moment."[2] For Bergson, "we are creating ourselves continually."[3] Biological change, in this rendering, may entail a lability of life so boundless that all we assume to be inherent in it could be transformed. How wonderful! If change is continual, and is also biologically expressed, then we can speculate with wild freedom. Boundaries between species, between individuals, could dissolve, making way for entirely new modes of existence that were perhaps no longer human.

As it is, evolution does not have the survival of the human species in mind. Hannah Landecker reminds us that "many kinds of living entities have emerged and will continue to emerge," and that this may in fact mean the death of our so-called species.[4] In her celebratory reading of Darwin Elizabeth Grosz writes, "Variations are crucial for the breadth, density and longevity of species, but these variations are the very mechanism by which differences in kind are born and species disappear."[5] If change is the principle of life, as Olamina believes, then what is to stop humans from evolving out of existence?

But in the *Parable* novels we encounter a humanist impasse. The idea of continual change exists in profound tension with Butler's belief, or at least as she wrote in her journals, that there are biologically determined instincts, drives, and behaviors endemic to the human species, and that these fundamentally heterosexual and hierarchical traits govern human potentiality. The hope for liberating change clashes with a biological essentialism found across Butler's work.

In most of Butler's novels, survival—the drive to "prevail" as Olamina writes in her verses—is a central instinct. (PS, 222; PT, 163) This includes a biologically dictated drive to reproduce. In the *Parable* books, Butler naturalizes possessive individualism in her particularly stern interpretation of Darwin. The human species is biologically wired to be fiercely and violently competitive. Any form of cooperation is based in self-interest. The will to dominate will thrive in chaos and often will turn into sadistic forms of cruelty. Butler's sense of humans' biological purpose—survival—and Olamina's commitment to a plan for species immortality do not fit with a Bergsonian model of constant and continual evolutionary change. Butler's biological imperatives foreclose the questions and possibilities the *Parable* novels' trope of change would seem to open up. Butler got stuck in a loop between her convictions about human nature and what radical evolution would look like as she struggled to complete the sequels to *Sower* and *Talents* she had planned. Later in this chapter I consider her plans for the first sequel, "Parable of the Trickster," as she struggled with them in her journals. Butler cannot settle on how to write about the efforts of the Earthseed colonists to terraform their new world, an extrasolar planet called Rainbow.[6]

Butler's journals describe what seems to be her personal belief in a kind of biological determinism, suggesting that her belief was not just a thought experiment. This is why the concept so fundamentally informs all of her novels. "The temptation to . . . show dominance, push the upstarts back into their 'proper place' is overwhelming when it is unacknowledged. It is in fact biological," she writes.[7] Yet she expresses hope that humans can suppress these tendencies once they are aware of them as biological. She continues in her journal, "The more we recognize the biological nature of the drive, the more ability we have to resist it."[8] What this resistance would look like is unclear, as in many of her works survival ultimately relies, at best, on forms of coerced submission and, at worst, on extreme forms of violence.

In the *Parable* novels, utopian possibility is curtailed by the human drive for "survival, position and power" (PS, 103). Humans by nature are hierarchical, biologically driven to struggle with each other for domination. One of Olamina's verses reads:

All Struggles
Are essentially power struggles.
Who will rule,

Who will lead,
Who will define,
Refine,
Confine,
Design,
Who will dominate. (PS, 94)

Butler situates this will to dominate as the drive shared by other animal species, and as humans' natural state. The world will descend into chaos without the tempering effects of a dominating leadership or some form of centralized discipline and control.

In some of Butler's notes this belief in the primacy of a drive to dominance naturalizes forms of oppression. Patriarchy remains a tenacious form of domination in her novels, with rape one of the most common forms of maintaining control. Heterosexuality and the binary system of gender among humans are biologically determined and, in her thinking, therefore naturalized. "The fact that male and female are two halves of a whole is obvious and inescapable, and yet the oppression, abuse, and denigration of women by women [sic] is a commonplace to one degree or another everywhere on Earth. Us and Them."[9] Butler does not envision other possibilities for human gender systems, and for her, male-dominated heterosexuality is fundamental to human existence.

Human species integrity and the possibility of human extinction is an obsessive theme in Butler's works. In her novels' biological explorations, the discrete boundaries around what it means to be human are compromised, and the loss of personal and species integrity causes intense anxiety.[10] This loss, so terrifying in Butler's work, involves touching and being touched. In much of *Black Utopias* permeability between people—the "melting times" spent within communities—is seen as potentially liberating, as a process that creates new ways for people to form collectivity and new forms of ethical care. Melting suggests connectivity to a wider universe and the decentering of the human in it. But for Butler, this permeability is horrifying. Touch is violating, hence the intensity of violence in the *Parable* novels. Violence is the extreme manifestation of the wider theme of "boundary violation" in Butler's work.[11] This violation of personal integrity involves encroachment upon individuals' emotional, mental, and physical cohesion. In *Clay's Ark* and in the *Xenogenesis* trilogy (*Dawn*, *Imago*, and *Adulthood Rites*), the violation of individuals' boundaries is also analogous to the violation of a species' definability as such. In the Patternist series (*Wildseed*, *Mind of My Mind*, *Clay's Ark*, *Survivor*, and

*Patternmaster*) the encroachment is mental, often violently so. In the *Parable* novels, the violation is mental and physical. As a result of her mother's use of a drug called Paracetco, Olamina is born with hyperempathy syndrome, a condition that causes her to empathize with others' physical experiences, to feel what other people feel. Sometimes this is pleasurable; most of the time, however, it is painful. Either way, this is a nonconsensual invasion of her sensual experience, a violation that challenges her individuation. In many of Butler's novels the dissolution of human integrity is involuntary; it is both violent and erotic.

Boundary violation, between individuals and between species, is often at once horrendous and compelling. Forms of interpenetration are a central fascination and obsession in Butler's works. Often these events are simultaneously repulsive and desirous. They are sites of ambiguous consent.

There is a central (im)possibility in the *Parable* novels, a hoped-for sea change in what interpenetration can mean beyond the question of coercion. Touching and being touched, malleability between the material and human worlds, are at the core of Olamina's concept of God. Yet how is it possible to step away from the troubles of the human long enough for the change to happen?

## God Is Change

God is a material force in the *Parable* novels. As Butler describes in her notes, Olamina's belief system is "odd, obvious, hardly religious at all, and yet less than wholly scientific."[12] Olamina's God does not come to her in bolts of lightning, as God does for Rebecca Cox Jackson, but gradually, as a set of rational ideas. Once at Acorn, there is no worship per se but, instead, reason and rational interchange based in shared purpose. "Gatherings" are enactments of democratic governance in which all are encouraged to speak. The presence of members called Shapers—those committed to manifesting humankind among the stars—is the only sign of religious organization. In the *Parable* world we are far from the ecstatic rituals, the melting times practiced by Jarena Lee's and Zilpha Elaw's prayer bands.

Olamina is not sanctified; she does not undergo a transformative moment in a flash of suspended time. Still, she is self-authorized and the recipient of God's word. At the age of twelve, Olamina begins compiling a collection of aphoristic verses to articulate these ideas as they come to her. As Olamina travels up the California coast, she begins to consciously use her verses to "gather students, teach" (PS, 125). She begins "fishing that river" with the aim of forming a community whose purpose will be to prepare for the ultimate journey into extrasolar space (PS, 223). Olamina claims her verses not as inspiring fictions of her own creation but as truths. One verse she calls "the right one, the true one." It is the verse "I keep coming back to," she says, and "the literal truth" (PS, 25):

God is Power—
Infinite,
Irresistible,
Inexorable,
Indifferent.
And yet, God is Pliable—
Trickster,
Teacher,
Chaos,
Clay.
God exists to be shaped.
God is Change. (PS, 25)

This verse will remain Olamina's leading verse throughout both novels as well as inspire the projected titles of Butler's never-completed sequels. The description "trickster, / teacher" is the only instance in which Olamina personifies God in her verses. Otherwise, God remains a kind of interface, both affecting, and being affected by, the material world.

God is not separate from matter, animate or inanimate; as Olamina writes, "Whether you're a human being, an insect, a microbe, or a stone," God is change (PS, 79). In Olamina's concept of God there is no separate spiritual realm apart from scientifically analyzable processes and phenomena. As Olamina's husband, Bankole, explains, "Some of the faces of her God are biological evolution, chaos theory, relativity theory, the uncertainty principle, and of course, the second law of thermodynamics" (PT, 46). For Olamina, belief is not based in blind faith but in the processes by which matter is composed and composes itself. "Change is ongoing," she tells a fellow traveler. "Everything changes in some way—size, position, composition, frequency, velocity, thinking, whatever. Every living thing, every bit of matter, all energy in the universe changes in some way" (PS, 218). The concept of change, as Olamina explains, is already present in both religious and scientific philosophies. "From the second law of thermodynamics to Darwinian evolution, from Buddhism's insistence that nothing is permanent and all suffering results from our delusions of permanence to the third chapter of Ecclesiastes . . . change is part of life, of existence, of the common wisdom. God has been here all along, shaping us and being shaped by us in no particular way or in too many ways at once like an amoeba—or like a cancer" (PS, 26). Shaping and being shaped is to touch and be touched, with inexorable effect, implying a permeability between beings and their environment.

In her notes, Butler voices a powerful critique of dichotomies by which man separates himself from his material body and environment:

> Just as we keep learning that we are not the center of the universe (even though we keep finding ways to reassure ourselves that we are just that) we keep learning that the dichotomies that become important to us are false. Mind and body for instance. Consider how a small chemical change or neurological disconnection or misconnect [sic] can radically change the "mind". . . . There's the appalling "man and nature." As if humanity could stand apart from nature. That makes as much sense as one of a man's arms trying to distinguish itself from the rest of the man's body and seek its fate with only the most superficial and effemeral [sic] consideration for the rest of the body.[13]

This would seem a promising philosophy, reflecting the best of what a materialist approach has to offer. But the material world of the *Parable* novels is understood through heteronormative metaphors of biological reproduction, and temporalities are organized around the common and individualist idea of what an organic life cycle is. According to Olamina's "God-is-change belief system," named while she is weeding in the garden, humans are seeds from earth, with a "Destiny . . . to take root among the stars" (PS, 76, 84). Earth is rendered a "dying place" (PT, 78).

The concept of shaping God, of changing the universe, is ultimately defined by the biological imperative of reproduction. "We are Earthlife maturing, Earthlife preparing to fall away from the parent world. We are Earthlife preparing to take root in new ground, Earthlife fulfilling its purpose, its promise, its Destiny" (PS, 151). Olamina's concept of Destiny is based in fulfilling the cycle of life, on understanding a species as also having a life cycle. However, if this is the case, then what of the phase of death? At some point Olamina's vision is conflictual. A species cannot fulfill its evolutionary destiny to keep changing and adapting and preserve itself at the same time. The very concept of a Destiny is at odds with Olamina's principal tenet: that life is unceasing change. Change, as per Olamina's verse, implies an infinite malleability, contingent on infinite variables of indeterminate ends (as Bergson would say) or, more accurately, on no ends at all.

The ultimate aim of Destiny, then, is to not to fulfill the cycle, although Olamina uses the metaphor. There is a central tension between Olamina's repeated insistence that "we must prevail" (lest humans become, as she repeatedly warns, "smooth-skinned dinosaurs") and the call to unceasing change (which would eventually evolve humans into what could be called another species or into another existence unrecognizable to us from here) (PS, 222, PT, 163). Olamina's plan for how to shape God aims to "[offer] . . . a kind of species adulthood and species immortality" (PT, 144). Bankole succinctly sums up her vision: "Earthseed is Olamina's contribution to what she feels should be a species-wide effort to evade, or at least to lengthen the specialize-grow-die evolutionary cycle that humanity faces, that every species faces" (PT, 48). He quotes Olamina: "We can be a long-term success and the parents, ourselves, of a vast array of new peoples, new species," she says, "or we can be just one more abortion. We can, we must, scatter the Earth's living essence—human, plant, and animal to extrasolar worlds" (PT, 48). It is unclear whether Olamina's vision of "new peoples" and "new species" implies discrete life forms genetically manufactured by humans themselves or the evolution of the human species into new forms of life. Both raise a host of questions and exciting possibilities. What would humans be capable of creating, and how? Or, if evolving, what would humans look like as they adapted to new environments? Where does species individuation end, and how do we define a discrete species in the first place?

Change or Prevail

At a certain point, changing and prevailing cannot coexist. Adaptation is a conundrum in the *Parable* novels. We must adapt to survive, but species are never stable over time if they successfully adapt. If God is change, then species survival is not possible. Thinking widely, then, the evolution of the human species spells its own demise. If species survival is the ultimate aim, then Olamina's concept of change does not stretch this far as it does not reach beyond the preservation of the species.

Despite the materialist tendency in her concept of God, Olamina's vision is deeply humanist. The overall principle of change affects life forms as it does the inanimate, but humans are assigned stewardship of the Earth. "We are flesh—self aware, questing, problem solving flesh. We are that aspect of Earthlife best able to shape God knowingly," reads a verse (PS, 151). Humans will be responsible for the survival of other earthly life forms as they are taken as the most evolved species, the one most capable of conducting change.

Olamina upholds the fundamental humanist claim that humans are the preeminent and most evolved species among what she calls "Earthlife." In Butler's texts it is intelligence that separates humans from other species. In order to avoid becoming smooth-skinned dinosaurs, humans must combine the evolutionary need for adaptation with this intelligence. Olamina writes, "Intelligence is ongoing, individual adaptability. Adaptations that an intelligent species may make in a single generation, other species make over many generations of selective breeding and selective dying" (PS, 29). Unlike other animals, so it goes, humans are capable of shaping their own adaptation and evolution. Olamina's idea of adaptability here has little to do with Darwin's theory of natural selection. Natural selection is the gradual change in an organism's biological makeup, which depends on endless variation, on the accidental and the unexpected. Olamina's idea actually resonates with the Lamarckian concept that acquired characteristics can be inherited. The trajectory of her ideas leads to the concept of eugenics, of artificial selection and intentional breeding for certain traits. But, surprisingly, the novels do not include much thought of biological manipulation or social engineering as part of a utopian urge.

The belief in humans' preeminent intelligence is a transhumanist one. In 1957 the biologist Julian Huxley coined the term *transhumanism*, excited over the future possibilities for new types of existence and as part of his bioreligious philosophy (TRANS, 13). But for Huxley as for his friend the paleontologist and priest Pierre Teilhard de Chardin, all change would aid and accompany a higher stage in human evolution. It was through conscious control of his own evolution that mankind would become a "new type of organism, whose destiny it is to realize new possibilities for evolving life on this planet."[14] Just how much of the humanoid form these new organisms would maintain is ambiguous. For Chardin, "man will have so far transcended himself as to demand some new appellation."[15] But for Huxley this being would transcend itself only through perfecting its human potential and would remain organized around a perfected quality of "humanness." Transhumanism is based on "man remaining man, but transcending himself, by realizing new possibilities of and for his human nature" (TRANS, 17).

In Huxley's ultimate formulation of evolution, the universe is of one fabric, but "Man" is the most evolved life form on earth. As Man has evolved, he has developed a "cosmic self-awareness" (TRANS, 13) and has a solemn cosmic duty; mankind has the "responsibility and destiny—to be an agent for the rest of the world," and "he is in point of fact determining the future direction of evolution on this earth" (TRANS, 14). Man has developed only a miniscule amount of his latent ability, and "the human race, in fact, is surrounded by a large area of unrealized possibilities, a challenge to the spirit of exploration" (TRANS, 15).

Huxley's ideas of evolution were not limited to a Darwinian theory of natural selection. As Huxley puts it, Darwin did give us the knowledge that "we were made of the same energy as the rest of the cosmos," and Man was linked by "genetic continuity with all the other living inhabitants of his planet . . . [which were] all parts of one single branching and evolving flow of metabolizing protoplasm."[16] But, as the most evolved life form on the planet, Man was different. Man could exert "*conscious control of evolution*," instead of leaving it to "the previous mechanism of . . . blind chance [my italics]."[17] As Huxley saw it, humans could improve and elevate themselves to a higher state of being, becoming superhuman.

This higher state of being was accessible only through improving the physical, intellectual, and moral capacities of the human species. In the introduction to his *Essays of a Biologist* Huxley writes, "The possibilities of physiological improvement . . . is no utopian silliness, but is bound to come about if science continues her current progress."[18] According to Huxley and many of his contemporaries, including his brother Aldous Huxley, the most effective way to improve humankind was through eugenics; like Aldous, Julian Huxley was a lifelong eugenicist.

Actual eugenics is all but avoided in Butler's vision of species perpetuation in her *Parable* novels, for she is suspicious of its ethical and political ramifications. Butler does begin to speculate on the use of biological manipulations in human social formation on Rainbow, or Bow, the name given to the settlement planet in her notes for "Trickster." The possibilities in such manipulation is part of her main interest in how humans would adapt to their new environment. "The people who travel to other worlds must use molecular biology to enable themselves to adapt to the new world and adapt the world to them," she writes.[19] But humans are rendered as inherently conservative, fearing—not embracing—change. "Those who are visibly different will suffer most;" humans who appear the most "normal and human will be the upper crust."[20] Yet Butler does speculate on human-originated biological change:

CONSIDER: What is "normal" will change slowly without most people noticing it. For instance, the number of fingers and toes might change and seem too small a thing to bother about except for purists who are foolishly un-Earthseed. But a small visible change may be a marker for something else—a greater sense of smell, or none at all. Agility that is unusual, longings and obsessions that are unusual, you name it. The children who are different will have differences that may not be defects as a result of mistakes.[21]

Butler does not spend much time, however, considering biological manipulation. She is mostly concerned with what humans would do when faced with a cruel environment and with the effects of indigenous microorganisms on humans. Blindness and hallucinatory states are her two main ideas about how such microorganisms would impact humans.

There would also be a natural culling based in people's ability to adapt. In Butler's final speculation on life on Bow, before she abandons the "Trickster" project altogether, humans must learn to live with the effects of extraterrestrial microbes, which cause humans to suffer particularly powerful hallucinations. "Those who cannot find accommodation with the hallucinations will die. . . . Those who learn to go slow, help one another, always work together, who accommodate rather than fight or deny, who begin to understand the essential changes, they will live," she writes.[22] Here we have a glimmer, found every so often in her thoughts, of the possibility that humans could learn to foster cooperative forms of relationality but, ultimately, only as a means to survive.

For the most part, Butler's speculations on the effects of technoscience are brief and do not shape the narrative trajectories in her published *Parable* novels. She does speculate on enhanced forms of reproduction, but these play a small part in Olamina's vision of species perpetuation. In *Talents*, Olamina remarks on the successful birth of a human infant, gestated in an "artificial womb" (PT, 82). She foresees a time when "human surrogates are replaced by computerized eggs" and "eggs combined with cloning technology," but she is skeptical (PT, 83). "Radical change or just one more option among the many?" she asks (PT, 83). In the *Parable* books Butler has a suspicion of the effects of biotechnology. Part of this is her understanding of scientific and technological advances as designed to serve only privileged first worlders. And she doubts that reproductive technologies would catch on as long as poor women are available and "willing to serve as surrogate mothers" to the wealthy (PT, 82). In *Parable of the Talents*, Olamina considers the use of artificial wombs in the settlement of the space colony. "Perhaps the eggs may be useful for us . . . in the long run. But what they'll do to human societies in the meantime, I wonder" (PT, 83). Enhanced forms of reproduction do show up tangentially in Butler's ideas for "Trickster," but these are not developed as part of its central conflict or plot in any version. "Consider: the second generation may well be mainly egg children," she writes. "They're brought from Earth as fertilized eggs and may not be related to the few adults who care for them and teach them. Genetic diversity demands that as many different kinds of human beings as possible be represented in the children, lest some *essential trait* be lost [my italics]."[23] Butler's speculations do feature some form of social engineering, then, at least in reproduction. Elsewhere in her notes Butler states that she is "fascinated by most things biomedical."[24] Still, Butler is much more interested in human behavior and relations when confronted with natural environments than in contemplating the effects of biotechnology.

How, then, do humans accelerate species evolution in the *Parable* novels? Unlike in Huxley's ultimately eugenicist philosophy or in Butler's novel *Wild Seed*, there is no suggestion in her published *Parable* books, and little in her "Trickster" notes, of outright biological engineering. Instead, there is the vague idea of a type of awareness, the importance of a sense of reproductive purpose, and dedication to moving to the stars. Conscious Earthseed believers should redirect their otherwise self-destructive drives in order to fulfill the Destiny. Olamina says,

> The human species is a kind of animal, of course. But we can do something no other animal species has had the option to do. We can choose: We can go on building and destroying until we either destroy ourselves or destroy the ability of our world to sustain us. Or we can make something more of ourselves. We can grow up. We can leave the nest. We can fulfill the Destiny, make homes for ourselves among the stars, and become some combination of what we want to become and whatever our new environments challenge us to become. Our new worlds will remake us as we remake them. And some of the new people who emerge from all this will develop new ways to cope. They'll have to. That will break the old cycle, even if it's only to begin a new one, a different one. (PT, 321)

But Olamina's idea of change is not based in inevitable improvement. Movement to the stars does not mean humans will be able to transcend their species' drive for self-destruction. Her call to her followers to "make something more of ourselves," to "grow up," results only in her hope that at least some people, in relating to the challenge of a new environment, will adapt to new worlds and develop new strategies for survival. The Destiny, then, is to survive, to keep the species alive, with just the hope that they can overcome their ultimately self-destructive tendency for hierarchical domination. Here logic chases its tail. If survival is based in a competitive struggle for existence, then how can humans ever overcome what they are biologically wired to do? How can humans change *and* stay the same?

There is tension and ambivalence in the *Parable* novels and, in Butler's notes for "Trickster," about just how much humans can change as they remake themselves and are remade in their new world. "What are we about?" she asks in her journal. "All the civilizations of the past have died or changed so greatly as to have died in giving birth to their current selves."[25] But just what the cycles of life and death are capable of producing remains a question.

Butler affixes the human tendency to self-destruction to all animal species. "What are we about?" she asks again:

> We are about doing what all animal species do. We are about turning as much of the world into ourselves as we can. We are about distroy-ing [*sic*] those things which make our lives possible, and when we have done enough of this, we will have another population crash. The four horsemen will ride. This has happened many times in the past. It will happen again and again. It will happen once too often, and we will be extinguished. [26]

Yet a faint hope remains, at least for the perpetuation of the species: "Or we will go to the stars, and there become what we can or will become and either repeat the terrestrial cycle or do something different."[27] For Butler, the concept of growth is ambiguous and the chance for human improvement slim, for self-destruction is inevitable as long as the human drive for survival is based in hierarchical struggle.

Apocalypse Redux

Since the 1990s critical dystopian literature and film have taken on a new importance in response to the devastating effects of neoliberal free market capitalism.[28] Earlier Cold War dystopias and nuclear-era apocalypses have been followed by millennial parables illustrating the effects of unfettered globalization and ecological destruction. Although Butler makes no explicit reference to contemporaneous events, it is easy to see the horrific conditions of the United States in the *Parable* novels as the consequences of the sociopolitical context in which she wrote the novels in the mid- to late 1990s. In explaining the causes for the dystopian world in the *Parable* novels, her primary concerns were "the education problem" and "global warming."[29] These catastrophic times could easily be understood as the results of Reagan- and Clinton-era neoliberal social policies that led to widespread privatization of essential services: education, fire departments, water, power, health care, and economic welfare programs. In the *Parable* novels, the continuation and extension of these policies leads to widespread destruction, mayhem, and suffering. In *Sower*, Butler also envisions the future consequences of 1990s neoliberalist economic policies that saw the institution of NAFTA and the unfettered power of transnational corporations. Keeping her vision to the United States, Butler foresees these corporations beginning to establish "company towns"—basically a form of indentured servitude—on the West Coast of the United States and the reemergence of forms of slavery, realized more fully in *Talents*. The world becomes "half antebellum revival, half science fiction," as homeless and vulnerable people are captured, enslaved, and kept under control by electronic collars (PS, 122).

In most of Butler's work, systems of oppression and violence are not organized principally around categories of race. Her utopian communities, as much as we can call them that, are not a discretely black response. She is concerned with species behavior, with racism just one form of domination and cruelty. What makes people "prey," in Butler's world, is lack of protection by clan or community. Racist white people, like the families within the community of Dovetree, are present in the *Parable* novels, but they have a relative lack of power. Poor people, the homeless, are the most vulnerable, but those with the best ability to fight are the ones who survive, while the rich often fall prey.

Yet while race is not explicitly referenced as the central category by which oppression is organized, the structure of the book speaks to an African American topos of the apocalyptic nature of everyday life: desperate and fragile forms of survival, constant crisis, alienation, upheaval, and the trope of exodus. In Olamina we can trace the history of black women itinerant preachers and of Harriet Tubman; in the movement of Olamina and her people north and, ultimately, to the stars, we can see the history of escape from slavery and migration and the tropes of flight and fugitivity. The long history of brutality and murder of African Americans certainly provide a model for the gruesome forms of violence present in Butler's books. While the communities described in the *Parable* series are not solely African American, they are primarily people of color, and it is their realities that form the novels' central experiential framework. That black people are the normative subjects of the novels goes unspoken in the published works. In her journals, early in her conceptualizations of the novels, Butler refers to Olamina as "a black woman attempting to push people into space" and goes on to explicitly state "attempting to push black people into space."[30] Black life therefore exists as a formal structure rather than as an explicit category of investigation in the novels.

In apocalyptic narratives such as Butler's, people are stripped down to bare life, without state, law, or civil society. In these stories, without cohesive social infrastructure life is a constant state of crisis—a state of exception. In Butler's narratives a strong, unifying state, force, or religion is necessary to keep people from violent conflict and power struggle. "When apparent stability disintegrates . . . when no influence is strong enough to unify people/ They divide," reads one of Olamina's verses:

They struggle,
One against one
Group against group,
For survival, position, power.
They remember old hates and generate new ones.

They create chaos and nurture it
They kill and kill and kill.
Until they are exhausted or destroyed,
Until they are conquered by outside forces
Or until one of them becomes
A leader
Most will follow,
Or a tyrant most will fear. (PS, 103)

It takes a "strong influence," or power, to control humans' tendency to struggle for domination. The general assumption undergirding these narratives is that without some unifying element, humans become violent, individualistic, and predatory in their desire for dominance. Nevertheless, humans have a basic need for some unifying force to keep from self-destructing.

In her notes for writing the *Parable* novels, Butler considers a range of possible responses to the human need for social organization under apocalyptic conditions and gives an interesting list of what she sees as other strategies humans would develop. "I must show . . . [the readers] people searching for order and stability in their own ways," she writes, and gives a numbered list of possibilities.[31] What is notable is that all of these social structures are organized around people's need for some type of hierarchical dominance. Her list includes "martial law—areas in which people do as they're told or are harshly punished, but since most feel the need for order above all, there is little rebellion."[32] Most of the social orders Butler sees as possibilities adhere to systems of oppression based in race, gender, or ability, but some don't, as in communism and, most notably, Christian America, the organization she creates in the *Parable* books.

First on Butler's list of ways people would try to establish order is "racism and segregation—blaming other races for all trouble." Second on Butler's list is "sex—free sex or group marriage or plural wives set up." The list also includes "sexism—with women and children as property." Butler's is not a feminist thought experiment—certainly not in her pessimistic list of ways people would organize after the destruction of life as we know it. Apocalypse is not a disruption that can free us from biologically determined male domination.

The most notable organization Butler chooses from the list is Christian America, a reactionary fundamentalist religious sect organized under the leadership of the elected president, Andrew Steele Jarrett. Before she begins her list of possible forms of social order, Butler writes, "I must show these Christian America people climbing to the top of the heap by convincing the country that their way is 'the American way,' and that in order to be whole and great again, they must join all of Americans together as a single religious unit. Race, ethnicity, social class, age, and sex are all things we must live with. Those things divide us. Religion must unite us."[33] In Butler's vision, Christian America is not a white supremacist organization. In the published novels, the organization is open to "every nationality, every race" (PT, 24). The extreme wing of this organization besieges Acorn, killing, raping, and collaring the community's members, and turns it into "Camp Christian Reeducation Facility" (PT, 205). Acorn members suffer grueling and torturous work regimes and systems of punishment, as well as incredibly violent forms of abuse, likened to slavery, although the members of Christian America are of various races and ethnicities.

While it lasts, Acorn offers an alternative of sorts, albeit one that still sees the importance of a unifying force and leadership. Olamina—called, along with other original members, "Shaper"—is clearly the leader. The community is not unified around a political structure but around its religious belief system. Its fundamental structure is around the formation of "family bonds," usually heterosexual couples, either with children or matched with children who have lost their families (PT, 65).

After Acorn is destroyed, Olamina decides against regrouping into another community. Olamina sees the religion, or the movement, as spreading through the activities of "believers with missionary inclinations" (PT, 161). The religion is not conceived as an alternative to nation-state structures or capitalism but as a movement entirely focused on preparing to fulfill the Destiny. Olamina's initial vision for Acorn and future communities is based in a form of entrepreneurial capitalism. "I foresee a time when our settlement is not just a 'castle on the hill' but when most or all of our neighbors have joined us," she says. "I want them as allies and members, not just as 'friends.' And as we absorb them, I also intend to either absorb some of the storekeeper, restaurant and hotel clients that we'll have—or want us to open our own stores, restaurants and hotels. . . . I want us to grow into the cities and towns in this natural, self-supporting way" (PT, 69). Olamina's vision of seeing humans launch into extrasolar space is marginally grounded in this community-based model but realized through forms of investment capital. Earthseed becomes, as Olamina's daughter Larkin unsympathetically calls it, a "wealthy sect. . . . It owned land, schools, farms, factories, stores, banks, several whole towns. And it seemed a lot of well-known people—lawyers, physicians, journalists, scientists, politicians, even members of congress" (PT, 340). The novel, through Larkin, seems to critique the way Olamina's sect develops but cannot see an alternative.

In many of Butler's narratives, the central question is whether and how the unifying element becomes dominant and remains so. Many of Butler's novels center on the question of how much coercion is necessary and how much consent is given to the unifying force. Butler is fascinated by relations of power, which are brought into sharp relief when people are forced to give up what they consider their mental, emotional, or physical integrity. In *Mind of My Mind*, Mary's pattern forces telepaths, otherwise destructive to each other, to unite. But this unity is based solely in her directive; individuals must accept their tethered condition as there is no way to escape. Mary herself is coerced, by her ability, into tethering others to her. The condition of power as dominance therefore coerces everyone involved into some form of consent.

The *Parable* novels are less concerned with consent, although they do consider the depth and ethics of Olamina's powers of seduction and manipulation. Olamina insists that what she brings to the world is not her fabricated hope but a truth she sees clearly (PT, 73). She is willing to manipulate people's need for unifying purpose and belonging to reach what she considers humans' true purpose for living. Earthseed is not simply aiding an inevitable process but a project Olamina is consciously engineering. On the one hand, she claims Earthseed to be something she discovers. "Stumbling across the truth is not the same thing as making things up," she tells Bankole (PS, 261). But, on the other hand, the religion is her orchestration. "I mean to guide and shape Earthseed into what it should be," she says (PS, 262). While on the road, traveling North, Olamina's entries in her journal lead us to believe the process of building the community is organic, as was her initial discovery. Yet, in some passages, it is her intention. "Earthseed is being born right here on Highway 101," she writes. "I've come to think I should be fishing that river even as I follow its current" (PS, 223). By the end of *Talents*, Earthseed is less about the formation of innovative communities and almost solely focused on extrasolar immigration. The reason for Earthseed to be a religion is almost purely functional. Butler writes, in her notes for a talk at MIT, "The main character in my new book *Parable of the Talents* believes that only some form of religious passion can cause us to take on in a serious way, the fantastically expensive difficult possibly multicentury effort to establish human settlements in extrasolar planets."[34] Utopia resides not in the development of communal structures but in the anticipatory state of preparation. Any utopian possibility is deferred to the future.

Although Olamina remains a benevolent leader, relying on consent, we are meant to feel the edges of possibility for firmer rule. Butler writes, "*Parable of the Talents* is the story of Lauren Olamina's struggles to seduce, scare, lash, her people on to the fulfillment of the Earthseed destiny."[35] Her relationship to her community and to Earthseed is also conceived as parental. "She must, in motherhood, in love, guide and direct, teach, seduce, coerce, scare, and goad her child as does any mother."[36] The *Parable* novels offer a different, softer version of coercion and consent than do her other novels.

Yet overall the *Parable* narratives are no less governed by violence than Butler's other works, as she renders violence as inherent to human nature. Sarah Outterson writes, "If all violence is biologically determined and necessary, then no action is possible—hardly a utopian world."[37] This limits Earthseed's ability to actually change the inherent tendency for destructive behavior in the human species. At best the urge for violence and domination can be suppressed but never fully lost. As Olamina sees it, keeping people focused on the stars will keep humans from their self-destructive tendencies. She organizes Earthseed, then, around an ultimate purpose. "*We need purpose!*" she tells Bankole. "We need the image the Destiny gives of ourselves as a growing, purposeful species. . . . When we have no difficult, long term purpose to strive toward, we fight each other" (PT, 163–64). In the *Parable* novels, the urge to "divide" and "kill and kill and kill" is the human response to unfettered, uncontrolled, and decentralized power, and throughout Butler's work humans indulge in incredibly brutal and gruesome forms of violence against each other. Outterson writes, "[Butler] engages the problematic idea that unity in community is a utopian project. The community structures she presents are soaked with explicit and implicit violence, inherent in both their origins and in the way their structure is controlled by determined, essentialist elements—whether genetic, pathological, or technological."[38] Some forms of violence are linked to the need for survival. In the *Parable* books, Olamina acknowledges that the group may be forced to forms of violence and theft in order to protect themselves and stay alive. At one point, her group comes across a group of children engaged in cannibalism. These acts are on some level understandable as forms of survival, according to a particular interpretation of Darwin's model of evolution. But much of the extreme violence in the *Parable* novels goes beyond the need for survival and is in excess of what will insure maintenance of domination. Olamina's brother is skinned alive, "cut and . . . cauterized" repeatedly, most likely by the drug dealers he had stolen from (ps, 113). Seeing a girl walking filthy and naked, with blood running down her legs, Olamina must shield herself against the pain she feels.

When Butler was writing the *Parable* books, Los Angeles and other cities were blighted by an epidemic of crack cocaine. Butler makes no direct reference to crack; instead, she invents a drug called Pyro, "short for pyromania" (ps, 143). Unlike crack, which particularly affected poor communities, Pyro is the drug of choice for wealthy and middle-class youth. This drug made "watching the leaping, changing pattern of fire a better, more intense, longer-lasting high than sex" (ps, 144). Synthesized on the East coast, once in "dry-as-straw California" the drug sets off a "real orgy of burning" (ps, 144). The effects of the drug seem to go beyond the desire to set fires. Shaving their heads and painting their faces, Pyros wage campaigns of torture, death, and rape. Rape is a common act of violence in the *Parable* world. It is an act of dominance but also reveals, as does the ecstasy felt by the Pyros, the ways violence and other forms of violation are often associated with erotic pleasure in Butler's fiction. In *Clay's Ark*, infecting another being is irresistible for the already infected. The infected yearn to touch those unaffected by the extraterrestrial microbes, and to do so "feels sexual . . . almost as good as screwing."[39] In the world of *Xenogenesis*, the Oankali have the biological imperative to mix genetic material with humans through sexual reproduction, and the line between consent and coercion is where its violence lies. As species survival is a paramount drive, the pleasurable experience of sex with the Ooloi is so highly compelling it is sometimes likened to rape in the text.

Violence is an expression of a wider affective terrain. It is the extreme manifestation of a wider theme in Butler's work that Outterson calls "boundary violation."[40] This violation of personal integrity takes shape in many ways throughout Butler's novels. This process involves encroachment upon individuals' emotional, mental, and physical cohesion. In *Clay's Ark* and the rest of the *Xenogenesis* trilogy, violation of individuals' boundaries is also analogous to the violation of a species' definability.

There are no utopias in Butler's novels. Her characters make it to the stars, but we never get there, as she was never happy with, and eventually abandoned, her plans for four sequels, to begin with "Trickster." Nevertheless, we are meant to feel Olamina's conviction that change—the breaking of old cycles—is possible through faith. And there is a draw in her work to forms of community, however fraught and conflictual those communities are. "Her return to her characteristic boundary-violating communities suggests that they carry some trace of whatever utopian hope may exist for her," Outterson writes.[41]

Butler is much more hopeful in her early conceptualizations of what was to be the sequel to *Parable of the Talents*. Arriving and settling on the new planet is not a utopian realization but the struggle of humans to adapt to their new environment. "Trickster" was meant to be the first in a four-book series.[42] "In book one, the struggle is to come to terms with the planet and with change itself," and there are a range of human responses.[43] Butler's initial vision believes in the possibility that humans could develop new, nondestructive ways of being not governed by the drive for dominance in their efforts to survive. She writes in 1989:

> The struggle is from unexpected chaos to a new balance, a new steady state of humans and world <u>not</u> distroying [*sic*] one another. . . . Smashing and dominating simply do not work. They must find ways to <u>live with</u> what is, to control it without smash and grab tactics. . . Book One is the story of how one small group of human beings are forced by the terrible consequences of their own behavior to ease into more viable, more mutual partnership.[44]

But, when she starts to plan "Trickster" almost ten years later, Butler struggles in her notes to find traction and voices great ambivalence about the project from the beginning. First, she struggles with envisioning the central character, Larkin, Olamina's daughter. Butler is distracted for a good while with the prospect of making the story a murder mystery. She settles on the concept of blindness (the question being what would happen if the colonists lost their eyesight) and titles the prospective novel "Eyes." Butler spent some time on it, until José Saramago won the Nobel Prize for Literature for his apocalyptic dystopian novel *Blindness*. "I would have continued if Saramago hadn't won the Nobel. But now, I must stop. . . . I hate giving up an idea that I like. I hate letting EYES go. It's a good idea. I still want to do it. But it's ended. EYES are closed," she writes.[45] Butler spends the longest time with the concept of microorganism-induced mass hallucination but, dissatisfied, abruptly abandons the project in frustration. "This piece of garbage I've been working on and writing different versions of is, ad [sic] usual, going nowhere," she writes.[46]

Before she gives up, Butler's notes include descriptions of what trades and occupations will be necessary and what the physical landscape and settlement will look like. She also gives glimpses of human social organization, which doesn't seem to have evolved. "Normal live [sic] and crime goes on. . . . People still beat their wives and kids. People still have babies. . . . People still steal, blackmail one another, fight, cheat on husbands or wives. . . . People still fall in love, marry, have in-law troubles. . . . People still divorce."[47] Notably, Butler's vision remains heteronormative and couple oriented. Gone are the communal innovations found in Acorn and the profound religious purpose. Gone are the tenuous hopes for any true change in species behavior. Her speculations on social structure and terraformation are curtailed by the desperate need for survival in a harsh terrain. Butler is unclear whether change—adaptation—could be willful or would be reliant on dire necessity. But in her notes, survival does not become the impetus for species adaptation and change but elicits a rigid desire to return home. Rather than an exploration of what change could look and feel like, we get a homesick society facing a terrible physical condition. It seems as if Olamina's dream has led us to a sad and miserable repeat of a vision of life on Earth.

Butler's *Parable* novels struggle with and against the concept of change. Olamina hopes that a full break with Earth could lead to an accelerated rate of human evolution and adaptation beyond humans' current biological predisposition for violent self-destruction. But the extent to which the texts can imagine evolutionary possibility is ultimately held back by a concept of change beholden to heteronormative ideas of a biological imperative. Species perpetuation, Olamina's goal, leaves ambiguous just what about the human species should be preserved, and how, and why. Wonder at the complexity of the universe, and the importance of interconnectedness within it, are arguably part of Darwin's observations in *On the Origin of Species*. These branches of thought in Darwin's concept of evolution, however, get lost in the novels' Spencerian interpretation of the struggle for life. This interpretation misses out on the power of variation and of the unexpected in evolution, which destabilize the very concept of species.

Alexandro Segade and Malik Gaines explore this possibility in their 2019 opera "Star Choir: Founding, Dissolution and Reconstitution of the Colonies on Planet 85K· Aurora." In this work they speculate where the ideas Octavia Butler was playing with for "Trickster" could have ended up, if she had not abandoned the project. As in Butler's notes for her sequel, when the colonists settle on their chosen planet (named Rainbow in "Trickster" and Aurora in "Star Choir"), they are quickly infected with microbes that, entering the colonists' brains, cause extreme hallucinations. In Segade and Gaines's speculation, we are privy to the perspective of the microbes as well as that of the colonists. The microbes are able to sing through one voice as they are organized according to a completely different ontological framework than the colonists, who can only sing through multiple voices. The microbes tell us they have sustained alien invasions before, and that they have turned other species away by "twisting neurons" and causing the "aliens" to become overwhelmed with extrasolar awareness (SC). The libretto reads:

> I know the way into the brains of these new invading two-legs
> I know how to make them see
> thinker
> see why they do not belong
> see what they have done
> see what has happened. (SC, 11)

The colonists who can accept them and survive the microbes' presence discover they have expansive stellar perception, telepathy, and awareness of their connectiveness across the universe. Humans bodies are transformed by their environment, as well as the new species coexisting with them, as the microbes reengineer the invaders' bodies for their homes. From the libretto comes this explanation:

> Our bones hollow from gravity, our eyes shaped by its force, our
>     brains inhabited, we've changed to telepathy
> two species living together in the same body
> live together all of us
> the humans the microbes
> connected by telepathy. (SC, 12)

Segade and Gaines have imagined a new kind of symbiosis or biological formation. Do we have an inter-special relationship or a new species? Segade says,

> We hit a wall in the imaginary, in terms of what these organisms would actually become. We realized that the two species together made a new mind. What would it be like if you could literally be in constant contact with all other life forms on the planet? In the universe? What kind of mutation would that be? What would it look like? We couldn't see that.

**Figures 3.2 and 3.3** The Star Choir from Alexandro Segade and Malik Gaines's opera "Star Choir: Founding, Dissolution and Reconstitution."

It seemed beyond the human mind's capability to imagine outside the idea of a single species entity. We left it up to the audience to decide how it would work out.[48]

Segade raises an important point. To carry the speculation further, we may have to let go of the very idea of single-species existence, of the idea of species itself. But we are not that far afield, if we look inside our own bodies. If we consider the number of bacteria and small organisms already living inside of us now, we could see we actually are not so much a single species as we think.

Butler was fascinated by inter-special possibilities, particularly in her *Xenogenesis* trilogy. For her, inter-special relations were a site of anxiety and power struggle based in the idea that biological organisms' first imperative is species survival. The Ooloi and humans mix, but there is always an element of fear and shame attached to such inter-speciality. Segade and Gaines's vision brings us out of the individualist version of the idea of survival and out of the idea of domination as a necessary element in this survival.

In the next chapter I think further about change. I ask, What if our ideas about biological existence were more plastic? What if we denatured the very category of species itself, understanding it to be the product of historically specific scientific discourse? How would broadening our conceptions of life—rescaling both spatially and temporally—bring awareness to the ways in which being human has been conceived as a category of exclusion? What if our concept of utopia could look past what we think of as human altogether? Timothy Morton, in his conception of ecological thought, is "deeply disturbed" by some deep ecology that "anticipates a day when humans are obliterated, like a toxic virus or vermin."[49] My provocation is not a concession to the deep ecologists or to a nihilistic notion of human obsolescence. It is instead a desire to destabilize the human, to unsettle commonsense notions of species exceptionalism and biological determination, to let ourselves teeter on the brink of the unknown. Can we imagine evolving into something new and unexpected? Are we brave enough to imagine dispersing into, as Frantz Fanon calls it, the "cosmic effluvia" of the universe?

# SPECULATIVE LIFE

Utopia Without the Human

# 4

I want to take up questions left suspended in the last chapter about the idea of change in relation to the possibilities for biological life. The tensions between human/species transformation and their/its preservation, between accepting change or fighting to prevail, resonates past a reading of Butler's novels to how we conceive of the alternative worlds we seek to make. I suggest that consideration of the strange and miraculous lability of living matter, when untethered from the anthropocentric idea of species exceptionalism, allows for alternative epistemologies of existence to emerge. I am profoundly interested in the possibilities, real and imagined, for "utterly new mode(s) of existence for human matter" and in the potential for alternative versions of life and liveliness.[1] I would like to press Wynter's call for new genres of the human and ask what it means to be "completely outside" all assumptions of what the human means, including the attendant, but not synonymous, idea of species.

What I propose is that consideration of the infinite changeability of biological matter potentially shifts ontological ground. It means to dream of the possibility of different modes of being, alternative understandings of existence, and different kinds of entities. This is particularly powerful, I argue, for those positioned as deviating from the dominating, hierarchical norms by which the human is defined. Such considerations dissolve the notion of universalism and give us license to envision, and practice, other forms of belonging and relationality. I argue that being categorized as inhuman, or not quite human, is a privileged position from which to undo the assumptions not only of race thinking but of the other systems of domination with which race thinking is linked. When not served by the category human/man, we can detach from our investment in belonging to such categories and instead marvel at the potential modes of existing as biological entities such exclusion opens up. We can foster the ways of being alive some of us on the planet already tenaciously practice in the spaces of our exclusion. Macarena Gómez-Barris's argument for the "submerged perspectives" of indigenous peoples of Central and South America reveals a radically different episteme for understanding humans' relationship to the planet's ecologies—one based in immersion rather than domination.[2] It is important for those of us who have been and continue to be excluded and dislocated to imagine such immersion past the boundaries of what we think distinguishes our species from the rest of the organic, and inorganic, universe. To think of material processes of life itself is to lose ourselves completely. Life itself becomes less our possession and more a flow of self-organizing and relational forces. My provocation is that utopia may not include humans at all. This may not be a bad thing.

Hannah Landecker asks, "What is the social and cultural task of being biological entities—being simultaneously biological things and human persons—when the 'biological' is fundamentally plastic?"[3] An explosion of possible inquiries follows Landecker's question. What comprises the distinction between biological thing and human person? What conceptual categories stabilize this distinction? Moving from "person" into "entity" invites us to think of the possibility for radical change in ontological understandings. But in Landecker's question the idea of an entity still retains some kind of notable distinction, implied by the notion of the "task." In the case of such retention, the idea of biological plasticity inherently invites ethical problems. When imaginings of biological plasticity retain notions of human superiority, they lead to the transhumanist dream of species perfectibility and other virulent eugenicist fantasies.

Moving away from an anthropocentric paradigm means to denaturalize the hierarchy of life forms. Life forms are categorized into species, with Homo sapiens situated as the most evolved, according to criteria that privilege a set of cognitive and physical functions, from feeling to language. Epistemologies of the human are weighed against the notion of species, with racial, gendered, and ablest hierarchies inherent. Humans, then, judged according to these criteria, are granted the right of stewardship over all other life forms (including those ranked as inferior and/or tenuously within the fold of the human) and ownership of all inanimate materials in the known as well as yet-to-be-discovered worlds. I argue that when we estrange our perceptions of life itself away from the sanctity of the human, we can think expansively about what it means to be biological entities. As work in queer theory and science studies suggests, expanding our thinking temporally, as life forms transform across greater expanses of time than we can see, and in noncontiguous and unexpected formations helps us think of the notion of species and selfhood in new ways. Working spatially, if we move away from the belief in molar stability and individuation and think instead on the level of cells, molecules, and epigenetic phenomena, the idea of the possessive individual is diffused, the boundaries between life forms blurred. When we look to protons and electrons, we can begin to trouble the carefully inscribed lines between organic and inorganic matter and perhaps gain awareness of the ways we can think of what "we" means for self-organizing entities.

Utopia is a part of a continual becoming, an embrace of change itself. Resituating our perspective to the scalar in our consideration of life is one form of estrangement from the idea of the human as a discrete entity. In laying out his theory of durée in relation to the material world, Henri Bergson shifts the physical scale of his analysis: "We should thus descend to the molecules of which the fragments are made, to the atoms that make up molecules, to the corpuscles that generate atoms to the 'imponderable' within which the corpuscle is perhaps a mere vortex."[4] Durée connects the "smallest particle of the world" to the sun, the planets, and their satellites, he elaborates. "[Durée] means invention, the creation of forms, the continual elaboration of the absolutely new."[5] Bergson's concept of change has informed strains of new materialisms that expand our sense of time, make porous the boundaries between species, and destabilize our sense of individuality.[6] To think of change as a continual becoming leads us to consider the fundamental connections, and relations, between all forms of molecular makeup and the ecological urgency of recognizing those connections and relations.

In this chapter I explore the idea of life itself and look to the ways a number of speculative narratives engage in thought experiments that reach outside our present biological paradigms. I open with the troubling utopian worlds of H. G. Wells, in his trilogy of nonfiction works culminating in *A Modern Utopia*, and the bio-spiritual world imagined by the biologist Julian Huxley. Both authors begin with expansive and wildly creative ideas of human plasticity and life itself, but because they are centered on human supremacy, their speculative worlds quickly become particularly vicious forms of eugenicist thinking.

In conversation with the work of Mel Y. Chen and Sylvia Wynter, I then consider the "hierarchies of sentience" that distinguish Homo sapiens as a species set apart from and above other biological entities. I argue that the category *species* is a leaky construct, a fiction designed (as Chen says, quoting Giorgio Agamben) "for producing the recognition of the human."[7] Race, gender, and ability figure into this production, and this recognition as human is not equally granted to all of those classified as Homo sapiens.

I then read Samuel R. Delany's early science fiction novel *The Einstein Intersection*, as it offers playful as well as painful speculations on life's malleability, on species, and on the normativizing force of the concept *human*. In the novel the life form that has come to inhabit Earth cannot fit within the norms set forth by particular notions of the human. Thinking of the capacious potential of biological matter can easily denature the human by leading us to the stretch points, gaps, and fissures the term cannot breach. I suggest that surrendering to the complex, expansive, and relational world of biological life makes new forms of sociality and subjectivity available and opens up new ethical landscapes.

Many science scholars exploring the malleability of biological matter think of it in relation to scientific manipulation. In *The Politics of Life Itself*, Nicolas Rose articulates the ways by which we have reached a new paradigm for thinking about life through scientific development.[8] In *Culturing Life*, Hannah Landecker is interested in what happens to biological matter in a scientific medium. But the politics of biological science, particularly in relation to race and sex, have never been neutral. Techniques and philosophies of the natural sciences are historically based in a model of colonial discovery, conquest, mastery, and human stewardship with intimate ties to capitalism and militarism. I don't wish to be reductive about the range of possible scientific approaches and whether or not there is a space for productive scientific inquiry and advances that do not rely upon, or are at least aware of, these fundaments and ties. But as Bruno Latour argues in *We Have Never Been Modern*, science is never free and objective, never set apart from cultural and political context.[9]

Some scientific methodologies insist on a teleology of progress. What is unknowable will inevitably be knowable in the future. In *What Should We Do With Our Brain*? Catherine Malabou's claim is that once we are conscious of our brain's plasticity, we will have "the capacity to form oneself otherwise, to displace, even nullify determination: freedom."[10] She argues provocatively that we can "think new modalities of forming the self, under the name of "plasticity."[11] But just what this process of self-formation would look like is unclear. If indeed we could control biological plasticity, is there a way to think about plasticity of life that is not bound up in problematic ethics? I suggest that it is possible, if we accept the unknowable, the unexpected activity of biological life, and if we decolonize what life means to us.

Rather than the tangled problem of scientific manipulations, I am interested in the unpredictable and unexpected ways that living entities act. Malabou, before she suggests we conquer what we don't know about our brain's functioning, argues for what she calls "neuronal creativity," explaining that, in fact, the brain, far from being a central computer for the body, is instead notable for its plasticity.[12] That plasticity, she argues, is in the cut, the void, the gap between synapses: "Between two neurons there is a caesura, and the synapse itself is gapped. . . . The cut plays a decisive role in cerebral organization. Nervous information must cross voids, and something aleatory introduces itself between the emission and the reception of a message, constituting the field of plasticity."[13] I am interested in the "something aleatory," in what remains unknown. What happens as the nerve cells transmit across the synaptic leap? What happens by chance or by accident? What remains beyond (Western) scientific control?

No one knows why the cancer cells from Henrietta Lack's body were and remain so vigorous and prolific. Not only do they flourish in artificial medium, but they are hardy enough to survive in the air, to ride dust motes, to enter and exit the laboratory on collars and on the tails of researchers' coats. Before development of the technology used to transport biological matter, batches of her cells were put in vials and carried in coat pockets or sent by post.[14] Perhaps there is a limit to science's reach, an unknowable region beyond its control that is accessible only from an entirely different ontological paradigm.

"The Limits of Individual Plasticity"

The concept of biological plasticity captured scientific, philosophical, and fictional imagination from at least the late nineteenth century. The speculations on biological life in the works of science fiction writer H. G. Wells and his colleague, the biologist Julian Huxley, were full of both marvelous and terrifying possibility. I focus on Wells because he is revered as a foundational figure in science fiction while his frightening and horrific eugenicist ideas are ignored or minimized. I consider the understudied Huxley because his expansive biological fantasies had utopian reach. Huxley believed that humans could be released from their limitations into a whole universe of bio-spiritual potential. Both men thought creatively about existence, consciousness, the mind, and the universe in their theoretical and fictional writing. But their theories of utopia held dreadful consequence; while there are moments in their writing that portray new paradigms of earthly inhabitance, these trajectories are terminated by their deeply entrenched transhumanist notions of human superiority and species perfectibility. Accompanying their leaps toward an expansive future were disturbingly calm calls for forms of social engineering and eugenicist policy.

For many, including Wells, what was interesting about the phenomenon of plasticity was not what happened in the gaps—the stretch points—of life-forms. What was most important to Wells and his colleagues was that plasticity made life-forms potentially manipulatable. Wells best articulated this fascination in 1895 in his article "The Limits of Individual Plasticity." Wells was not a trained biologist, having attended just one class with T. H. Huxley ten years earlier at the Normal School of Science in London before he began to write science fiction short stories and novels.[15] Wells's claims to speaking as a biologist shows the blurred lines between fiction and nonfiction in his era of natural science. In "Limits" Wells wrote, "We overlook only too often that a living being may also be regarded as raw material, as something plastic, something that maybe [sic] shaped and altered, that is, possibly, may be added and . . . eliminated and the organism as a whole developed far beyond its apparent possibilities."[16] The strength of Wells's assertions was not in their biological accuracy, but in his articulation, in a clear manner, the scientific potential to stretch the limits of what we could think of as a discrete living being. "There is in science . . . some sanction for the belief that a living thing might be taken in hand and so moulded and modified that at best it would retain scarcely anything of its inherent form and disposition; that the thread of life might be preserved unimpaired while shape and mental superstructure were so extensively recast as even to justify our regarding the result as a *new variety of being* [my italics]."[17] As Landecker suggests, the possibility of a new variety of being could be considered quite radical as it destabilizes the concept of species itself. The possibility for a new variety of being pulls away from the goal of ultimate human perfection. But in Wells's fiction, particularly *The Time Machine* and *The Island of Dr. Moreau*, the prospect of a new variety of being is a terrifying prospect. Wells's nonfiction eugenical writing is concerned with preserving the species and keeping it from "degeneration."

Julian Huxley followed Henri Bergson in believing in the continuity of all matter, both inorganic and organic. As Huxley puts it, "We were made of the same energy as the rest of the cosmos," and man is linked by "genetic continuity with all the other living inhabitants of his planet . . . [which are] all parts of one single branching and evolving flow of metabolizing protoplasm."[18] This perspective is exciting as it invites us to situate Homo sapiens as one of many manifestations of cosmic effluvium or even to dispense with the idea of a discrete species altogether. But Huxley does not do this; instead, he affirms the idea of species exceptionalism—that man is the most evolved life form on the planet. As Huxley saw it, humans could improve and elevate themselves to a higher state of being, but this higher state of being was only accessible through "improving" the physical, intellectual, and moral capacities of the human species. "The possibilities of physiological improvement . . . is no utopian silliness, but is bound to come about if science continues her current progress," Huxley writes in *Essays of a Biologist*.[19]

Once humankind was perfected, Huxley had utopian plans. The mind was inseparable from the body and so was evolving along the same progression to a higher level of consciousness. Phases of evolution would progress from the purely biological to what Huxley calls the "psychosocial" phase, in which man is "no longer steered by . . . instincts" but by "rational, knowledge-based imagination."[20] This third evolutionary phase was to the spiritual; for Huxley (like Octavia E. Butler's Olamina), there was "no basic cleavage between science and religion."[21] Huxley drew on William James's ideas of religion stripped of its supernatural origin and understood instead as superposed on the biological. Huxley was particularly inspired, after 1946, by Pierre Teilhard de Chardin and his ideas of the "nöosphere," the world created by the bioconsciousness of evolved humans.[22] This new spatial dimension is an "organised web of thought" formed as a planetary sphere.[23] Man could develop the abilities of the mind, including extrasensory perception. Huxley's utopianism takes us to an abstract cosmic elevation, inaccessible from where humans currently exist.

The idea of existence in a new spatial dimension is creative and compelling, but with Huxley it is linked to the hierarchical notion of human superiority and so cannot be a fully expansive release into a new paradigm of life. Huxley was a lifelong eugenicist. The language of eugenicism drew lines in stark and bloody terms between who was deemed human and who needed to be excluded from the category. For Huxley, some should live and others die. In "UNESCO: Its Purpose and Philosophy," a speech Huxley delivered upon acceptance of the UNESCO directorship in 1946, eugenics should work to relieve the "dead weight of genetic stupidity, physical weakness, mental instability, and disease-proneness."[24] It is clear that the science of eugenics was white supremacist, particularly in its Malthusian manifestations, which rendered non-Europeans as uncontrollably reproducing "inferior types." In his address before the Galton Society in 1962, Huxley's solution to improving mankind was not only in "discouraging genetically defective or inferior types from breeding" but also in general population control, "reducing over-multiplication in general and the high differential fertility of various regions, nations and classes in particular."[25] While Huxley doesn't use the language of race, the idea of race is implicit within the notions of "regions, nations and classes."

Wells and Huxley together supported the practice of sterilization, commenting on the success of the practice in America, "Six thousand such operations have been performed in California alone and it would be difficult to find fault with the results," they write in 1932 in *The Science of Life*.[26] As well as negative eugenics, Huxley had ideas for positive measures that he believed would result in increased health and intelligence. While certain populations were to be controlled, certain individuals would be encouraged to reproduce. "Quality of people, not mere quantity, is what we must aim at," Huxley writes in his 1957 treatise "Transhumanism."[27]

While the shadow of race is everywhere in their work, Huxley and Wells are careful to distance themselves from what Huxley termed the "crude racism" of racial science.[28] In his UNESCO acceptance speech, Huxley clearly delineates an ethical eugenics from the policies of racial extermination enacted by the Nazis. Any attempts at racial or national purity, he maintained, were "scientifically incorrect."[29] Eugenics should hold dear "human variety" while it worked to raise the "mean level of desirable qualities. . . . healthy constitution, a high innate general intelligence, or a special aptitude such as that for mathematics or music."[30]

Huxley was careful to distinguish between his eugenicist theories and racial science, and the work of Wells and Huxley shows that eugenics does not map evenly onto scientific racism. Both argue against discrimination on the basis of race and against any belief in racial purity. Statistical methods, Huxley argued, showed that a certain range of intelligence and strength could be found in any race and that raw potential could be developed through education and improved environment.[31] "There is no more evil thing in this world than Race Prejudice," Wells spoke out forcefully in an 1893 article.[32]

Yet, as their work shows, they both retained a hierarchical racial scale informed by their colonialist perspective. Huxley's ideas of racialized people may not be the "crude racism" of the American eugenicists, but they still retain what Huxley calls a "liberal imperialism," another branch of race thinking based in European superiority.[33] "UNESCO should aim at securing the fullest contribution to the common pool from racial groups which, owing to their remoteness or their backwardness have so far had little share in it," Huxley writes.[34] There is a geopolitical dimension to the global carving of racial difference crafted through Huxley's work. There is a separation for Huxley between the science of race and the social arrangements of colonialism But it is clear in his calls for population control that these policies would be aimed at the populations of Europe's colonies. While Huxley claimed to be above vulgar racism, he did not actually transcend racialized thinking. This is because of the hierarchical ways in which the concept of *race* is constructed in the first place and, as Chen eloquently argues, because of its association with disability.[35]

Wells's and Huxley's denials of crude racism were accompanied, and occluded, by their assumptions of racial hierarchy. Theirs was a historically specific racism.[36] This affects how they see the potential for biological plasticity. It is implied that Europeans would be improved while racialized populations would be tolerated.

Wells contradicted himself about race, as in his article "Race Prejudice." By no means did Wells believe all men to be equal. "Obviously in no measurable or estimable personal quality are men equal," he writes. "It is far more acceptable to suggest that some individuals are on the whole superior, others inferior to the average."[37] Wells states that race or class was not a factor in evaluating the quality of a person. "These superiorities are too various and subtle to admit of class and race treatment," he writes.[38] But in his non-fiction criticism and commentary Wells was self-professedly anti-Semitic and antiblack. After complaining that he cannot help himself in the case of the "aggressive Jew," he writes that the necessary civilities demanded in a democracy "must not blind one to the real differences of personal quality, to such a fact as that a negro is usually simpler, kinder, and stupider than a Beacon street Bostonian. One has to keep one's head in these matters."[39]

Wells contradicts himself in speaking out against race discrimination. In the same article, he referenced his rather strange friendship with the soon-to-be president of the National Association of Colored Women, Mary Church Terrell. "Certainly it would be difficult to find any purely white American woman more level-headed and capable than that admirable public speaker, Mrs. Church Terrell," he writes.[40] Wells's perspective on race is fissured and inconsistent but profoundly reveals how race itself is hierarchically conceived. Wells can think of exceptions to the rules of racial inferiority, but they prove the rule.

Some critics defend Wells against accusations of racism, calling Wells's critics "biased and selective" in their criticism and insisting that they distort Wells's thought. Despite the contradictions, Wells's own copious words belie any defense. Contradicting his earlier and later protests against discrimination based on race, he is virulently racist in his 1901 utopian treatise *Anticipations of the Reaction of Mechanical and Scientific Progress upon Human Thought*. "Over the Southern States the nigger squats and multiplies. It is fairly certain that these stagnant ponds of population will go on stagnating till drained," he writes.[41] "The young negress degenerates towards the impossible," and "rabbits and negroes" breed with "*abandon*" [Wells's italics].[42] Despite his claims of race neutrality, in Wells's mind the "negro" in particular—here Wells refers specifically to African Americans from the South—is predetermined to be overly fecund and incapable of civilization. Negros are paired with rabbits, showing the ways in which the lines between racialized peoples and animal species judged as distant from Homo sapiens insistently remain blurred in the dominant epistemology of the human.


Wells's New Republic

Wells's utopian fantasies are unequivocally eugenicist. For Wells, unlike for Huxley, species perfectibility did not mean the total transcendence of the species but the regulation of social structures, rid of the "people of the abyss," as he calls them, who could not be assimilated into his hierarchical and authoritarian model of social and political organization.[43] In three books published between 1901 and 1905, Wells laid out his utopian vision of an ordered world, an unfettered authoritarian state free to regulate populations, issuing and enacting educational and eugenicist policies. "This grey confusion that is democracy must pass away inevitably by its own inherent conditions . . . as the embryonic confusion of the cocoon creature passes, into the higher stage, into the higher organism, the world state of the coming years."[44] Wells's eugenicist plans are at their cruelest in his 1901 treatise *Anticipations*. In this world, the "unadaptable" must be eliminated. "Euthanasia of the weak and sensual is possible," he writes.[45] Of the "people of the abyss," some may be educatable, but the bulk of them would need to be removed. He consistently advocated specifically negative eugenics throughout his works. In a response to a lecture given by Francis Galton at the founding meeting of the Sociological Society in 1904, Wells writes, "It is in the sterilization of failures, and not in the selection of successes for breeding, that the possibility of an improvement of human stock lies."[46] The nation that will be the "dominant nation before the year 2000," he writes in *Anticipations*, will be "the nation that most resolutely picks over, educates, sterilizes, exports, or poisons its people of the abyss."[47] Some may dismiss these declarations as examples of his fantastical excess. Others discount them as the isolatable flawed reasoning of an otherwise brilliant mind. Still others argue that Wells was no exception in his eugenical thinking among scientifically minded men of his time (an argument repeatedly stated to me in response to my criticism). What is interesting to me here is this kind of selective historical and scholarly memory. I wonder at the man-of-his-time argument, for there were plenty of scientific and politically minded people expressly opposed to such fascist visions. My interest in Wells's biological speculations is not meant to be celebratory but cautionary. What scholarly examples of forgetting or diminishing his cruel calls for extermination and control show us is just how embedded ideas of hierarchical assessment and biological determinism are to the notion of the human.

Throughout his nonfiction work, Wells is clear that social hierarchy is not determined by class or inheritance but by the innate quality of individuals. In this he disagrees with Galton. "I am inclined to believe that a large proportion of our present day criminals are the brightest and boldest of families living under impossible conditions," he writes in *Sociological Papers*. "That fact that the sons and nephews of a distinguished judge or great scientific man are themselves eminent judges or successful scientific men, may after all be far more due to social knowledge of the channels of profession advancement than to any distinctive family gift."[48] Yet this hardly implies that Wells thinks all humans equal. In his ideal world, explicitly called forth in his 1905 treatise *A Modern Utopia*, "Education is uniform until differentiation becomes unmistakable."[49] It is the people in whom the marks of deficiency are recognizable that make up Wells's "people of the abyss." In his first utopian treatise, *Anticipations*, the leaders of Wells's new republic will be merciless:

The alternative in right conduct between living fully beautifully, and efficiently will be to die. For a multitude of contemptible and silly creatures, fear-driven and helpless and useless . . . feeble, ugly, inefficient, born of unrestrained lusts, and increasing and multiplying through sheer incontinence and stupidity, the men of the new republic will have little pity and less benevolence. . . . I do not foresee any reason to suppose that they will hesitate to kill. . . . The men of the new republic will not be squeamish in facing or inflicting death, because they have a fuller sense of the possibilities of life than we possess.[50]

In his next installment in his trilogy for a new world state, *Mankind in the Making,* Wells modified his cruel mandates of *Anticipations.* But Wells never explicitly repudiated his earlier statements. *A Modern Utopia* is the most cited in his trilogy outlining a new republic. In this volume he further develops his plan for an iron-willed World State run by men of science. "We of the twentieth century are not going to accept the sweetish, faintly nasty slops of Rousseauism. . . . We know that order and justice do not come by nature," he writes.[51] The state therefore would regulate all marriages, but, responding to criticism of the cruelty in his previous volumes, he is very careful in this utopia to repudiate his earlier calls for pitiless extermination of the "incurably melancholy or diseased or helpless persons."[52] Controlling and engineering the rest of society required "resort[ing] to a kind of social surgery,"[53] but in this version of utopia the strong ruling class would not kill but send away and isolate its weak and diseased members. Remote island enclaves would be established to quarantine drunks and other exiles and keep them from reproducing. "Perhaps," he suggests, "it might be necessary to make these island prisons a system of monasteries and nunneries. . . . Around such islands patrol boats will go. . . . It may be necessary to have armed guards at the creeks and quays."[54]

Like Aldous Huxley's caste-centered world in his 1932 novel *Brave New World,* Wells's World State model is based on the organization of classes of men. Unlike Aldous Huxley's world, where the classes are conditioned according to a behavioral modification system, Wells's classes are not learned; neither are they hereditary nor assigned according to wealth or status. Instead, "they are classes to which people drift of their own accord."[55] The hierarchy, consisting of four classes, was natural, according to Wells.[56] A "voluntary nobility" made up of the first two classes will run the state.[57] "We reject men who are fat, or thin and flabby, or whose nerves are shaky," the citizen of Utopia explains to a time-traveling Wells.[58]

Wells devotes an entire chapter to race in *A Modern Utopia* and directly contravenes his earlier position on race in *Anticipations*. Because Wells's Utopia is a World State, it takes the entire planet, and Wells makes clear it will be composed of myriad races all employing a common language. "White and black, brown, red and yellow, all tints of skin, all types of body and character, will be there," he writes in his first chapter.[59] Despite his earlier racist claims against "negroes," here he criticizes the systems of colonialism and slavery, the turn to race science, and a "grotesque insistence upon Anglo-Saxonism."[60] In Wells's Utopia, eugenicist policies would not discriminate along racial lines: "Extinction need never be discriminatory. If any of the race did, after all, prove to be fit to survive, they would survive—they would be picked out with a sure and automatic justice from the over-ready condemnation of all their kind."[61]

Inconsistencies and gaps remain in Wells's work; it is unclear if the "lower races" are indeed capable of advancing. He is ambivalent about what to do with the "rejected white and yellow civilizations and the black and brown races . . . who cannot keep pace" with civilization.[62] These peoples are not synonymous with the "people of the abyss" he is so sure should be eliminated or, in his more leavened later views, shipped to a guarded island.[63] Yet these people of the warmer climes may inevitably be erased in the tide of forward-looking biological manipulation. But Wells retains the streak of cruelty evident in *Anticipations*, as he still considers extermination the most efficient way of controlling the quality of the population. "Suppose . . . for a moment, that there is an all-round inferior race; a Modern Utopia . . . would . . . exterminate such a race as quickly as it could." But Utopia could cleanse itself "without any clumsiness of race distinction, in exactly the same manner, and by the same machinery, as it exterminates all its own defective and inferior strains."[64]

Wells retains a patronizing tone in describing the "queer little races," who may indeed have their "little gifts" to contribute to utopian civilization. "The black-fellows, the Pigmies, the Bushmen, may have . . . a greater keenness, a greater fineness of this sense or that, a quaintness of the imagination or what not, that may serve as their little unique addition to the totality of our Utopian civilization," he writes. "Cannot we imagine some few of these little people . . . may have found some delicate art to practise, some peculiar sort of carving, for example, that justifies God in creating them? Utopia has sound sanitary laws, sound social laws, sound economic laws; what harm are these people going to do?"[65] Racialized peoples may not be by nature defective enough to sterilize or exterminate, but they definitely are by nature not equal to Europeans. Wells kindly allows the possibility that these "quaint . . . little people" may have something, some small thing, worthwhile enough for the superior European civilization to keep them alive. His condescending assent here occludes any claim he makes elsewhere to race neutrality. And Wells leaves open the question of whether a race is inferior or not. If inferiority were the case, his eugenical solution would assure its eradication. If a race were inferior, Wells assumes "it would follow that in Utopia most of them are childless, and working at or about the minimum wage, and some will have passed out of all possibility of offspring under the hand of the offended law."[66] Notions of race and ability are intimately a part of biological notions and evaluative processes of worth and legitimacy.

Optimistic fantasies about the plasticity of life in contemporary speculative thought ignore the history of race and eugenics and its own investment in these same ideas to the discipline's peril. Remembering how plasticity of life was imagined and scientifically practiced through race and ability is key as scholars go forward in the project of decentering the human. A trust in Western scientific knowledge must be interrogated, and the "we" of new materialist thinking situated historically. Diana Cole and Samantha Frost, in the introduction to their anthology *New Materialisms: Ontology, Agency, and Politics*, urge us to "rediscover older materialist traditions while pushing them in novel, and sometimes experimental, directions or toward fresh applications."[67] Materialist studies need to attend to the ways in which systems of inequality are embedded in our understandings of that materiality and the processes by which scholars theorize it.[68] While they focus a scientific eye, scholars must retain a political, cultural, and historical memory.

On Species

Western natural science has classified and categorized biological life into species and imagined the species Homo sapiens as the end point of a hierarchical and linear evolutionary schema. Those critical of such species supremacy, especially as a rationale for domination, call this hierarchical assessment *speciesism*. Race, gender, and ability do not disappear in the designation of the species category. Species designations are given to living beings judged along an evolutionary timeline, in ascending order from amoeba to Homo sapiens. Historically there are gradations of evolutionary development with race, class, gender, and sexuality as deviations from the linear process of evolutionary development. Those putatively within the definition of the species can still be judged according to stages of development. Racialized subjects are less evolved, while others are throwbacks to more primitive moments in the evolution of humankind. Species are a type of animal, but humanness, as opposed to belonging to a species, is assessed by an individual's or group's distance from the "animal"—the latter term, as Chen argues, being an equally specious category. As Chen elucidates, "the biological ramifications wrought by these separated categories is extremely complex, since 'humans' are not all treated one way and 'animals' uniformly treated another way."[69] The lines between species are set along a continuum, making them potentially porous.

The base unit used to define all life forms is the concept of sentience: the ability to feel, to have a subjective perceptual experience. To be sentient is to have an individuated inner life defined by sensation and, according to some definitions, emotion. But there is a categorical hierarchy of sentience; assessment of an animate entity's sentience is measured by a specific set of physical and cognitive functions. Race, gender, and ability are judged by levels of sentience, levels of these abilities. Remnants of nineteenth-century debates around whether or not black people, or women, could feel—either physical pain or the "higher" emotions—remain today. The idea of disability also rests on the hierarchy of sentience. Debates included, with effects that persist, whether or not the subject was educable, civilizable, or rehabilitatable.

Above all other criteria, the slide from Homo sapiens to human finds its proof in the development and use of verbal and written language. Mel Y. Chen writes of language, "As a register of intelligence, judgment, and subjectivity it is a key criterion by which lay, religious, and expertly scientific humans afford subjectivity—and sentience—to animate beings both within and beyond the human border."[70] Language use, then, is a sign for the ability of the species to think abstractly, and to be self-aware—that is, to be able to represent the self. This understanding of written language as the most complex form of communication does not acknowledge the many other forms of perception, communication, and expression practiced by animate beings. Beings may have other forms of sentience humans cannot assess according to human criteria, or other epistemes of life not registerable in the concept itself.

As Sylvia Wynter's sociogenic principle suggests, humans are only capable of self-awareness through epistemic frameworks, and through practicing what Walter Mignolo calls "epistemic disobedience,"[71] other "genres/modes of the human" are possible.[72] I am inspired by this call for disobedience but wish to push it further. While Wynter sees the biological as a category by which racialized subjects were "dysselected"—excluded from the category of human—she nonetheless retains biological assumptions about species.[73] In her thinking, species furnishes the unchangeable substrate of the human. Species criteria is what will be retained in new genres of the human.

For Wynter, the principle criteria differentiating the human from other species is the idea that the species is distinguishable, and exceptional, by its use of language. "Humans have been preadapted, primarily through the co-evolution of language and the brain, to be a symbolic and, therefore, a self-representing species."[74] Wynter's ideas of change are centered in humans' use of language and self-awareness, ostensibly unique from other biological entities. Only through individuated abilities of self-representation can there be an epistemological shift. Wynter writes, paraphrasing Aimé Césaire, "Only the elaboration of a new science, beyond the limits of the natural sciences . . . will offer us our last chance to avoid the large-scale dilemmas that we must now confront as a species. This would be a science in which the "study of the Word"—or our narratively inscribed, governing sociogenic principles—will condition the "study of nature."[75] For Wynter, the study of nature refers here to the study of the biology of the species, understood as the basis for what is possible for humans. The study of nature is "of the neuropsychological circuits/mechanisms of the brain that, when activated by the semantic system of each principle/statement, lead to the specific orders of consciousness or modes of mind in whose terms we then come to experience ourselves as this or that genre/mode of being human."[76] In her concept of human subjectivity, Wynter retains a Cartesian mind-body split, locating consciousness purely in the mind, and considers possibilities for the human as biologically determined, according to specific criteria.

Wynter argues that the process by which we come to "experience ourselves" is "outside our conscious awareness, thereby leading us to be governed by the 'imagined ends' or postulate of being, truth, freedom that we lawlikely put and keep in place, without realizing that it is we ourselves, and not extrahuman entities, who prescribe them."[77] But why not extrahuman entities? Wynter is calling for us to become aware that we can only understand ourselves through particular epistemes and, with this awareness, shift them. As with Butler's conceptualization in the *Parable* novels, exactly how we would do this is unclear. I am tickled by the idea of extrahuman entities residing among us. These entities are not responsible for the ways the genre of the human is currently understood and practiced. Rather, in my imagination these entities are suggesting, perhaps in a register we are not attuned to, that other forms of being are possible if we begin to reach for, or practice, forms of interchange, relationality, and communality based in immersion in the nonhuman world.

Throughout his science fiction, Samuel R. Delany explores the malleability of biological matter and frees it from normative determination. His humans enjoy an infinite number of predilections and pleasures and practice myriad forms of relationality and bodily expression. The idea that there might be a normative set of criteria by which to measure the human becomes an easily dismissed absurdity. His fiction foregrounds the sensorium; smell, touch, and sound are as important to the texture of the world as sight. His early science fiction novels, *Babel 17* and *The Einstein Intersection*, published in 1966 and 1967 respectively, experiment with the idea of the human, playing with notions of biological species, sentience, and the concept of subjectivity.

As well as embodiment and sensation, Delany's fiction considers language, including how it works, how we use it, and the complex discursive systems of self-representation. "Who is this animal man?" asks the General at the beginning of *Babel 17* (B17, 3). The novel plays with this ontological inquiry and ostensibly makes the assumption that the species, at its base, is defined by the use of language. It also seems to be affirming the idea that subjectivity—the ability to reference the self—is based in this language use. An entity needs to be situated around a core sense of being before it can communicate. Yet even as it seems to be making these claims, it imagines different forms of communication, selfhood, and ways of conjoining that destabilize the possessive individualist model for subjectivity.

Set in space, the novel's central character is Rydra Wong—poet, telepath, and code breaker—out to solve the mystery of a disruptive radio transmission accompanying acts of sabotage against the Alliance (which the author leaves undescribed). Through her augmented abilities, Rydra deduces that the transmissions are not a code but a language, which she names Babel 17. To find out who speaks the language, she assembles a starship and crew to chase it down.

To recruit her crew Rydra visits the rowdy heterotopia of Transport Town with a reluctant customs officer in tow. Here stellarmen and roustabouts drink, fight, and carouse. Transport Town is heterotopian in two senses of the word; *heterotopia* refers to a kind of utopian enclave but is also a medical term referring to skin grafting, the coexistence of one tissue type with another. The town is filled with humans who have modified their bodies in a variety of ways. Here biological lability is not in the name of supporting a norm or a regularized idea of superiority, as it is in the dreams of Wells and Huxley. Instead, "cosmetisurgery" affirms a heterogeneity of imaginative fleshly formations. Rydra and the officer are greeted at the door of a basement café by a man, "ebony-skinned, with red and green jewels set into his chest, face, arms, and thighs . . . white teeth needle-filed . . . [with] pointed ears" (B17, 25). In the bar "amphibian or reptilian creatures argued and laughed with griffins and metallic-skinned sphinxes" (B17, 27). Brass, the entity Rydra hires as captain, has modified himself into a leonine beast, with "ivory saber teeth . . . brass claws . . . yellow plush paws . . . mane [and] barbed tail" (B17, 35). The captain must be strong, with quick reflexes, for "his nervous system will be directly connected to the [ship's] controls" (B17, 35). Play and aesthetic pleasure are the ethos of such bodily modification.

Delany plays with the lines between man, animal, and plant. As illustrated through the ship's crew, Delany experiments with forms of relationality and subject formation. He disrupts the distance between the living and the dead, and the heteronormative notion of the couple. A typical ship's crew consists of a range of entities, including a navigating triad called Ears, Eyes, and Nose, an inseparable tripling who are sexually, emotionally, and sensorially connected to each other. On Rydra's ship, Navigator One is a "discorporate," a type of being who has been awakened after death. Another of the navigators has a rose implanted to grow out of his shoulder. To mind the platoon of children on a ship, assigned to "do the mechanical jobs," the ship must have a chaperone, called a Slug (B17, 36).

While on their quest, Rydra and her crew discover the saboteur to be a brutal, beast-like man called the Butcher. Through her telepathic abilities, Rydra conjoins with the Butcher and helps him discover his own subjectivity, as the language he knows, Babel 17, has no word for *I* or *you*. With a newfound sense of self, the Butcher is able to remember that he is the son of a weapons manufacturer who, to make him an ideal soldier, had doctored his brain. The plot plays with the conventions of the space opera but contemplates the possibilities for other states of being and forms of communality. Rydra teaches the Butcher that the word *I* can only exist in relation to the word *you*, for both are relational categories. There is no individuation without plurality.

Delany's next novel, *The Einstein Intersection*, is also about language and contemplates the grand narratives through which the idea *human* is organized. It is about the stories that provide origin and definition. It is about how narratives, or myths, universalize themselves and create normative, and normativizing, figurations. The myths invoked in the novel are primarily Greek myths (Theseus and the Minotaur, Orpheus and Eurydice); iconic figures from a European tradition (the shepherd, the dragon slayer); settings and story lines from Hollywood films, Westerns, and popular music, and icons of

US popular culture, including Elvis, Billy the Kid, and Marilyn Monroe. Notably missing are myths and figures drawn from African American culture.

The book brings these myths into relief as we are profoundly estranged from the concept of the human in this novel. Extraterrestrials of some kind, the characters of *Einstein Connection* are not human. They are not biological; they are a psychical species, composed according to alternate, noncorporeal laws of existence. These extraterrestrials have been drawn to Earth following the extinction of the human species, who have all died most likely from radiation poisoning. *Einstein* is a painful critique of normativity: for some unexplained reason the extraterrestrial species is attempting to abide by a human template by adopting an idea of the human from (Western) myths and stories. Although these entities are not biological, they are straining to become so; they are struggling to conform to a biological existence even though the template does not fit. The species' struggle to conform to a human set of norms involves a complicated politics of becoming biological entities, which involves often-failed genetic mixing.

There is a "net of caves that wanders beneath most of the planet," perhaps created by humans, which those in our story call the source cave (EI, 112). The lower levels of the cave "contain the source of the radiation by which the villages, when their populations become too stagnant, can set up a controlled random jumbling of genes and chromosomes," explains Spider, whom our hero, Lo Lobey, meets on his travels (EI, 112). "Though we have not used them for almost a thousand years, the radiation is still there. As we, templated on man, become more complicated creatures, the harder it is for us to remain perfect" (EI, 112).

As a result of "the terribly risky genetic method of reproduction [they've] taken over" (EI, 48), there are many entities with a range of different mutations. The entities are assessed according to how close they are to the "total norm" and hierarchically categorized. Those found physically or mentally distant from the complete norm are called "nonfunctional" and kept in "kages." Some are missing fingers or toes or have gills. Some entities without limbs or human physical features, drooling and gibbering and in worlds of pain, are sometimes killed by those who tend the kages. Those who are physically close to the human norm, although sometimes with slight aberrations, are called "functional." Those deemed functional are also given gendered articles before their names which may or may not fit with the species' own system of sexes: Lo for male, La for female, and Le for their third sex.

Those with mental and psychic abilities—to move things and read minds—are called "different." Some are rendered nonfunctional and relegated to the kage. Those who are functional enough to be of use are expected to keep their differences quiet and to stay on the move.

Our main character, and our narrator, Lo Lobey, is a functional, although not a total norm. His physical attributes include very thick skin and toes with opposable digits. These he celebrates with delight in their usefulness as he journeys on his quest. He is also different in that he has incredible musical ability and telepathic powers, including those that reach beyond death. Music goes with him everywhere, as he carries with him a machete that doubles as a flute-like musical instrument.

The story opens in a village, of which we are told very little. Unlike Delany's other often heavily detailed prose, *Einstein* is cryptic and incomplete in its storytelling. We are unsure of the fate of humans, and we are told very little of the new species' origins: where they came from, why, and how. While we are placed carefully in the sound, smell, and feel of the immediate surroundings, the larger map of this dystopian world remains opaque as we travel from jungle to seashore.

In the village there is much debate about how the lines between functional and nonfunctional are drawn and how difference should be judged. Those of a previous generation remember when the nonfunctionals were killed off in droves. Lo Hawk, an elder in the village, remembers. "You don't *know* what they did to them when I was a boy, young Lo man. You never saw them dragged back from the jungle when a few did manage to survive. You didn't see the barbaric way complete norms acted, their reason shattered bloody by fear" (EI, 15).

Even with his critique of the cruel policing of an earlier generation, Lo Hawk is concerned with preserving a rigid normative human template. He maintains, "In my day, La and Lo were reserved for total norms. We've been very lax, giving this title of purity to any functional who happens to have the misfortune to be born in these confusing times." But other members have a different approach to life and its plasticity. Another elder, La Dire, replies, "Times change, and it has been an unspoken precedent for thirty years that La and Lo be bestowed on any functional creature born in this our new home." The real issue, as La Dire points out, is just how to draw the line between function and nonfunction through the template of the human. "The question is merely how far to extend the definition of functionality," she says. The novel brings into relief the arbitrary nature of policing the edges of what gets deemed human. Does one born mute, with six fingers and the ability to shift objects without touching them, get a title reflecting their gender? La or Lo or

Le? According to whose criteria do potential assets—extra fingers, telepathy, kinesthetic abilities—become liabilities?

The conversation between Lo Hawk and La Dire occurs during the assessment of a being named Friza, to determine whether to consider her functional and grant her the gendered article La. As a baby, she had been put in the kage as she refused to move. When it was discovered Friza could indeed move, she was taken out of the kage. But when she refused to speak, they took away her La. Lo Hawk and La Dire disagree about the use of language as an assessment for judging a being as functionally human. "Is the ability to communicate verbally the *sine qua non*?," La Dire asks, questioning the use of language and verbal communication as the gauge by which to measure someone's worth or ability. Lo Hawk believes so.

Their opposing perspectives are summed up in this conversation:

> "The beginning of the end, the beginning of the end," muttered Lo Hawk. "We must preserve something."
> "The end of the beginning," sighed La Dire. "Everything must change."
> Which had been their standing exchange as long as I remember" (EI, 4).

Lo Hawk and La Dire's ongoing debate speaks to the questions of the human at the heart of the novel and of central interest to me. It speaks to the arbitrary system of species definition and the exclusionary nature of how the human is defined. It is ultimately about what change means, and about the ability to accept fundamental transformation.

As the story opens, Lo Lobey is herding sheep with others of his kind, those with abilities useful on the job. While herding, they meet Friza, and soon she and Lo Lobey are companions. When Friza is killed, Lo Lobey goes on a quest to find what killed her and avenge her death. This quest weaves together several mythical journeys central within European and American origin stories: Theseus and the minotaur, Orpheus in his quest for Eurydice, the myth of the cowboy on the range, the story of migration to the city. While looking to find answers about Friza, Lo Lobey's first test is to hunt a bull-like creature, mutated from radiation, through the maze of the source cave and consult an oracle, a computer called "Psychic Harmony and Entangled Deranged Response Associations," or PHAEDRA, one of those that "still chuckled and chattered throughout the source cave" (EI, 30, 26). In the second phase of his journey Lo Lobey wrangles dragons with a gang of herders, ending up in a city, Branning-at-Sea, where he meets his final oracle, a third-sex entity called Le Dove, who embodies the iconography of a Hollywood star. All the while he is in search of Kid Death, who has killed Friza. In the ultimate test, he must face the Kid and learn the truth of his own power, the ability to bring back the people the Kid has killed. It is Lo Lobey's musicality that brings the end to Kid Death. "There is no death, only rhythm," we are told, and throughout the novel Lo Lobey brings the force of such vibration (EI, 78). Death ceases to be an end, but another state of being.

Each of the oracles Lo Lobey meets speaks to him of the limits of the species' endeavors to live circumscribed by human norms. "You're a bunch of psychic manifestations, multisexed and incorporeal, and you—you're all trying to put on the limiting mask of humanity," chides the computer oracle PHAEDRA (EI, 129). Le Dove exclaims, "Lobey, we're not human! We live on their planet, because they destroyed it. We've tried to take their form, their memories, their myths. But they don't fit" (EI, 128). Ultimately, the call is for change. "We're worn out trying to be human, Lobey," Le Dove tells him. "To survive even a dozen more generations we must keep the genes mixing, mixing, mixing" (EI, 124).

Change is not self-willed but a larger process that the species can either accept or fight against. "Something's happening, Lobey, something now that's happened before when the others were here," says Spider. "Many of us are worried about it. We have the stories about what went on, what resulted when it happened to the others."

But the stories inherited from the humans are insufficient. Lo Lobey replies, "I'm tired of the old stories . . . their stories. We're not them; we're new to this world, this life. I know the stories of Lo Orpheus and Lo Ringo. Those are the only ones I care about" (EI, 78).

Lo Lobey's musical gift is to hear the music running in others' thoughts and produce it on his machete. He can reproduce the old rhythms, the old melodies, from the templates of others' minds. While in Branning-at-Sea with Le Dove he is finally able to risk playing an original tune, to compose a new vibration, a new melody for life.

"Earth . . . fifth planet from the sun—the species that stands on two legs and roams this thin wet crust: it's changing," says Spider. "We have taken over their abandoned world and something new is happening to the fragments, something we can't even define with mankind's leftover vocabulary. . . . It is indefinable; you are involved in it; it is wonderful, fearful, deep, ineffable to your explanations, opaque to your efforts to see through it; yet it demands you take journeys, defines your stopping and starting points, can propel you with love and hate, even to seek death for Kid Death—" Lobey interrupts Spider, "—or make me make music" (EI, 110). Newness, the embrace of a continual becoming, begins with a different frequency, a new tune.

We return to the conversation between Lo Hawk and La Dire:

"The beginning of the end, the beginning of the end," muttered Lo Hawk. "We must preserve something."
"The end of the beginning," sighed La Dire. "Everything must change."

Is it about the end, and therefore we need to preserve the human? Or is it the beginning, and we need to embrace change? What would it look like to take as our provocation the idea that we embrace our inhumanness? Can we let go of our old myths? What would it mean to let go of the assumption of human superiority and open up to new forms of sociality and modes of being?

# PART III
# SENSE AND
# MATTER

# IN THE REALM OF THE SENSES

**5**

Heterotopias of Subjectivity, Desire, and Discourse

Desire says: "I should not like to have to enter this risky order of discourse; I should not like to be involved in its peremptoriness and decisiveness; I should like it to be all around me like a calm transparence, infinitely open, where others would fit in with my expectations, and from which truths would emerge one by one; I, should only have to let myself be carried, within it and by it, like a happy wreck."—MICHEL FOUCAULT, "The Order of Discourse" (1977)

Estranging ourselves from common notions of the human frees us to think differently about how we are with one another and with/in/as part of a wider, unknowable universe. This process of estrangement involves recognizing, imagining, or inhabiting other states of being, both psychic and physical. At their limits, these forms of existence are not wedded to species nor at the center of the universe. But imagining who "we" are when humans are decentered and denatured is difficult. What then would be the basis of subjectivity? Does subjectivity depend on individuation? Can individuation be separated from a possessive individualist epistemology?

Questioning liberal humanism's individualist politics in the search for a new sense of collectivity—a utopia—means to face a tension between exploring alternative forms of subjectivity apart from the idea of sovereign control and creating the good life. Utopia, in a humanist sense, is about creating a world without want based in the fulfillment of people's needs and desires. Locating these needs and desires would seem to require an autonomous subject, human fulfillment necessarily predicated on sovereignty over the self. But can the subject ever be an unconstrained author, unified, knowing, and autonomous? Do our desires make us whole and stable entities? Are they truthtelling? Or are they culturally and politically constructed according to particular epistemic frameworks? Can we articulate desires outside established circuits of knowledge (discourse)? Is selfhood predicated on this articulation? These are the questions I explore in the context of the utopian worlds found in science fiction writer Samuel R. Delany's novel about utopia, *Trouble on Triton: An Ambiguous Heterotopia,* and in early-nineteenth-century social utopianist Charles Fourier's voluminous *Oeuvres complètes de Charles Fourier* [Complete Works of Charles Fourier], particularly Volume 5, *Le nouveau monde amoureux* [The New Amorous World].[1] This may seem a strange coupling, but these texts read well together as both envision utopias predicated on the fulfillment of all passions and predilections, with an emphasis on the physical senses. As such, they both provoke questions of desire and subjectivity. My central exploration is how desire and its fulfillment both form and diffuse the individual self. Letting our desire—our physical desire—loose, I propose, allows for the self to be in motion, in transformation, in becoming. Transgender and transsexuality theories point us to this idea, taking *trans* to mean the relaxation of the need for set and fixed gender and sexual identities and the embrace of fluid and expansive modes of being.

Neither of the texts I analyze takes desire in a Hegelian sense—as negation, or lack, as Lacan would have it. Instead, desire is understood in a Deleuzian sense—as effulgent, "a productive and generative activity."[2] Gilles Deleuze takes desire as a multiplying and playful set of forces not so much about power but "an exchange that intensifies and proliferates energy and power into a state of excess."[3] Desire is foundational to subjectivity but not the result of a dialectical process meant to lead to a unified self. Desire is not unifying. Understanding this, "once the requirement of discrete identity no longer governs the subject, difference is less a source of danger than it is a condition of self-enhancement and pleasure," writes Judith Butler.[4] There is a place for subjectivity, just not one governed by an originary and ahistorical center prior to language. Subjectivity is more a matter of a relational practice, always in motion and always already becoming, always in response to the worlds around us.

Selfhood need not be dependent on a hard kernel of truth, a solid, unchanging core centered in the mind. The ideal of the human is that the species has a superior form of sentience based in a relationship to language and abstract thought. But, in a beautiful passage from his essay "Shadow and Ash," Delany qualifies selfhood not as mastery but as selfhood held in a gentle, flexible web of desire:

> "I am the sweeping tapestry of my sensory and bodily perceptions. I am their linguistic reduction and abstraction, delayed and deferred till they form a wholly different order, called my thought. I am, at the behest and prompting of all of these, my memory, which forms still another order. I am the emotions that hold them together. Webbing the four, and finally, I am the flux and filigree of desire around them all."[5]

Delany's delicate and graceful articulation of "I am" points to a supple sense of the self, one not bound by hard edges but by a fluid lacing of desire.

In *Triton*, as in many of his works, Delany is interested in the nature of discourse. Michel Foucault is an overarching presence in this book, and the novel questions the relationship between discursive ordering and what remains elusive about sensual worlds. Delany's critique is of the ways desire disrupts discourse, and of the way this disruption shows the constitution of subjectivity to be ambiguous. Language, taxonomies, and categorizations fail us if we try to classify and stabilize our passions. The novel's central tension is between the static force of discourse and the fluidity of the feeling self. Reading *Triton* next to Fourier's *Le Nouveau Monde Amoureux*, I explore how desire, lust, and their gratification refuse language. But I also find, in Delany's theoretical metanarrative and in Fourier's eccentric and grandiose opus, that attempting to capture the desiring subject also causes language to proliferate, to explode into a million pieces.

The Triton of Delany's novels is a moon circling Neptune, settled by humans from Earth and Mars. It is a utopian enclave set up to honor each of its citizens' desires and proclivities and to develop social structures to gratify every propensity. The utopian society's organizing principle is to make "the subjective reality of each of its citizens as inviolable as possible" (TT, 225). The libidinal pleasures of Triton's citizens are paramount, and Triton's sexual

**Figure 5.1** Samuel Delany, circa 2003. Photograph by Laurie Toby Edison from *Familiar Men: A Book of Nudes* (San Marino, CA: Shifting Focus Press, 2003).

freedom is the "golden myth of [the] two worlds [Earth and Mars]" (TT, 105). This world would seem one of infinite freedom, but the text holds an implicit critique of the ordering of this world. Triton society is built around classification, on the hardening of predilection into fixed, categorizable identities. Desires and proclivities define identities, dividing them into "type[s]" (TT, 5). There are "forty or fifty basic sexes, falling loosely into nine categories" (TT, 99). Subjects can change their bodies and objects of sexual desire at will through processes of medical and psychological refixation. But in order for one's reality to be inviolable, the subject must choose, must be fixed in place and discursively determined with firm boundaries around itself. Such fixation occludes the mutability of human passions and their tendency to be fluid and protean. There is crisis between such protean surfaces and need for fixation. Does the self need a bounded wholeness in order to be? Or can it thrive in the effluent?

Delany troubles the idea that desires can be fixed and categorized and that our identities can be identified in this way. Desire cannot be contained. Desire disrupts discourse, marking "the limit to language itself."[6] These limits are what *Triton* explores: the ways in which a discursive parameter around a self is ambiguous, clouded by desire and its pleasurable gratification.

This is also the main problem that the discipline of metalogics, the founding philosophy of Triton, is trying to solve. Metalogics' central purpose is the "rigorous mapping of the Universe of Discourse" (TT, 52). One of metalogics' most brilliant theorists was Ashima Slade, whose story and theories furnish appendix B following the main story. This appendix is written in the form of a critical biography, parodying academic writing. Slade's quoted theories are a profusion of mostly indecipherable equations and suppositions. The disruption of discourse shows language to be insufficient to capture desire or pleasure. But this disruption is also one that causes a profusion, rather than a negation, of language—a cacophony ignited by sensation.


Fourier's Passions

Such is the case with the absurdly complex ordering and logic of Charles Fourier's utopian plan, spelled out in eight volumes. I focus particularly on his vision of sexual utopia, outlined in the suppressed volume *Le nouveau monde amoureux*. In it Fourier insists that the repression of desire is the source of all inequality and corruption. He envisions utopia as the complete fulfillment of all human passions. Fourier was adamantly opposed to the ideas of the Enlightenment philosophes, particularly Rousseau and Voltaire, for whom reason and moderation were key. For Fourier, any philosophy calling for the restraint of humans' desires had it wrong.

Fourier is an important figure, underrecognized by queer theory. He was an ardent feminist and polyamorist with an open and flexible understanding of sexuality and gender and an embrace of polymorphous sexualities and familial structures. Like Delany's satellite Triton, Fourier's world lets us see what fantasies can be spun when the fulfillment of human desires is the fundament of a social world. At the core of Fourier's utopia is what he called the "passions."[7] The passions are immutable and unchangeable urges at the core of every person, but also, according to what Fourier calls "universal analogy," passions are the primary principle of all of the cosmos, with the laws of "passionate attraction" generating the entire universe.[8]

As on Triton, in Fourier's world the passions necessitate forms of classification. Fourier's utopian vision, published in his *Oeuvres Complètes* in 1817, was shaped by the zeitgeist of his time to chart and order everything into a world system. Fourier called his system, by which the properties of passionate attraction could be ordered applying mathematical and physical laws, a science. According to him, these laws are in "complete accord with the laws of material attraction, as explained by Newton and Leibniz."[9] Yet Fourier's systematic rendering of the entire universe is a bewildering and complex labyrinth; his series and lists and taxonomies follow their own rules of association. There are also interesting parallels between Fourier's relentless calculations and classifications and the metalogical theories of Ashima Slade, which I will explore later in the chapter.

Fourier's system for ordering the world identifies the passions as twelve in number. Individuals are dominated by one or more of these essential passions, which form a series. The passionate series falls into three categories. The first, the "luxurious" passions, are governed by the five senses; these are not base urges but basic needs.[10] The second category includes the "affective passions: friendship, love, ambition, and familism."[11] The third category contains the "distributive passions," which organize the other two. These include the tendency to intrigue and rivalry and the "butterfly" passion, which is the need to "flutter from pleasure to pleasure, every two hours."[12] The highest distributive passion is the desire for a perfect balance of physical and spiritual gratification.

Unlike Triton's designer utopia of the individual, with fulfillment defined simply as the satisfaction of personal proclivity, Fourier's vision of utopian fulfillment is a larger concept with collective scope. For Fourier, a world ordered around the passions was anathema to "Egotism" or "the mania for subordinating everything to our own individual convenience"; the aim of his plan is "happiness . . . the full development of 'Unityism'."[13] In Fourier's sexual universe, pleasure is the collective obligation of all of the society's citizens. Most importantly, the senses of taste and touch are essential, the bare necessities of life, and all citizens are guaranteed by collective obligation to receive a minimum level of gratification for these senses. "The sexual needs of men and women can become just as urgent as the need for food," he writes. "It follows that society should grant a minimum of satisfaction to the two senses of taste and touch. For the needs of these two senses can become much more urgent than those of the other three."[14] In a system of "sexual philanthropy," Harmony, the name of his utopia, has a social organization, headed by a supremely enlightened group called the Angelics, that will meet the needs of everyone, from rejected lovers to the elderly and the disabled. Collective sexual expression is an integral part of Harmonian society. Orgies of various types include "introductory orgies and farewell orgies, fortuitous orgies and bacchanalian orgies." Some orgies are, like dances, choreographed; others, called "museum orgies," are for visual stimulation only. Orgies are part of the ways in which the different passions are organized.[15]

Fourier's utopian mandate is that the sexual desires of every person in Harmony's phalansteries are to be fulfilled. Fourier himself was an enthusiastic lover of lesbians. He writes, "I was thirty five years old when by chance a scene in which I was an actor made me realize that I had the taste of mania of Sapphianism, the love of lesbians and the eagerness to aid them in every way possible."[16] Harmony particularly values those with tastes condemned as "perversions. . . . Lesbians, sodomites, fetishists, and flagellants all figured prominently in his descriptions of amorous life in the higher stages of what he called Harmony."[17] Those with multiple sexual proclivities have reached the highest stages of enlightenment.[18] Fourier critiques de Sade: cruelty and a "taste for atrocities is simply a consequence of the suffocation of certain passions."[19] Manias such as "heel scratching" are not aberrations but particular needs for certain people that have to be honored.[20]

Fourier rejected marriage, monogamy, and compulsory heterosexuality as unnatural social impositions that repressed the variety and fluidity of human sexual inclinations. "Polygamous penchants are universal," he proclaimed.[21] Fourier inspired feminists in the 1840s, as he was adamantly critical of the patriarchal family household and marriage. Marriage, for Fourier, was a "mercantile calculation" and a woman "a piece of merchandise, offered to the highest bidder."[22] He writes, "Their conjugal system only tolerates that form of love which is strictly necessary for propagation. It would be impossible to conceive of a social order any more drastic in its restriction of love."[23] Instead, Fourier proposed "eighty to a hundred people, [living] together in 'progressive households' in which members of both sexes would benefit from flexible arrangements concerning lovemaking and the performance of domestic chores."[24]

For Fourier, passionate attraction is the "central element in a comprehensive vision of the universe."[25] Like his amorous world, his exceptionally creative cosmological theories were suppressed by the many followers of his economic and social model of the phalanstery. In Fourier's cosmological vision, the planets themselves are heavenly creatures, each with their own life cycles. The movement of celestial bodies is the result of stars and galaxies drawn to each other; some are "androgynous organisms" with distinctive "aromas that allowed them to copulate with each other at a distance."[26] Fourier writes, "All stars can copulate: 1. With itself like a vegetable, the north pole copulating with the south, 2. With another star by means of outpourings from contrasting poles, 3. With the help of an intermediary."[27]

Fourier's work has its intersections with science fiction. Once humankind has adapted itself to Harmony, great changes will occur on earth. Animal species will change, continents will shift, and the sea will turn to lemonade. But, most importantly, the human species will mutate, growing to seven feet in height and living for 144 years. Humans will become amphibious and, after sixteen generations, develop an "archibras," a prehensile tail with a small, strong hand at its end.[28]

## Delany's Heterotopias

Fourier's world-making project, with its endless charts and taxonomies, seems just the type of planned utopia Delany would reject. Delany satirizes such blueprint utopias by constructing Triton's society as based in an absurdly endless labyrinth of types and categories of desire. In an interview, "Of *Trouble on Triton* and Other Matters," Delany dismisses in no uncertain terms the idea of a planned utopia—or at least the use of the concept in writing or interpreting science fiction. He specifically damns the concept in the reading of *Triton*. "I've always seen SF thinking as fundamentally different from utopian thinking: I feel that to force SF into utopian templates is a largely unproductive strategy," he says.[29] "To look for *any* critique in [*Triton*] in utopian/dystopian terms will, I suspect, doom you to disappointment and/or distortion."[30] Yet there is no denying an explicit conversation between *Triton* and utopian thought, as Delany chose as *Triton's* subtitle *An Ambiguous Heterotopia*, after Ursula K. Le Guin's utopian novel *The Dispossessed*, which is subtitled *An*

*Ambiguous Utopia*. Delany finds Le Guin's novel a rich exploration of the possibility and failure of utopia because it troubles the idea itself. Delany writes, "It's only by problematizing the utopian notion, by rendering its hard, hard perimeters somehow permeable, even undecidable, that you can make it yield anything interesting."[31] Delany explains that he could never detail the world of Triton completely, for any sociopolitical structure must remain supple, open to change and experimentation, and its boundaries porous. A totalizing plan for social engineering cannot account for the shifting quality, the permeability, of people's propensities and their gratification.

It would seem that Delany adopted the concept of *heterotopia* to disrupt the totalizing claims of a utopia. Various fields, including architecture and literary criticism, have taken up the concept of heterotopia, defined by Foucault in a lecture given in 1967. Foucault introduces his concept of heterotopia as "something like counter sites, a kind of effectively enacted utopia."[32] In this lecture utopia and heterotopia are not mutually exclusive terms. Foucault states, "I believe that between utopias and these quite other sites, these heterotopias, there might be a sort of mixed, joint experience."[33] Most critics have defined heterotopias as spaces of "resistance and transgression" and described them as having an exclusively subversive function, particularly in relation to urban spaces.[34] Foucault states, "A society, as its history unfolds, can make an existing heterotopia function in a very different fashion. . . . [Heterotopia functions] as a sort of simultaneously mythic and real contestation of the space in which we live."[35] Gardens, libraries, festivals, and Scandinavian saunas all are on Foucault's list of heterotopian spaces. In popular parlance the term has therefore come to refer solely to liberatory enclaves, permissive spaces that are free from oppression and outside a (particularly sexual) hegemonic normative. In other sections of his lecture, however, Foucault designates distinctly oppressive sites as heterotopian—old-age homes, brothels, and prisons—and sites whose function is to preserve societal structures are painfully dystopian spaces for some. In Foucault's lecture the term *heterotopia* also refers to colonies and imperial spaces like "Polynesian villages that offer a compact three weeks of primitive and eternal nudity to the inhabitants of the cities."[36] Here Foucault seems to miss the oppressive function these spaces serve. Imperial spaces evoke the history of primitivist fantasies of utopia, such as adventurers, missionaries, naturalists, and merchants' accounts of travel, in which they happen upon ideal societies whose primitive inhabitants lead lives of leisure and abundance. The ship, for Foucault, is also a heterotopia. It is included at the end of his lecture as it sails "from port to port . . . from brothel to brothel . . . as far as the colonies in search of the most precious treasures they conceal in their gardens."[37] I am not sure what Foucault expects us to understand about heterotopias here or how those critics evoking the term as sites of resistance account for these particular examples. For these instances—especially for those forced into the hold of the ship or those living under imperial rule in the colony—don't seem liberatory or counterhegemonic at all.

As we shall see, heterotopia operates in more than one sense for Foucault, and the term takes on a number of meanings in *Triton*. On the one hand, heterotopian spaces, in terms of urban planning, architecture, and social organization, are consciously structured in the novel as "effectively enacted utopias" around the desires and proclivities of the population. There are various heterotopias within the novel by which personal and collective desire and gratification are organized, from communal living arrangements and religious sects to performance theater and work environments.

But Delany references another meaning of the term not found in Foucault. *Heterotopia* is also a medical or biological term, as Delany states, referring to the coexistence of one tissue type with another: "skin grafts" and "sex change . . . are one meaning of the word."[38] In *Triton* the body itself is a primary heterotopology. Heterotopias operate at the level of the body or, more accurately, the flesh, from the self-mutilation of religious sects to the sex and race reassignments the novel's characters undergo. Body-modification practices feature in a number of Delany's early science fiction novels. In this sense the conceptual terrain of Delany's novels predates the work of William Gibson, credited with ideas of body modification in what was termed *cyberpunk*.

On Triton, characters modify and remodify their bodies and refix their objects of desire at will. Identities based in race, gender, or sexual and spiritual desires are a matter of changing preferences. Through refixation, sexual predilections can be reset from straight to gay; race changed from black to white; gender altered from woman to man—and back again. On Triton bodies are plastic—if you are unhappy with your body, you can have it altered. You can dress in ordinary clothing or in costume—or go naked—as you choose. Every preference you may have is considered part of the sanctity of your subjective reality:

> If you want to manacle an eighteen-year-old boy to the wall and pierce their nipples with red-hot needles . . . you can always drop in [after work] to a place where eighteen-year-old boys who happen to be into that sort of thing . . . have all gotten together in a mutually beneficial alliance where you and they, and your Labrador retriever, if she's what it takes to get you off, can all meet one another on a footing of cooper-

ation, mutual benefit, and respect . . . If you aren't satisfied . . . you can make an appointment to have your preferences switched. . . . If you find your own body distasteful, you can have it regenerated, dyed green or heliotrope, padded out here, slimmed down there. . . . And if you're just too jaded for any of it, you can turn to the solace of religion and let your body mortify any way it wants to while you concentrate on whatever your idea of Higher Things happens to be, in the sure knowledge that when you are tired of that, there's a diagnostic computer waiting with soup and a snifter in the wings to put you back together. (TT, 99)

The predominant heterotopias on Triton are articulated through the body. These articulations are based in desires but also, the novel seems to say, on the self-indulgent whims of the individual. *Triton*'s critique is of a world designed around the sanctity of an individual's preferences devolving into self-indulgence. Delany published *Triton* in 1976, in an era marked by utopian thinking and communing, in the years of a historical moment when utopian possibility had been the daily practice for sub- and countercultural first worlders. Part of the critique available in *Triton* is of what happened to the healthy hedonism of the 1960s and 1970s. What had begun as a liberatory movement based in philosophical commitment could, without collective vision, devolve into solipsistic self-gratification and egotism.

Trouble on Triton

At the beginning of *Trouble on Triton* we are introduced to a range of heterotopian spaces and modes of being. As the novel opens, Bron Helstrom, Delany's main character, strides through the streets of Triton's principal city, Tethys, on his way home from work. Bron's is the first heterotopia we meet: he was, in his younger days, a prostitute (as indicated by the arc of gold that replaces one eyebrow) in the city of Bellona, on Mars, where he is from. Male prostitution on Mars, we learn, was "a highly taxed and government approved job" following its legalization by Mars's female president (TT, 79). Bron no longer works in that field. We join Bron on Triton as he is walking home from his job as a "metalogician" for a giant computer company.

A religious sect is the second heterotopia we come across in the novel. Near Bron the Poor Children of the Avestal Light and Changing Secret Name, or mumblers, walk the streets, chanting endlessly. The Poor Children is a self-abnegating sect in daily practice of purification, an example of extreme asceticism as heterotopia. Yet they are less extreme than other sects on Triton who maim in self-mortification. Some of the most graphic heterotopian body modification we encounter is in followers of the many religious sects on Triton. Next, Bron encounters a follower of a self-mutilating sect called the Rampant Order of Dumb Beasts. The man is "filthy" and heavily mutilated, "the flesh high and to the left of his nose was so scarred, swollen and dirty, Bron could not tell if the sunken spot glistening within was an eye or an open wound" (TT, 12). The man inexplicably jumps out of the dark and slugs a woman walking by, then tells Bron he is safe. This woman turns out to be "the Spike," who will play a central part in the narrative. But even these extreme examples of human suffering appear composed. "The things people will do to their bodies," Bron judges, in a later encounter with another member of this sect. "Just as the outsized muscles were conscientiously clinic-grown . . . so the filth, the scars, the sores, the boils that speckled the grimed arms and hips were from conscientious neglect" (TT, 95). The Rampant Order of Dumb Beasts has as its creed, as the Spike explains, "putting an end to meaningless communication. Or is it meaningful?" (TT, 12). The Dumb Beasts, the mumblers, and other sects on Triton all reject language, speech, or education in some way, their ascetic and spiritual desires refusing discourse.

On Triton there is a heterotopology of communal living arrangements, each organized and classified by familial, sexual, and gendered desires. After walking through the unlicensed district, Bron makes his way back home to a room in Serpent's House, an all-male, sexually nonspecified co-op. On his block are a gay male co-op, a straight male co-op, and three mixed co-ops (male/female/straight/gay); a heterosexual female co-op is four blocks away. Some, like Bron's lactating boss, Philip, live in "complex family communes," many of which are found in and on the more affluent ring surrounding Tethys (TT, 57). At Serpent's House we meet Bron's friends: Sam, a former white lesbian who has become a black straight man, and Lawrence, a seventy-two-year-old white gay man. Disability and age are also accounted for on Triton. As well as Sam and Lawrence, we meet Flossie, a twenty-three-year-old man with neurological defects, and Freddie, his ten-year-old son. Technological assistance through crystalline memory units in the form of rings supplement both. Ideas of age, childhood, and adolescence are also denaturalized. At Bron's workplace we meet the seven aged sisters, members of a cult that formerly shunned literacy, retrained and now employed, and the twelve-year-old twin sisters Tristan and Iseult, former managers of the entire Tethys wing of the hegemony.

Bron Helstrom walks home through what is called the city's unlicensed (u-l) sector, a set-aside area where "no official law held" and anything was permissible; these u-l heterotopias were established in cities on each of the satellites, as they "fulfilled a complex range of functions in the cities' psychological, political, and economic ecology" (TT, 8). Although there are no official laws, unofficial laws develop here, and the u-l has very little crime. There is a "definite and different feel in the u-l streets," which is why Bron decides to walk through the sector on his way home (TT, 8). While walking through the u-l sector, Bron encounters the Spike, now in a gold cape and with gold eyes. She leads him without his knowledge to another heterotopian space, an experimental theater event in the streets of the u-l. For the experience to be immersive, Bron must be led in unawares, and so the Spike brings him to a small street square. Here a blazing fire fills a trashcan, lighting the face of a girl strumming a guitar. Another girl suckles a baby and yet another figure slides down a long rope. The figures begin swaying and singing to the music, and an acrobat performs magnificent flips. Bron, stimulated by a mild psychedelic, is enveloped in ecstasy and brought to tears, with his entire body tingling. It is only later that the Spike tells him that the troupe is a theatrical commune "operating on a Government Arts Endowment to produce micro theater for unique audiences" (TT, 17). This theatrical commune, which will be with us through the rest of the novel, is one of the text's utopian sects that create heterotopian spaces with their shows.

This encounter illustrates the body as heterotopia—but it also shows the body, especially in relation to other bodies, as a site of utopian expression— acrobatic, rhythmic, melodic, full of sensation. Most importantly, this utopian moment is built on reciprocity and is beyond a merely individual experience; it is based in a sense of fulfillment among fellows, in this particular example between Bron and the actors. The utopian body is not fixed but illusive and, unlike in the case of heterotopian body modification, expressed relationally.

In "Of Other Spaces" Foucault's definition of heterotopia primarily has to do with the use and organization of social space. In this respect he allows utopia and heterotopia to coexist. This bears out in another lecture Foucault gave in 1967. In "Utopian Body" [*Le corps utopique*] he says, "For me to be a utopia it is enough that I be a body. . . . The human body is the principal actor in all utopias."[39] Foucault's lyrical, almost romantic tone in this lecture contrasts with his otherwise quite analytical voice in the rest of his work from that year. It also seems inconsistent with his critique of the idea that there is a locus of self that exists prior to language. He continues, "The body . . . is at the heart of the world. This small utopian kernel from which I dream, I speak, I proceed, I imagine, I perceive things in their place, and I negate them also by the indefinite power of the utopias I imagine. My body is like the City of the Sun. It has no place, but it is from it that all possible places, real or utopian, emerge and radiate."[40] It is almost as if there were an ontological truth, a centered self, a "small utopian kernel" at the heart of the body that governs action. Yet Foucault's declaration is a recognition of the generative power of our senses as they work together.

Reading another passage Foucault wrote, also in 1967, about utopia and heterotopia in *The Order of Things: An Archaeology of the Human Sciences*, it would seem that for him there are contradictions around these concepts. When applied directly to the subject of discourse, heterotopia takes on another meaning. In *The Order of Things* Foucault adamantly differentiates between the two. This sense of the relationship between the concepts is important, as it is quoted by Delany at the end of the novel, before *Triton's* crucial appendix B.

> *Utopias* afford consolation: although they have no real locality there is nevertheless a fantastic, untroubled region in which they are able to unfold; they open up cities with vast avenues, superbly planted gardens, countries where life is easy, even though the road to them is chimerical. *Heterotopias* are disturbing, probably because they make it impossible to name this *and* that, because they shatter or tangle common names, because they destroy "syntax" in advance, and not only the syntax with which we construct sentences but also that less apparent syntax which causes words and things (next and opposite one another) to "hold together." This is why utopias permit fables and discourse: they run with the very grain of language and are part of the fundamental *fabula*; heterotopias . . . dessicate speech, stop words in their tracks, contest the very possibility of grammar at its source; they dissolve our myths and sterilize the lyricism of our sentences.[41]

Heterotopias rupture discourse; they distort and tear apart what would be held together by it. They interrupt order and are unruly. They stop language. Like and as desire, they show its limits. They open to a space not reachable by language, to an ineffable and seemingly confusing place.

### Fourier's Profusion, or, The Cycloid

Charles Fourier's endless classification would seem part of what Foucault criticizes about utopia: that it "runs with the grain of language." Yet the sheer magnitude and creativity of Fourier's ordering of the world are fascinating, as is his dedication to recognizing every single passion, desire, mania, or fetish that could exist. His systems are illogical, of another order altogether, and create their own rules. Here desire disrupts discourse and could be thought of as heterotopian. Yet it does so not with silence; language is not stopped but *meaning* is—by an ungovernable profusion. Order and meaning are torn apart, established myths destroyed. We are in and of language, but a language ordered differently.

Fourier designed systems, categories, and series to delineate the various connections and associations between the passions, be they animal, vegetable, mineral, material, emotional, or sexual. He devised his own bizarre yet strangely poetic "passional grammar with its own declensions, conjugations and syntax."[42] Obsessed with associating everything in the entire universe, including emotions and sexual behavior, Fourier designed his own discursive logic based in his own associative patterns. Numbers, colors, flavors, shapes, and proclivities correspond and are ordered into categories major and minor, into ascending and descending wings, phases, and combinations, and are organized into charts and tables. Fourier calls the laws of the four movements "hieroglyphs," as he devises his own semiotic world.[43] For example, passionate attraction is ordered into groups and series:

| *Type* | *Symbol* |
| --- | --- |
| Major Group of Friendship | Circle |
| Group of ambition, cooperative tie | Hyperbola |
| | |
| Minor Group of Love | Ellipse |
| Group of paternity or family | Parabola |

Fourier's "wild system" fascinated Roland Barthes, and Barthes's fascination opens up a new appreciation for Fourier's obsessive naming, numbering, and listing.[44] Barthes gives us a post-structuralist analysis of Fourier:

The hieroglyphic, different from the symbol as the signifier is from the full, mystified sign. . . . The hieroglyph . . . postulate[s] a formal and arbitrary correspondence . . . between the various realms of the universe, for example between forms (circle, ellipse, parabola, hyperbola), colors, musical notes, passions (friendship, love, parental, ambition), the races of animal[s], the stars, and the periods of societal phylogenesis. The arbitrary obviously resides in the attribution: why is the ellipse the geometric hieroglyph for love? The parabola for parenthood? Yet this arbitrary is just as relative as is that of linguistic signs.[45]

Fourier's language reveals the arbitrary relationship between signifier and signified. His alternative discursive world shows that desire cannot be fully captured, and his attempt to do so shows the limits of language. Yet, as Barthes observes, it does not shut language down but causes it to proliferate. Rather than criticizing Fourier's system as an absurd attempt to control the entire universe, Barthes revels in Fourier's "adorable detail":

> Fourier's petty calculation is the simple lever that opens up the phantasmagory of adorable detail. . . . Detail (literally: *minutia*) magnifies, like joy. It is a fury of expansion, of possession, and in a word, of orgasm, by number, by classification: scarcely does an object appear that Fourier taxonomizes (we are tempted to say: sodomizes) it. . . .
>
> Perhaps the *imagination of detail* is what specifically defines Utopia. . . . This would be logical, since detail is fantasmatic and thereby achieves the very pleasure of Desire. In Fourier, the number is rarely statistical. . . . It is, through the apparent finesse of its precision, essentially quantitative. Nuance, the game being stalked in this taxonomic hunting expedition, is a guarantee of pleasure (of fulfillment). . . .
>
> The integral soul, a tapestry in which each nuance finds utterance, is the great sentence being sung by the universe: it is, in sum, the Language of which each of us is but a word. [46]

It is as if desires do not so much disrupt discourse as reconfigure it. They do not silence it but cause it to proliferate in phantasmagoric ways. While discourse, for Foucault, begins as a form of control and order, the passions' expansiveness demands we loosen our hold, lift off into a cloud of signs. Barthes writes, "Fourier . . . calls for an integral freedom [of tastes, passions, manias, whims]; thus, we could expect a spontaneistic philosophy, but we get quite the opposite: a wild system, whose very excess, whose fantastic tension, goes beyond systems and attains systematics, i.e. writing: liberty is never the opposite of order, it is *order paragrammatized* [Barthes's italics]." [47]

Barthes's paragrammatization resonates with Triton's philosophy of metalogics, which seeks to capture the nuance between desires and discourse. "Nuance," as Barthes writes, "is the acme of number and classification." Metalogics, the founding philosophy of Triton, is a "rigorous mapping of discourse," yet the mapping is far from able to capture the vaporous quality of the subject. The problem of this ambiguity is what metalogics is trying to illuminate.

It is in the field of metalogics that we encounter an allusion to Foucault, in the form of one of the field's authors, Ashima Slade, who writes thick volumes "full of dense and vaguely poetic meditations on life and language . . . outlining the mathematical foundations of the subject"(TT, 11). Bron's job as a metalogician is the classification, the attempt to approximate language and meaning, a kind of magic in itself. Bron explains an aspect of metalogics to his would-be assistant, Miriamne, thus:

> Language is parametal, not perimetal. Areas of significance space inter-mesh and fade into one another like color-clouds in a three-dimensional spectrum. They don't fit together like hard-edged bricks in a box. What makes "logical" bounding so risky is that the assertion of the formal logician that a boundary can be placed around an area of significance space gives you, in such a cloudy situation, no way to say where to set the boundary, how to set it, or if, once set, it will turn out the least useful. Nor does it allow for two people to be sure they have set their boundaries around the same area. (TT, 50)

This passage is partly understandable and partly not, as it is bound by Delany's fictional technical language. Bron's description accompanies his sexual advances toward Miriamne and can be seen as about desire. This cloudy situation seems the unsolvable ambiguity at the heart of the sexual heterotopias of Triton: how to set boundaries around desires. What if an individual can't firmly identify themselves? Or doesn't want to have to choose? In another section, Bron complains to the Spike, "Somewhere, in your sector or in mine, in this unit or in that one, there it is: pleasure, community, respect—all you have to do is know the kind, and how much of it, and to what extent, you want it. That's all. . . . But what happens to those of us who *don't* know?" (TT, 103). This is Bron's problem: that he thinks having a firm, stable sense of self based in the truth of one's desires is essential. This is the final and absurd tragedy of a rather unlikeable character. Ultimately discourse, either insufficient or proliferating, cannot encompass the sensing flesh. Desire is embedded in the visceral, composed of a decentralized relationality.

Bron is convinced that he needs a stable, unambiguous self, and that setting the parameters of his desires will provide that surety. Yet the novel ends with a return to indecision, to an overarching ambiguity. Following catastrophic events across the galaxy and the effects of the war on Triton, Bron has an epiphany based in a strange illogic of his own. Searching for surety, Bron impulsively undergoes a full gender reassignment as well as a refixation of his sexual proclivity. This is his attempt to embrace the body as heterotopia. The text turns satirical; as he goes between doctors, the scientific facts of the differences between genders are rendered absurd, the lines blurred, the ground made unsure:

> She was sure, sure for thirty-seven seconds . . . sure in a way that implied volumes on the rotation of the planets, on the entropy of the chemistry in the sun itself . . . sure with a surety which, if it were this subjectively complete must be objectivity (and wasn't that the reason why, her scrambling mind careened on . . . in these ice-and rockbound moons, the subjective was held politically inviolable . . . ? Then, as suddenly, sureness ceased. . . . She *had* been sure!), sure would never come. (TT, 278)

What Bron cannot come to terms with is what doesn't work about Triton: the attempt to render desire static, containable. Desire refuses, or diffuses, discourse; it resides in an outside to disrupt any ordered sense of the self. But it also forms the self: sensations giving us a soft, shadow-like shape. Perhaps fulfillment needn't rely on ourselves as bounded so like a brick. Perhaps we can imagine a calm opacity of meaning to ourselves, a softly binding flux and filigree of our desires.

# THE FREEDOM NOT TO BE

## Sun Ra's Alternative Ontology

**6**

This is the why of the music I represent; and this is the why of the image of a better world: the alter-life for the alter-life is different from the life of this world.—SUN RA, "My Music Is Words," in *Sun Ra Collected Works* (2005)

Omniverse
Is
The totality
Of all the universes
And you
Are welcome
To
Be citizens
Of
The Omniverse
—SUN RA, "Omniverse," in *Sun Ra Collected Works* (2005)

On what looks like a warm day in Egypt, in December of 1981, Sun Ra and his Arkestra dance and chant among the pyramids—vocalist June Tyson leading the way, with fabric fluttering behind her in the warm breeze. Tyson passes through an archway, followed by dancers and musicians including John Gilmore and Marshall Allen, who twirl, circle, and worship, arms outstretched. At the end of the procession strides Sun Ra. He pauses, stretching his arms wide to touch the piers of an archway, and then passes through it to the other side. It's as if he is floating between the present and the past, between this dimension and another, space- and time-traveling right in front of us. This is truly beautiful theatre, a graceful and bold invitation to expand our sense of time, space, and beingness. What happens if we unmoor ourselves from this world? these artists ask.

The musician and director of his group's performance, Sun Ra believed, as does Olamina, that the place for humans was extraterrestrial. But, unlike Olamina, he held that that "place" is also extrahuman. To be transported to the stars is to become a "cosmic multi-self," to join in a diffusion of cosmic elements.[1] Sun Ra's philosophy did not jive with the idea of subjectivity as a self, organized around a solid core or with the idea that liberation means being restored to a rightful sovereignty over the self. Joining in the nothing, jumping into the endless void, is to relinquish the self, to join in a multidimensional universe as "cosmic multi-selves."[2] Ra's philosophies reached toward a sense of beingness beyond a politics of earthbound inclusion.

In contrast to the world-building ethos of desire and passion found in Samuel Delany and Charles Fourier, Ra was an ascetic: for him, desire—earthbound passions—distracted from the discipline that was essential for transcendence into other planes of existence. To vibrate according to another frequency, to travel to other planets, meant adhering to very strict rules of self-denial and training. Sun Ra and his Arkestra operated according to stringent artistic principles that, while homosocial, did not include the usual sexual bravado of his male contemporaries in the world of jazz.

In other ways Ra's work can be read in the context of US black politics of his time. His frame of reference is often Afrocentric in that it refuses Eurocentric knowledge formations, seeking instead black ways of knowing which have been occluded by such formations. With deference to ancient Egypt glittering in the gods' heads of his elaborate headgear, his iconography evoked the trend in 1970s black politics and culture of reconnecting Egypt and Ethiopia to Africa, severed from the rest of the continent by Western Egyptology. But the scope of Ra's vision reached beyond black nationalisms or a struggle for representation in a US or global body politic. His call was not for civic or hu-

**Figure 6.1** Sun Ra.

man rights, recognition, reparation, or a nation on earth. "What is the world to me?" he writes. "It is truly nothing; I have sought to bypass it rather than become part of it, because it has no known diplomatic relations with the Creator Creater [*sic*] of the infinity universe."[3] As Zilpha Elaw, Sojourner Truth, Jarena Lee, Rebecca Cox Jackson, and Alice Coltrane did with their utopian visions and worship practices, Ra reached through his poetry, music, and performance for a utopianism that helps us recalibrate, or expand, conventional models of black political radicalism.

Looking at and listening to Sun Ra's written and spoken words, and the music and theater he created with his Arkestra, I consider his expansive philosophies of time, space, and existence as I continue my exploration of radical worlds and subjectivities. I argue that Ra's philosophical framework conceives of human life as a simple, limiting, and troubled dimension of an infinite beingness. His call is for us to tune in to an alternate frequency, to join the "omniverse," to become the "multi-self" of infinite nothingness.[4]

This chapter continues an exploration of beingness beyond the boundaries of what we know as possible, beyond the binding ideas of political engagement, organized religion, and biological evolution. My conversation is with utopian studies, Afrofuturism, and queer theory as I respond to concepts of the future and futurity in those fields. I share with all three a challenge to normative time, as they look to temporal disruptions as a key way to intervene in dominant regimes of power.

To call Sun Ra an Afro*futurist* may be inaccurate, for Sun Ra's relationship with time was fraught. "Me and time never got along so good—we just sort of ignore each other," he states.[5] *Time*, as Ra uses the term, refers to concepts of a linear, narrative, or evolutionary time that orders itself according to the past, present, and future. However much we trouble these terms, they are temporal markers tied to the human life span and irrelevant to a larger ontology of existence.

As well as not being concerned with the future, Ra was not concerned with the past. "The past is a fabrication-thing / Some fictitious one-dimension fantasy," he writes in his poem "The Past Is Like a Dream."[6] Ra also rarely references the present, as it is as binding as the past and future. The present is what we live and this, for Ra, is a dreadful state of being that must be traveled away from. For Ra, the temporal, at least as it is rendered by history, was not the primary axis of being or potential.

Queer theory and black studies have given us powerful arguments for the revolutionary force of alternative conceptions of time, notably ideas of futurity. But the concept of the future is often fettered by notions of progress and, even in its more liberated definitions, still limited to a particular understanding of time. "Somewhere on the other side of nowhere there's another place in space beyond what you know as time," Ra says.[7] His ideas of time and space rescale the idea of existence itself, asking us to think dimensionally and vibrationally.

I am also engaging in conversation with black studies about the valuation of the human. Zakiyyah Jackson has powerfully argued against (post)posthumanism's call to think beyond the human. While I agree we do not want to leave a politics of liberation behind in an apolitical backwash from such a call, I find in the poetry of Sun Ra another approach to the very idea of existence. His radical modes of existence take a Wynterian "new genre of being human" out into the cosmos.[8] Ultimately, we are no longer human at all but radically decentered, destabilized, dispersed as particles, energies, and vibrations. The effect of such radical disorientation is a powerful provocation. It may appear to be pure escapism—or it may spur new forms of relationality, communality, and collectivity, new paradigms of what we mean by freedom. To redefine the idea of human emancipation is not the goal; instead, it is complete abandonment of very limiting paradigms of life and self. In their profound alienation, their illegibility, black people have the "freedom not to be."[9]

The utopian energy of Ra's poetry and music enlivens the concept of the impossible. He writes, "The future is obvious, but the potential impossible is calling softly and knocking gently."[10] The future is what can be seen, or imagined, in our current epistemology, but the impossible exists outside the knowable world. As Brent Edwards points out, "Sun Ra's use of the word impossible is the recognition that . . . a radical alterity is inconceivable, and yet paradoxically exactly that which must be conceived."[11] The term *alterity* is a much more useful term than *futurity*. Alterity is nonlinear and multidirectional and suggests altogether different relationships to time and space. It implies an entire paradigm shift, a jump into the unknowable.

Rather than with metaphors of time, Sun Ra's poetry and spoken word ring with spatial metaphor and imagery. "Space is the place," the Arkestra chants, and Ra proclaims, "Time is officially ended." I think about how the spatial, instead of linear, narrative time, works as a central category in Ra's vision. I focus on the ways his philosophy reaches into space, as he thinks of alternative worlds in terms of ratio, dimension, and vibration. He thinks beyond the bounds of past, present, and future, death and life, into an infinite universe of multidimensions. Like Rebecca Cox Jackson's and Alice Coltrane/Turiyasangitananda's visions, Ra's science offers a geometry of the cosmos and presents the possibility of a utopia taking place on alternate planes of existence.

Ra's omniverse extends beyond the human form while remaining in the material realm. For Ra, as for Lauren Olamina in Octavia E. Butler's *Parable* series, our place is among the stars. But, unlike Olamina, Ra is not concerned with preserving the human species. In fact, he seeks to "get away from the earthman" and leave the human form altogether.[12] "I am not a human being anyway, so don't treat me like them," he says in a lecture from a class, "The Black Man in the Cosmos," that he taught at the University of California, Berkeley, in 1971. "I express God [and say] I am a different order of being, I am not man. What does man mean? According to the good book Man means filthy and abominable. Now who wants to be that?"[13] I consider Ra's ambivalence about the human and his concepts of beingness in which we are made of the same elements that articulate across an unknowable infinity. Ra lifted off and away from humanness into an infinite universe that included other modes of being.

Ra's philosophy cannot help but be universal, but this universe is not a humanist universe conceivable, and ultimately conceived by, human beings. It is unknowable in its vast endlessness. I use the term *unknowable* instead of *unknown*, for there is no hope that humans could master or conquer or classify this universe in their current epistemological condition. Ra refers to a bigger, wider concept he calls the "omniverse . . . the totality of all the universes."[14] But Ra's concept is not a new universalism *We* is an ambiguous referent in Ra. Most often his address is to black people, and his messianic journey is specifically for them. The terms *human* and *earthman* are synonymous with white people, who are not of the same molecular makeup as black people. "White people are an entirely different order of beings, God made them that way, and they are in a particularly ignorant state," he says.[15]

Blackness does not disappear in Ra's philosophy. In the terms set by the earthman, black people are "myths," not recognized as human; they "did not exist" according to human laws. But not existing is a liberatory condition. Black people are free to travel the spaceways; they have the freedom to move within the spheres of "other-greater-worlds:"

> If it was not slavery
> It was the freedom not to be
> In order to get ready for the discipline plane
> From other-greater-worlds.[16]

Untethered from human laws, with "the freedom not to be," black people have privileged access to the omniverse. With his Arkestra, Sun Ra will bring black people—the "shadows," the unrecognized—to other planes of existence.[17] There are many ways to get there, he explains in *Space Is the Place*; one of them is "transmolecularization" and another, as he explains in his poem "State of the Cosmos," is the "resynchronization of the shadow into / the living cosmic multi-self."[18] The concept of living takes on a deeper epistemological meaning beyond the cycle of birth and death. To be "cosmically alive" is to be an integral part of the material omniverse. Black people, the shadows on earth, will rematerialize as parts of larger molecular and vibratory phenomena.

For Sun Ra, transformation is made possible through the constant creation of music and performance. The Arkestra's performances are "not just entertainment. . . . They are tightly orchestrated rituals of emancipation from dominant, oppressive, sterile governance."[19] They are always more than the music. The motive power is in the ritual of the Arkestra's cosmodramas. These per-

**Figure 6.2** Sun Ra Arkestra.

formances depend on the participation of vocalist June Tyson, the twirling dancers, elaborate costuming, and special effects, like the Moog-synthesized organ connected to color projections.

While the show was key and included women, Sun Ra's center of gravity was the communal houses that he set up with his male musicians. With his houses in Chicago and New York City, Ra and his musicians formed a utopian community. The two houses were a complex homosocial space. The band members lived, rehearsed, and performed together twenty-four hours a day. While the house was a forceful space of creativity, Ra demanded a level of strict obedience and disciplined commitment from his musicians to the rules he set. Women could not live there, and musicians were forbidden to bring women around or use drugs or alcohol. Rehearsal at the houses was practically continuous as Ra barely slept. The home was like a monastery. "We lived like monks," remembers tenor saxophonist John Gilmore. Many musicians found the living conditions overly restrictive and confining, referring to the houses as the "Ra jail."[20] At the same time, they recognized the permission such discipline gave them and appreciated the houses' climate of focused—if enforced—productivity and creative freedom.

Sun Ra was an ascetic. Discipline was a philosophical principle and way of life, as important a tenet for Sun Ra as strict worship was for Alice Coltrane. With a mandate from the universe, Sun Ra demanded obedience and precision. "You watched and you were kept busy, you kept so busy until you'd just cry," says alto saxophonist Marshall Allen. "'Cause you was in the Ra Jail and you in with Sun Ra and he was a busy man."[21] Ra's leadership style was not democratic. He demanded complete attention and enacted weird forms of punishment for infractions of his rules. Yet he was an ill-fitted patriarch; the homosocial space of the Ra houses was not modeled on that of a heterosexual family or compound of families. While they were based in discipline, they were not based in hierarchical rank or competition. Other forms of male leadership also don't fit. Ra was no military leader as music and the experience of sound were not battles nor war; neither was he a king, as the forms of fealty he demanded were not solely geared to maintain his personal power. Acts of loyalty were to the music and to the equilibrium of the musical/theatrical community. Collectively lived music was the force; everything else was secondary. June Tyson sums up the ambiguity. "Sun Ra would whisper the lines to me on stage, and I'd have to sing," she remembers. "We were really doing as told. . . . It was fun!"[22] In some ways, the Arkestra posed an alternative form of collectivity, absent the militarism usually associated with such male spaces and not organized around the principles of the acquisitive individualist.

Sun Ra's organization allowed for alternative forms of masculinity. His apparent asexuality poses a challenge to the hypersexual braggadocio of many jazzmen. Ra seemingly was celibate or at least did not present a sexuality in any sense recognizable by normative strictures. He writes in his poem "The Planet Is Doomed":

all these squares with this
economic system and
sweatin' blood on the job and
runnin' after all this sex stuff . . .
sex ain't nothin' but a
ain't nothin' but a gimmick, man. . . .
like, man, they can have it
they can take it and shove it
every cotton pickin' lousy bit of it
all these sexual broads that're
commercializing minds
got 'em right in the bag

**Figure 6.3** Sun Ra Arkestra and June Tyson (left).

　　that's the earthman's bag
　　and like, man
　　I gotta break away from them.[23]

From this poem at least, Ra's opinions about heterosexual sex could be seen
as in alignment with contemporaneous forms of misogyny, which conflated
women with sex and blamed them for colluding with the masters under slavery and with capitalist exploitation. But there are ways to consider Ra's approach to sexuality as nonconformist. Ra did not participate in the culture of
masculinist posturing rife in the male jazz community. Instead of the favored
quartet, Ra believed in the collective structure of the orchestra, which did
not base musical innovation in a model of competition. While he may have
distrusted women, as John Szwed suggests in his biography of Sun Ra, he did
have women perform with the Arkestra and his attention was to their artistic contributions. Ra's philosophies and the kinds of music and performance
he and his collective practiced, coupled with his nonconformist relationship
to sexuality and social organization, offer a queer alternative to the virile and
heteronormative conceptions of jazz genius developed between musicians at

the time and in critical reception since. Like Samuel R. Delany, Ra cast out into the galaxies, beyond the realm of simple ideas like gender, sex, birth, and death, to an expansive kind of music.

## Cosmogenesis

Ra did mine the past—but he was not searching for origins or for some kind of return. He did not seek to remember the great gods, pharaohs, and kings of Africa simply for them to be recognized by white Western institutions. He looked instead to ancient histories for the hidden mysteries that could unlock access to other worlds. Ra's way of thinking was based in seeking out subjugated knowledge, hidden philosophies of beingness obscured by Western (white) dominant and dominating knowledge formations. His thinking is part of a tradition of African American intellectualism that seeks other ways of knowing, outside of and in between the cracks of white Western institutional control of knowledge. Ra's early broadsheets, written primarily in the 1950s, are like the work of other street corner preachers, aimed at revealing the mythical histories of black people.

The sources Sun Ra drew from were wide and esoteric. His theosophy is grounded in a mixture of sources, including nineteenth-century romantic spiritualist cosmologies found in Helena P. Blavatsky's *The Secret Doctrine: The Synthesis of Science, Religion and Philosophy*, the spells contained in *The Egyptian Book of the Dead*, phonetic readings of the King James Bible, and the works of early Afrocentrists like Theodore P. Ford. Ra composed, in curlicued and layered tangents, reinterpretations of history. He pulled from his sources an endless stream of minutiae, manipulating the concept of fact and blurring the lines between science and fiction. The effect is that we are estranged from and disoriented in our usual orbit.

Ra drew heavily on nineteenth-century spiritualism, blending various arcane sources. The works of Madame Blavatsky appear on his syllabus for the class he taught at Berkeley in 1971, and her *Secret Doctrine* was an obvious influence. Blavatsky's project is not based in spiritual revelation, conversion, or sanctification but in "the results of her own study and observation."[24] Blavatsky writes in *Cosmogenesis*, the first volume of *Secret Doctrine*, "What is contained in this work is to be found scattered throughout thousands of volumes embodying the Scriptures of the great Asiatic and early European religions, hidden under glyph and symbol, and hitherto left unnoticed because of this veil. What is now attempted is to gather the oldest tenets together and to make of them one harmonious and unbroken whole."[25] What she offers is nothing less than a "new genesis . . . rescuing from degradation the archaic truths which are the basis of all religions."[26] Ra was not looking to archaic truths for a new site of origin but had a similarly integrative approach to spirituality: he sought a portal to other worlds hidden in the words and hieroglyphs of earlier civilizations.

Divinity and God were key truths for Ra, but while his vision is one that integrates philosophy with divine understandings, Ra's universe, unlike Alice Coltrane/Turiyasangitananda's, is not God centered. For him, we humans are not in the body of a God or embroiled in a divine battle. Ra was also highly critical of organized religion: "I'm not in the least bit religious. I'm not interested in that. Because churches don't do anything but bring people . . . peace," he states in an interview.[27] As we will explore further, for Ra peace, along with equality and freedom, was only possible after death, and death marked an acceptance that human life was the only option. Ra was critical of church teachings. He speaks, in his early broadsheets, directly to black people through interpretations of the Bible. "THE BIBLE IS WRITTEN IN SUCH A WAY THAT IT HAS ONE MEANING FOR THE NEGRO AND ANOTHER MEANING FOR THE WHITE MAN," he writes. "THE AMERICAN NEGRO HAS THE KEYS TO THE HIDDEN MEANING OF THE BIBLE, IT IS BECAUSE THE NEGRO HAS NOT SOUGHT THE WISDOM THAT WILL FREE HIM THAT HE IS STILL IN CHAINS."[28] Nevertheless, Ra's philosophy and musical practice do hold within them structures resonant with the black Christian tradition. Ra uses Christian metaphor and myth; angels, devils, and references to heaven populate his poetry. Ra's central tropes could be interpreted as recalibrated Christian parables, interpretations of the Bible coming out of black Christian culture.

But it would be too easy to dismiss Sun Ra's mythos as purely derivative. His philosophy, theosophy, poetry, and musical practice refer to black vernacular tropes—like exodus and transcendence—that encompass but extend beyond a Christian framework. The performances of Ra and his Arkestra could be thought of as resonating with the performance of a church service—the interaction of preacher, choir, and congregation. But the orchestral structure of the Arkestra, the use of call-and-response, and the circling movement of the artists, often within the audience, reflected not so much a church service itself as the ineffable phenomena that a service ignites.

Ra's plan for an escape to the stars is often interpreted as based in the Christian story of Exodus. Sometimes Ra uses Christian references to illustrate his plans for escape to the stars, leading his people away from the horrors of this planet and away from the earthman. "If an angel led the exodus out of Egypt, why can't an angel lead some others somewhere else," he writes.[29] But Ra's philosophy and practices of escape are past the bounds of religious understanding, with the Hebrew exodus from Egypt in the Christian Bible a metaphor fitted to a deeper trope of black fugitivity.

The tale of Exodus from the Bible is one narrative of escape crucial to a black thematics of freedom beyond the bounds of a liberal humanist definition. "Perhaps constant escape is what we mean when we say freedom," Fred Moten writes. "Perhaps constant escape is that which is mistreated in the dissembling invocation of freedom and the disappointing underachievement/s of emancipation."[30] Ra critiqued these limited notions of freedom and emancipation bounded by Enlightenment ideals. Moten continues, "What does being sent into the terrible pathways and precincts of the human do of and for the human? What happens when we consider and enact the aesthetic, epistemological and ontological escape of and from being-sent?"[31] Reading Ra's poetry gives us an example of what a response to these hypotheticals could look like.

Ra was not interested in finding a homeland on an earthly plane, and his Heavens are much vaster than a Christian Heaven. Particularly in his later work, Ra is less concerned with a spirituality found on earth than with the mutability of human beings into a wider universe. To be is to be

> Celestially alive
> Beists of the endless
> Bottomless
> Abyss of the outer never no end endless
> Kingdom of The Eternal BEING.[32]

This celestial surpasses the idea of God; to be alive surpasses species definition and intellectual powers of perception.

This universe of Ra's is a material universe and his sense of God was as coolly scientific as Olamina's. Science in African American culture blends a creative range of ways of knowing and deducing—magical, telepathic, alchemical, intuitive. There is little distinction to be made between science and the spiritual; science is not incommensurable with what the Transcendentalists (via Hinduism) thought of, as William James writes in *The Varieties of Religious Experience: A Study of Human Nature*, the "immanent divinity of things, the essentially spiritual structure of the universe."[33] Music is therefore a science. To align with the vibrations of music is to join the elements and transform the self into a divine order of being. "Space music is an introductory prelude to the sound of greater infinity. . . . It is a different order of sounds synchronised to a different order of being," Ra writes.[34] Marxist utopian philosopher Ernst Bloch points out that music was once considered a science. "Music, together with arithmetic, geometry and astronomy, constituted a science. . . . Kepler connected it to the heavenly bodies, to the realm of purest revolutions. . . . Here it does not surge from feeling but pours down from the planets," Bloch recalls.[35] Science—in Ra's work the art of turning lost or innovative ways of knowing into new forms of existence—expands into the magical.

Ra was ambivalent about the system of life on earth. He found its cycle confining. He considered himself a "different order of being," and as a nonhuman, he rose above both birth and death.[36] He had great aversion to death as it was proof that someone was bound temporally to the system of earth life. Black life, that is to say black existence, did not have to be lived in death. To do so was to obey a false ontology of being. "I came to the conclusion that the only reason people died was because there is a God. . . . Death is a god . . . and all people are subject to it. . . . Should they be obedient to the god Death or should they be rebels? . . . If you rebel, then you move over into uncharted paths, and, of course they won't like it," he reflects.[37] Like a manmade God, the past is part of an epistemology of death that must be broken with for us to exist as cosmic beings. Life and death are part of the same system. "I command you, give up your death!" Sun Ra and June Tyson bellow. "Is *this* what you call life?"[38] Ra calls for us to refuse the limitations of the human life form, to rebel against the terms of being alive that would call for a beginning, middle, or end. These are part of "an equation set up that's fooling folks."[39] The past is associated with death, with a severance from the possibilities of time ordered differently. In his poem "Of the Day That Died," Ra writes:

> The Past always reminds me of the day that died
> It shall not come again
> Because it dwells in the realm of "been"
> And that which has been
> Is forever separated from that
> Which is to be.[40]

Ra's cosmology plumbs the past but is not mired there. "That which is to be" is not a continuation of the past nor is it in a foreseeable future. Rather, it requires a disaffiliation from such terms. That which is to be is the infinite possibility "beyond what you know as time."[41] We must jump into the break, the cut, into an entirely different paradigm.

Future

According to the most developed theories of utopia, inspired by the work of Ernst Bloch, we can't realize utopian totalities, for they will be the consequence of historically situated processes, and we are unable to imagine past our current epistemological frameworks. The "blueprinting" of utopia, the attempt to draw up a new world in its entirety, is impossible. Utopia is forever on the horizon. The future, in this sense, looks to ongoing processes that we can never bring to completion, as they exceed our own limited terms.

According to Bloch the future does not break away completely from notions of the past and present but dialectically transposes into the New. I suggest, alternatively, that anything we could call a future is "on the other side of time."[42] It is not the result of dialectical processes but is what would happen after a complete break with time as we know it. We are not held by a binary but instead proliferate into myriad relationalities.

For Ra, a utopian consciousness is synchrony with an infinite universe. It is the state achieved through jumping into the void and becoming part of a "gigantic atmosphere. . . . that tends to make you part of it."[43] This state of being requires activation through, as Bloch writes, an "extreme effort of will."[44] Ra's concept of discipline resonates with Bloch's concept of will. While Bloch's effort of will remains relatively unformed in *The Principle of Hope*, Ra's concept of discipline is complex. His concept holds within it an almost Victorian set of mores. When it comes to musical training, dedication, and precision, it is, above all, about a work ethic. Ra's adherence to a principle of discipline is reflected in his complex musical composition. He admonishes other musicians: "They got to change the way they write, they got to change the way they play, and of course it comes down to strict discipline."[45] Discipline is also about restraint from earthly bodily pleasures that would lead to dissipation and hedonism. Despite these tenets' apparent resonance with African American middle-class reformers' call to "lift as we climb," Ra's concept of discipline is not based in bourgeois notions of class deportment. Discipline's aim isn't to build a better future through adherence to social propriety; instead, it holds within it a deep and spiritual asceticism, a commitment to giving over the self to something bigger, to shedding human ties to earthly needs and wants. Discipline is essential to developing and releasing musicians' creative abilities. Strict adherence to the demands of musical precision provides the ground for creativity to be expressed. Discipline is essential to accessing other realms. It is essential to be able to face the vastness of the universe. It is required of those who would do nothing less than travel into infinity. "The alternative to limitation is INFINITY. Yet, be warned! Infinity is precision discipline," he says.[46] The infinite is a key concept that appears throughout Ra's music and philosophy. The infinite is boundless and endless, the principle ordering all matter. It is unknowable, and it is this vastness beyond all vastness that Ra is concerned with.

Both Afrofuturism and queer theory play with temporality, allowing for a different relationship to ordering regimes. But both defer possibility to some kind of future. The very concept of the future itself works to compose a narrative of time and is bound to a relationship with the past and present. While the future is the contested ground for a plethora of political stances, it is still ultimately tied to a narrative of time; Ra's more radical ideas of temporality go unnoticed when put under the umbrella of the future, as they look more to scale and spatiality as the grounds for utopian imaginings. This is not to say that temporality disappears altogether; what the work of Ra does is point to an alternative sense of temporality, beyond even the bounds of the dialectical binary based in conflict or confrontation. Its utopian drive is a dispersive, centripetal impulse, infinitely multiplying and relational, as we become "cosmic multi-selves."[47]

Vibratory Ratios

Ra does not come from a mythical past, the present, or the future but from another planet. He has unwillingly come to Earth (sometimes from Saturn) at the Creator's behest. His planet is "nothing like the earth," as he explains in the poem "In Orbit." Time, at least as ordered according to the human life span, does not exist on his planet. "There's no past, there's no future," Ra writes in "In Orbit":

> there's actually no present
> because everything moves in an
> infinite number of dimensions
> infinite number of vibratory ratios.[48]

With "In Orbit," Ra suggests an alternate order for understanding time and space. The universe moves not according to chronological earthly time but according to dimensions and vibrations: all the elements in the cosmos move in coordinated relation to each other. The concept of dimensionality appears in Ra's poetry, as in science fiction writing, as a fantastic disorientation. "There are other dimensions and the equation of it is every other world in the infinite universe," he writes.[49] To imagine dimensions opens up a plethora of speculative possibilities for marveling at existence. There are an infinite number of alternate spatial and temporal dimensions to which travel may or may not require time or may operate according to a time ordered by a different set of laws. Imagining dimensions and dimensionality is one of the instances in which science fiction blurs with science fact, destabilizing both.

In his poetry and philosophy, Ra uses the language of various sciences, particularly quantum physics and mathematics. These sciences radically shift the scale by which to consider the universe. Decentering our common-sense understanding of a molar, human-ordered world, the basic principles of quantum physics invite philosophical exploration. Quantum physics brings us to the level of the molecule, the atom, the electron, and the photon. At these levels matter does not operate according to the same laws as in the macroscopic world. Matter can travel from one place to another without moving through space. At the level of the electron and photon, perception itself becomes unstable. According to Werner Heisenberg's uncertainty principle, what we think of as matter becomes unknowable, immeasurable. Karen Barad explains in *Meeting the Universe Halfway*:

> According to Heisenberg's analysis, the key issue is the discontinuous change in the electron's momentum, that is, the fact that it is *disturbed* by the photon in the attempt to determine the electrons position. This analysis, based on the notion of *disturbance*, leads Heisenberg to conclude that the uncertainty relation is an *epistemic* principle—it says there is a limitation to what we can *know*. . . . We remain *uncertain* about [the electron's] value, owing to the unavoidable disturbance caused by the measurement interaction [Barad's emphasis].[50]

The universe becomes an "immeasurable equation." Science fictions rub up against what gets called science fact, revealing the limitations of human perception. The results are ontological and epistemological thought experiments that call the known world—or the very knowability of the self, matter, and the universe—into question.

Matter does not stay still. "Everything moves," as Ra writes, "in an infinite number of dimensions / infinite number of vibratory ratios."[51] To acknowledge this constant motion of all matter, we must also recognize its temporality, as movement takes time. As G. William Barnard explains in his exploration of the work of Henri Bergson, "The inside of atoms resemble not small inert chunks of matter, but an intricate dance of vibrating motion, a dynamic structure of rhythmic patterns. . . . Particles are not tiny, unchanging 'objects,' but rather, are intrinsically dynamic, fluid processes, involving, on the one hand, a spatial dimension (the material, cloud-like 'particle' form) and on the other hand, an equally prominent temporal dimension (the energetic pattern, the wave-like flux)."[52] To think of matter in this way, as a constantly moving set of interacting elements, is to think of time outside notions of linear, chronological measurement. "From the perspective of quantum physics, the understanding of the universe as a type of giant Clock has been smashed, not into tiny bits, but rather into a vortex of interconnecting vibrations and fields. . . . Empty space is now considered to be a vibrant ocean of potentiality, a matrix from which countless numbers of particles emerge and disappear."[53] Thinking of the self as a set of relationalities in space is to merge the self with the universe.

Bergson's concept of durée predates discoveries of quantum physics. For Bergson, time is immeasurable and cannot be translated by mathematics or science. Durée is Bergson's complex understanding of the "temporal flux of our consciousness" in the context of a vast vibratory fluidity we call the universe.[54] We do not experience existence as a succession of static states, in linear progression. Instead, conscious experience of time is as a constant swirl, with no linear coordinates, no beginning, middle, or end. Our conscious perception is a filter, electing what it wants to perceive out of the swirling potential, creating as it does the illusion of past, present, and future. Bergson uses melody as the primary metaphor to illustrate the ineffable quality of durée, the "uninterrupted humming of life's depths."[55] One reaches into the impossible not forward into the future, but spatially and energetically.

## The Human

It would be easy at this point to claim Sun Ra as an antihumanist, for he troubles the bedrock most humanisms rest upon. He critiques a humanism that sees humans as the penultimate form of life and that holds the belief in the universal human potential to evolve into something better, to progress, to achieve an ideal of liberty and equality. His call is not for these tenets of humanism to be fulfilled, for inclusion in the brotherhood of man. It is not a plea to earthmen for a Hegelian moment of "mutual recognition." It is not a fight to the death, a hand-to-hand struggle dependent on a negative and binary relation of power. Ra critiques a humanism that elides its own contradiction and obscures its basis in the oppression and exclusion of vast numbers of people. Ra's musical agenda is not, as Kodwo Eshun says of commercial R&B, a "drive to banish alienation, and to recover a sense of the whole human being;" Ra would seem to agree with Eshun's assertion that "the human [is] . . . a pointless and treacherous category."[56] For Ra, being human is a state of ignorance and not a status we should be fighting for. Instead, black people should embrace our conditions of alienation, dislocation, and exclusion.

Ra troubles a humanist framework that calls on concepts of peace, freedom, and equality, concepts driving what he sees black activists fighting for. He writes, "If I was ruling, I wouldn't let the people talk about freedom. . . . I wouldn't let them fight for it, I wouldn't let them speak of it. . . . I wouldn't let them talk about peace, I wouldn't let them picket for it, I wouldn't let them have anything to do with peace. Because the whole thing is very simple: they're free when they're dead, and they're at rest, and at peace when they're dead. . . . The only equality they got too is that all of them die."[57]

Peace, freedom, and equality—fundamental principles to a humanist politics—cannot be lifted out of these determinations. To speak of them, to picket for them, is to ask to be human. Ra's play with words here acknowledges *human* as an always exclusionary term. Peace, freedom, and equality are unachievable for black people here on earth as the *human* they refer to is the earthman, another order of being altogether. Black people have to let go of the idea of the human, which Ra sees as inseparable from the liberal terms that have defined it. The human dimension is therefore a limited notion of existence. While Sun Ra talks of leaving the earth and transmolecularizing into another state of being, he never uses the term *freedom* as it has been determined through Enlightenment discourse. "When I speak of freedom, I do not speak of freedom of the land of liberty or the freedom of any land of this plane of existence, for this plane of existence is only a temporary illusion."[58] The aim, then, is to disengage completely from the illusory system that made, and delimits the meaning of, the word *freedom* in the first place. Sun Ra is only here, temporarily, to help us leave.

As Sylvia Wynter elucidates, *Man* is a European invention, defined in contrast to non-European peoples.[59] For Wynter, there is a distinction between *Man* and *human*, and there is something recoverable from moments in the development of ideas of humanism. In reply to interviewer David Scott's question, "Why not abandon humanism?," Wynter replies, "Because we have to recognize the dimensions of the breakthroughs that these first humanisms made possible at the level of human cognition, and therefore of the possibility of eventual emancipation, or our eventual full autonomy, as humans."[60] Some version of the human can be created if we "complete the partial emancipatory breakthrough at the level of human cognition that the voyages [of Columbus] had made possible."[61] Autonomy—freedom for the individual—is a precept she wishes to retain. Completion, for Wynter, is through the breaks these moments make possible, the ability for humans to "effect the deconstruction of the mechanisms by means of which we continue to make opaque to ourselves . . . the reality of our own agency with respect to the programming and reprogramming of . . . ourselves."[62] Wynter's call is for a renewed universalism.[63] Humans can progress, and improve, by pulling back the ideological deceptions that have blinded us, by making conscious the processes by which "we . . . come to experience ourselves as this or that genre/mode of the human."[64] Upon achieving this there is the possibility of imagining the human differently.

For Ra, *Man* is also a construct, although he does not distinguish it from the term *human*. "The word man is but an image symbol," Ra writes, with a "manufactured history."[65]

> What is called man when first created was
> Given an invented memory:
> A storehouse of manufactured, unschooled
> conceptions,
> conclusions and beliefs . . .
> How comes this manufactured history?
> Because of the void . . . The manufactured history was
> Substituted for the void in order to keep man from feeling empty and
>     without foundation.[66]

Ra's philosophy would seem to overlap with Wynter's hoped-for ability for humans to see their own ontological foundations, to untie themselves from ideas of Man. Ra's agenda could be assessed as one of creating a new genre of the human, one completely outside an ontology based in dominant notions of the human. But Ra does not share the agenda of reenchantment. *Man* and *human* are damning terms. "'Man is a horrible word to galactic beings," Ra exclaims.[67] He proposes a rescaling of the human past the bounds of recognition. For Ra the aim is not a reformation or even a transformation, but a *complete break* with the human. Ra's call is not for a new genre of the human but a new genre of *existence*, an entirely new mode of being. This different mode of being is not to leave the material world behind but to disperse into the universe. Black people must let go of ideas of the (earth)man and not only face but join the void, the nothing, a place we cannot know.

To become a citizen of Sun Ra's omniverse is to leave behind a limited and oppressive earthly mode of existence—remaining part of the material world but detached from earthbound ideas of the human. Joining the omniverse is to become a diffusive self, one that is decentered, destabilized. "I belong in a space where / you just ain't got no identity / you're just exploring and exploring," Ra continues in his poem "In Orbit."[68]

> But no earthmen here
> Matter fact
> Ain't no man here
> Ain't no woman there
> Ain't nobody there
> It's just a hyperdimension of a concurrent coplanar force that
> Tends to make you
> Part of the universe
> Part of a gigantic atmosphere which
> Intermixes and becomes
> Becomes something big and frightening
> And
> Tends to make you
> Part of it[69]

Ra's vision is of a total loss of self, a diffusion into an infinite, terrifying vastness that swallows up the individual. We disperse into an "endless void." We become nobody, absorbed in total darkness. We become nothing, that is, total blackness. *Nothing*, the subject of many of Ra's poems, is blackness. But nothing is not the negation of being itself. Blackness is nothing—that is, anterior to ontological possibility, but only on earthly terms. *Nothing* is the "freedom not to be," the refusal to respect sovereignty or acquiesce to its terms.[70]

The void is a cypher, a central motif throughout Ra's work that is associated with nothingness. But the void, the nothing, is generative. It holds virtual worlds within it. The void is infinite potential; out of the void comes sound. Sound is a material force; out of it comes music. To release into the void is to tap into a utopian consciousness: "The music comes from the void, the nothing, the void, in response to the burning need for something else. And that something else is something else/this nothing, this outer nothing is out of nothing, it is the music of the spheres. The symbol for every sphere is the sign of nothing: O. . . . The spiral is another type of nothing. . . . It is of the onward reach."[71] The void, this nothing, remains unknowable, unperceivable. To join it is the ultimate form of disengagement from the effort of articulation, materialization, visibility, resistance, refusal, escape, accommodation, suicide, homicide, or any other assertion of self in a power structure that would equate blackness with negation. It is not based in recognition nor on conversation with the earthman, but it is not mute. Its tones and timbre come from where language cannot travel. Blackness is negation. But blackness is not abjection. It does not exist according to earthly laws.

For all his rejection of the state of humanness, Sun Ra's commitment, however unwilling, to staying on earth belies his seeming misanthropy. But he is ambivalent. Ra often has little more than cruel blandishment for his people. His ambivalence is expressed in the poem "like a universe":

> I look at people sometimes and I hate them
> I don't wish to destroy them
> I don't want to harm them
> Because I know that I'm a part of them
> That I am here for them
> And I belong to them
> That's why I hate them
>
> because you see, if I didn't belong to them
> if I wasn't placed here for them
> I would be a free spirit . . .
> but yet I am chained
> you see, it's a great joke on me, too
> then again, I look at people, and I love them
> I love them so very much until I turn my head in shame . . .
> then I look at them, then I hate them again
> I hate them because I love them so much
> and I don't know
> I don't know where hate begins and love ends
> I don't know how love ends and hate
> begins . . . [72]

This poem reveals Ra's ambivalence on a number of levels. His felt connection to people is ambiguous. Is he part of the species? Or is he simply in human form out of obedience to a cosmic directive? Hate and love keep him earthbound. But Ra's patient building and tenacious maintenance of a creative collective belies his hate. His adoption of relatively untrained musicians, his inclusive practice of allowing artists impromptu appearances, and the Arkestra's incredible longevity and prolificacy show a Ra dedicated to utopian practice.

Ra's philosophy is reflected in the Arkestra's performances. Its performances were more than jazz; they were cosmodramas—the enactment of a collective worldmaking that extends beyond the band. The Arkestra's perfor-

**Figure 6.4** June Tyson and Sun Ra. Album cover, *I Roam the Cosmos* (2015).

mances were an invitation to audiences to "be of our space world." At most concerts, Ra, the Arkestra, and dancers wound through the audience, engaging all with their invitation. "Sun Ra would . . . wade into the audience . . . and pick up people . . . lift them off the ground and scream into their face, 'are you willing to give up your death for me?' People would say, 'yes, yes, put me down!'"[73] Giving up death, for black people, meant release from the limiting and painful constraints of earthly existence under the human regime.

## Conclusion

In this age of extinction, there has been a turn in speculative aesthetic practices away from anthropocentric fears and fantasies of technological triumph
toward envisioning new modes of being as organic entities embedded within
larger ecologies. Finding ourselves floundering at world's end, the material
world shocks us out of the twentieth-century certainty that the universe can
be controlled and manipulated, that everything can be converted to code and
information. As we swim in the data streams and algorithms of high capitalism, we look to the possibility of radically new epistemologies and modes of
existence. There is no need for a nostalgic, wished-for return to a pretech-
nological era or condition. The world was never ours to run or husband or
protect or save, and we cannot control or direct the future of carbon-based
life-forms. We must be willing to consider models of relationality that see
past the presupposition of human supremacy, to consider forms of reciprocity
that bring into question the hierarchical systems of biological classification,
developed in the nineteenth century, by which life forms were, and still are,
assessed and categorized.

The versions of symbiosis, cooperation, and coexistence, the blurring of
boundaries between self and other in some contemporary speculative works,
are dark—stripped of the hope for sustainability, environmental justice, or
ecological preservation and the notion that anyone, anywhere, can engineer
any of that. Nothing is in the control, or in the interest, of human well-being
or survival. In Alex Garland's film *Annihilation*, a group of women scientists
and academics enter Area X, a geographical region separated from the rest
of Earth by a shimmering force field that formed as the result of classified
military/scientific experimentation. Inside the force field, called "the shim-

mer," all life forms are undergoing bewildering processes of genetic muta-
tion. Suddenly, epistemologies by which humans have defined themselves and
the world do not apply. All means of species classification—in fact, the very
nature of species individuation—are no longer relevant. The group comes
upon a house and garden filled with bushes shaped oddly like humans. Here
Josie (Tessa Thompson), the group's astrophysicist and sole black woman,
has a revelation that the force they are facing is causing life-forms to rewrite
each other's genetic codes on a subcellular level. After this revelation, she becomes strangely silent. "You want to face it," Josie says to the group's biologist,
Lena (Natalie Portman). "She wants to fight it," she continues, referring to the
group's leader, Dr. Ventress (Jennifer Lason Leigh). "I don't think I want either
of those things." As Josie walks away, branches begin to sprout from her arms
and she becomes a flowering bush.

Josie chooses another form of relation, one not associated with human
dominance over the environment, its classification into a dominant system of
knowledge, or its conquest, but one of radical dissolution. Her choice is not
a complete disappearance but a dismantling, a relinquishment of the idea of
gene ownership. They aren't ours in the first place, the film suggests. "It's in
me," Lena replies to Josie's insight, but she is misrepresenting the powerful
and intrusive force scrambling and merging biological systems. "It's in all of
us," Josie corrects her.

What this book has done, I hope, is to open up new imaginings, new forms
of beingness that instead of basing themselves in some dialectical struggle,
look to radical relationalities and qualities of sentience outside a human-
centric ontological framework. But many questions remain for me. What
does it mean to be ethical, if ethics is not predicated on the model of responsibility? What then, if the destination is not the preservation or restoration
of existing ecologies? A partial response presents itself in these pages: all we
can do is surrender to the unknown—the unknowable—and be open to vast
change. Perhaps we have within us a desire, a utopian urge, a radical longing,
to merge with the cosmos, to diffuse into the marvelous particles we understand so little about. Perhaps now is the time that we must join the awesome,
the unexpected, already present in the world.

# Notes

INTRODUCTION

1  Orlando Patterson, *Slavery and Social Death*, 5.
2  Sun Ra, in *Space Is the Place*, directed by John Coney written by Sun Ra and Joshua Smith, featuring Sun Ra and his Intergalactic Solar Arkestra (North American Star System, 1974) 85 min.
3  Muñoz, *Cruising Utopia*, 1.
4  June Tyson, in *Space Is the Place*.
5  Wynter, "Re-Enchantment of Humanism," 136.
6  Bergson, *Creative Mind*, 62.
7  Bergson, *Creative Mind*, 62.
8  Bergson, *Creative Mind*, 160.
9  Barnard, *Living Consciousness*, 11.
10 Bergson, "'Phantasms of the Living,'" 79.
11 Goodman, *Sonic Warfare*, xiv.
12 Bergson, *Creative Evolution*, 10.
13 Bergson, *Creative Evolution*, 4.
14 Bergson, *Creative Evolution*, 9.
15 Frank Manuel and Fritzie Manuel offer an exhaustive resource for the history of utopian thought in Europe. See Manuel and Manuel, *Utopian Thought*.
16 Braidotti, *Transpositions*, 14.
17 Gregg and Seigworth, "An Inventory of Shimmers," in Gregg and Seigworth, *The Affect Theory Reader*, 2.
18 Spillers, "Mama's Baby, Papa's Maybe," 67.
19 Spillers, "Mama's Baby, Papa's Maybe," 67.
20 Lee, *Religious Experience and Journal*, 24.
21 Braidotti, "Posthuman, All Too Human," 201.
22 "Forevermore Transcending: the Ashram Albums of Alice Swamini Turiya-

sangitananda-Coltrane." Dublab online radio program produced by Mark "Frosty" McNeill. Accessed July 8, 2018. http://dublab.com/forevermore-transcending-the]-ashram-albums-of-alice-swamini-turiyasangitananda-coltrane/. 60 minutes.

23 Landecker, *Culturing Life*, 140.
24 S. R. Delany, *Triton*, 269.
25 Ahmed, *Cultural Politics of Emotion*, 25.
26 Levitas, *Concept of Utopia*, 160.
27 Thompson, *William Morris*, 790–91.
28 Edward George in *The Last Angel of History*, directed by John Akomfrah (London: Black Studio Film Collective, 1996).
29 See Bersani, "Is the Rectum a Grave?," and Edelman, *No Future*.
30 Bloch, *Principle of Hope*, 1:11.
31 Geoghegan, *Ernst Bloch*, 37. "Anticipatory illumination" is one version in English translation for Bloch's concept *Vor-Schein*.
32 Jameson, "Islands and Trenches," 6.
33 Bloch, *Natural Law and Human Dignity*, 192.
34 Moylan, "Introduction: Jameson and Utopia," 4.
35 Moylan, "Introduction: Jameson and Utopia," 5.
36 Sun Ra, "My Music Is Words," in *Sun Ra Collected Works*, 1:xxxii.
37 Eshun, "Further Considerations on Afrofuturism," 298.
38 Eshun, "Further Considerations on Afrofuturism," 301.
39 Edelman, *No Future*, 1.
40 Muñoz, *Cruising Utopia*, 1.
41 Bloch, *Principle of Hope*, 1:11.
42 Bloch, *Principle of Hope*, 1:11.
43 Bloch, *Principle of Hope*, 1:4.
44 Bloch, *Principle of Hope*, 1:202.
45 Barnard, *Living Consciousness*, 7.
46 Bloch, *Principle of Hope*, 1:201–2.
47 Bergson, *Creative Evolution*, 139.
48 Bergson, *Creative Evolution*, 140.
49 Sun Ra, *Space Is the Place*.

CHAPTER 1. ALONG THE PSYCHIC HIGHWAY

*Abbreviations*

GP   Rebecca Cox Jackson, *Gifts of Power: The Writings of Rebecca Cox Jackson, Black Visionary, Shaker Eldress*, ed. Jean McMahon Humez (Amherst: University of Massachusetts Press, 1981).

JL   Jarena Lee, *Religious Experience and Journal of Mrs. Jarena Lee, Giving an Account of Her Calling to Preach the Gospel* (Philadelphia: printed by the author, 1849).

ST    Margaret Washington, *Sojourner Truth's America* (Chicago: University of Illinois Press, 2009).

NST   Olive Gilbert, *Narrative of Sojourner Truth: A Bondswoman of Olden Time, with a History of Her Labors and Correspondence Drawn from Her "Book of Life"; also, a Memorial Chapter*, ed. Nell Painter (New York: Penguin Books, 1998).

ML    Zilpha Elaw, *Memoirs of a Life, Religious Experience, Ministerial Travels and Labors of Mrs. Zilpha Elaw*, in Andrews, *Sisters of the Spirit*, 49–160.

1   *Chicago Daily Inter Ocean*, August 13, 1879. As noted in ST, 148 (n20p413).
2   Carl Carmer, *Listen for a Lonesome Drum: A York State Chronicle*, in Cross, *Burned-over District*, 3.
3   As contemporaries, Truth, Lee, Elaw, and Jackson's itinerancy overlapped. In this chapter I discuss the four women together, although there were great differences in their belief systems and strategies of worship. We have no mention from Truth that she knew of or interacted with any of these women, but there are interesting anecdotal overlaps between Lee's and Truth's narratives; it is easy to imagine that Truth had Lee's narrative, the first version of which was published in 1836, read to her during the four years she worked with Olive Gilbert on her own book. Lee and Elaw knew each other; Lee recounts that she and Elaw, with some competition, "enjoyed good seasons together" (JL, 88). Jackson only traveled the itinerant preaching circuit between 1831 and 1837. It is hard to imagine that Truth did not know her, or at least of her, as Jackson was in New York, just north of Albany, with a "little band" of Perfectionists until 1840 and then in the Shaker community of Watervliet. Jackson and Lee did know each other and had a rather contentious relationship. Jackson recounts an otherwise pleasant meeting they had, while at the same time she "look[s] back to the . . . times she was one of my most bitter persecutors" (GP, 262).
4   Smith, *Autobiography*, 116–17.
5   Mack, *Visionary Women*, 150.
6   Mack, *Visionary Women*, 178.
7   Martin R. Delany, "Political Destiny," 56.
8   Martin R. Delany, "Political Destiny," 53.
9   Martin R. Delany, "Declaration of Sentiments," 24.
10  Mack, *Visionary Women*, 62.
11  Massumi, "Autonomy of Affect," 102. Massumi, unfortunately, uses Ronald Reagan as a negative example of this embodiment.
12  Geyser, "Affective Geographies," 293.
13  Gregory J. Seigworth and Melissa Gregg, "Inventory of Shimmers," in Gregg and Seigworth, *The Affect Theory Reader*, 8.
14  Isaac Penington, qtd. in Mack, *Visionary Women*, 151.
15  Mack, *Visionary Women*, 151.
16  See Mack, *Visionary Women*; Taves, *Fits, Trances and Visions*; Brekus, *Strangers and Pilgrims*.

17  Cross, *Burned-over District*, 34.

18  Wisbey, *Pioneer Prophetess*, 11.

19  Wisbey, *Pioneer Prophetess*, 13.

20  Wisbey, *Pioneer Prophetess*,126.

21  Wisbey, *Pioneer Prophetess*, 189.

22  Brekus, *Strangers and Pilgrims*, 80.

23  Painter, *Sojourner Truth: A Life*, 4.

24  Paul Gaffney, "Coloring Utopia: The African American Presence in the Northampton Association of Education and Industry," in Clark and Buckley, *Letters from an American Utopia*, 243.

25  David Ruggles, "Northampton Water-Cure Electricity and Hydropathy." *Liberator* (Boston, MA), December 8, 1848, 196, col. E.

26  Porter, "David Ruggles, 1810–1849; Hydropathic Practitioner," 67.

27  Elaw, *Memoirs of a Life*. Cited as ML.

28  Johnson and Wilentz, *Kingdom of Matthias*, 95.

29  Johnson and Wilentz, *Kingdom of Matthias*, 118.

30  Vale, *Fanaticism*, 1: 8.

31  Vale, *Fanaticism*, 1:24.

32  Vale, *Fanaticism*, 1:9.

33  Vale, *Fanaticism*, 1:82.

34  Vale, *Fanaticism*, 2:91.

35  Johnson and Wilentz, *Kingdom of Matthias*, 142.

36  Jean McMahon Humez, introduction to GP, 28.

37  Mack, *Visionary Women*, 157.

38  David Ruggles, "Dr. Ruggles' Hydropathic Experience." *North Star*, February 4, 1848, col. E.

39  Ruggles, "Dr. Ruggles' Hydropathic Experience."

40  See Cayleff, *Wash and Be Healed*.

41  Hodges, *David Ruggles*, 188.

42  Ruggles, "Dr. Ruggles' Hydropathic Experience."

43  Ruggles, "Dr. Ruggles' Hydropathic Experience."

44  Ashcroft, *Spark of Life*, 4.

45  George Lomas, letter to a Watervliet elder, December 25, 1872, qtd. by Humez in introduction to GP, 40.

46  Braidotti, *Transpositions*, 14.

47  2 Corinthians 12:3. *King James Version of the Holy Bible*, 666. Accessed August 15, 2018. https://ia801704.us.archive.org/5/items/KingJamesBibleKJVBiblePDF/King-James-Bible-KJV-Bible-PDF.pdf.

48  See McGarry, *Ghosts of Futures Past*.

49  Braude, *Radical Spirits*; McGarry, *Ghosts of Futures Past*.

50  McGarry, *Ghosts of Futures Past*, 53.

51  James, "Case of Psychic Automatism," 277.

52  James, "Address by the President," 2.

53  James, "Address by the President," 9.

54  James, "Address by the President," 9.

55  James, "Address by the President," 9.

56  Bergson, "Phantasms of the Living, 87.

57  Deveney, *Paschal Beverly Randolph*, 15.

58  Hardinge, *Modern American Spiritualism*, 218.

59  Hardinge, *Modern American Spiritualism*, 219.

60  Andrew Jackson Davis, "The New Motive Power," *Telegraph*, June 1, 1854, quoted in Hardinge, *Modern American Spiritualism*, 223.

61  Hardinge, *Modern American Spiritualism*, 226.

62  Neil Burkhart Lehman, "The Life of John Murray Spear: Spiritualism and Reform in Antebellum America" (PhD diss., Ohio State University, 1973), 408ff, qtd. in Deveney, *Paschal Beverly Randolph*, 18.

63  Deveney, *Paschal Beverly Randolph*, 8.

64  Paschal Beverly Randolph, "The Anairetic Mystery: A New Revelation Concerning SEX!," qtd. in Deveney, *Paschal Beverly Randolph*, 317.

65  Deveney, *Paschal Beverly Randolph*, 27.

66  Deveney, *Paschal Beverly Randolph*, 27.

67  Hardinge, *Modern American Spiritualism*, 239.

68  Hardinge, *Modern American Spiritualism*, 239.

69  Hardinge, *Modern American Spiritualism*, 243.

70  Deveney, *Paschal Beverly Randolph*, 151.

71  Deveney, *Paschal Beverly Randolph*, xvi–xvii; Randolph, *After Death*, 21.

72  John Patrick Deveney, "P. B. Randolph," *Religio-Philosophical Journal* 3, no. 11 (December 8, 1866): 4, cited in Deveney, *Paschal Beverly Randolph*, 171.

73  Deveney, *Paschal Beverly Randolph*, 254.

74  Gerona, *Night Journeys*, 4.

75  Gerona, *Night Journeys*, 5.

CHAPTER 2. LOVELY SKY BOAT

*Abbreviations*

EW    A. C. Turiyasangitananda, *Endless Wisdom*, vol. 1 (Los Angeles: Avatar Book Institute, 1979)

FB    Franya Berkman, *Monument Eternal: The Music of Alice Coltrane* (Middletown, CT: Wesleyan University Press, 2010).

ME    Alice Coltrane-Turiyasangitananda, *Monument Eternal* (Los Angeles, Vedantic Book Press, 1977).

1   Radha Botofasina-Reyes in "Forevermore Transcending: The Ashram Albums of Alice Swamini Turiyasangitananda-Coltrane." Dublab online radio program produced by Mark "Frosty" McNelll, Accessed August 27, 2016, http://dublab

.com/forevermore-transcending-the-ashram-albums-of-alice-swamini
-turiyasangitananda-coltrane/. The Luaka Bop reissue offers these interviews
in its liner notes.

2   Sherrie Tucker, email to author, July 18, 2014.

3   Sherrie Tucker, email to author, July 18, 2014.

4   Sherrie Tucker, email to author, July 18, 2014.

5   Chalmers, *Conscious Mind*. See also Dennett, *Consciousness Explained*.

6   Dennett, *Consciousness Explained*, 16.

7   Chalmers, *Conscious Mind*, x.

8   Chalmers, *Conscious Mind*, ix.

9   Barnard, *Living Consciousness,,* xxxii.

10  Bergson, "Phantasms of the Living," 80.

11  Barnard, *Living Consciousness*, xxxiii.

12  Bergson, "Phantasms of the Living," 97.

13  Bergson, "Phantasms of the Living," 92.

14  Bergson, "Phantasms of the Living," 97.

15  Bergson, *Creative Mind*, 159.

16  Bergson, *Creative Mind*, 74.

17  Alice Coltrane, liner notes, *Journey in Satchidinanda* (Impulse! Records, 1971).

18  Alice Coltrane, "Alice in Wonder and Awe: Swamini Turiyasangitananda (Alice
Coltrane) on Jazz, God, and the Spiritual Path," interview with Clea McDougall,
*Ascent 29* (Spring 2006), 36–38, quoted in ME, 94.

19  Suriya Botofasina in "Forevermore Transcending: The Ashram Albums of
Alice Swamini Turiyasangitananda-Coltrane." Dublab online radio program
produced by Mark "Frosty" McNeill. Accessed September 8, 2017. http://
dublab.com/forevermore-transcending-the-ashram-albums-of-alice-swamini
-turiyasangitananda-coltrane/.

20  Watts, "Jesus vs. the Jesus Freaks," in Fairfield et al., *Modern Utopian*, 196.

21  Watts, "Jesus vs. the Jesus Freaks," in Fairfield et. al., *Modern Utopian*, 197.

22  Martin Kowinski, "Koinonia Means Community," in Fairfield et al., *Modern
Utopian*, 198.

23  Martin Kowinski, "Koinonia Means Community," in Fairfield et al., *Modern
Utopian*, 199.

24  Turiyasangitananda, *Endless Wisdom*, 2:259.

25  Steven Ellison, in "Forevermore Transcending: The Ashram Albums of Alice
Swamini Turiyasangitananda-Coltrane."

26  Steven Ellison, in "Forevermore Transcending: The Ashram Albums of Alice
Swamini Turiyasangitananda-Coltrane."

27  Steven Ellison, in "Forevermore Transcending: The Ashram Albums of Alice
Swamini Turiyasangitananda-Coltrane."

*Abbreviations*

OEB    Octavia E. Butler Archive, Huntington Library, Pasadena, California.

PS    Octavia E. Butler, *Parable of the Sower* (New York: Warner Books, 1993).

PT    Octavia E. Butler, *Parable of the Talents* (New York: Seven Stories, 1998).

SC    Alexandro Segade, "Star Choir: Founding, Dissolution and Reconstitution of the Colonies on Planet 85K: Aurora" (unpublished opera, 2019), Microsoft Word file.

TRANS    Julian Huxley, "Transhumanism," 13–17, in J. Huxley, *New Bottles for New Wine* (London: Chatto & Windus, 1957).

1  Bergson, *Creative Evolution*, 10.

2  Bergson, *Creative Evolution*, 4.

3  Bergson, *Creative Evolution*, 9.

4  Landecker, *Culturing Life*, 221.

5  Grosz, *Nick of Time*, 25.

6  According to Butler's journal, "Parable of the Trickster" was to be followed by "Parable of the Teacher," "Chaos," and "Clay." Octavia Butler, journal entry, Thursday, November 26, 1998, box 58, file 1054, OEB.

7  Octavia E. Butler, journal entry, Friday, November 27, 1998, box 58, folder 1054, OEB.

8  Octavia E. Butler, journal entry, Friday, November 27, 1998, box 58, folder 1054, OEB.

9  Octavia E. Butler, journal entry, undated, box 58, folder 1069, OEB.

10  We see this in the invasion of extraterrestrial microbes in human bodies in Butler's *Clay's Ark*, the poisonous symbiotic relationship between microorganisms and humans in her planned book "Parable of the Trickster," the troubling versions of symbiosis in short story "Bloodchild," the processes of gene mixing in her Xenogenesis series, and the DNA-based desires for human blood in *Fledgling*.

11  Outterson, "Diversity, Change, Violence," 437.

12  Octavia E. Butler, journal entry, undated, box 98, folder 1823, OEB.

13  Octavia E. Butler, journal entry, undated, Box 58, folder 1069, OEB.

14  Huxley, introduction to Chardin, *Phenomenon of Man*, 20.

15  Huxley, introduction to Chardin, *Phenomenon of Man*, 13.

16  Huxley, *Humanist Frame*, 19.

17  Huxley, *Essays of a Biologist*, x.

18  Huxley, *Essays of a Biologist*, viii–ix.

19  Octavia E. Butler, journal entry, Saturday, December 12, 1998, box 58, folder 1054, OEB.

20  Octavia E. Butler, journal entry, Saturday, December 12, 1998, box 58, folder 1054, OEB.

21  Octavia E. Butler, journal entry, Saturday, December 12, 1998, box 58, folder 1054, OEB.

22 Octavia E. Butler, journal entry, Thursday, July 6, 2000, box 59, folder 1091, OEB.

23 Octavia E. Butler, journal entry, Sunday, January 3, 1999, box 58, folder 1064, OEB.

24 Octavia E. Butler, journal entry, Saturday, December 12, 1998, box 58, folder 1054, OEB.

25 Octavia E. Butler, journal entry, undated, box 58, folder 1069, OEB.

26 Octavia E. Butler, journal entry, undated, box 58, folder 1069, OEB.

27 Journal entry, undated, box 58, folder 1069, OEB.

28. Moylan, *Scraps of the Untainted Sky*, 183–186.

29 "There is [sic] the effects of drugs on the children of drug addicts. There is throwaway labor, the rich-poor gap, the literacy problem (make it the education problem), and the various problems resulting from or exacerbated by global warming. For instance again, food-price driven inflation, erratic, extreme weather, sea-level-rise, decrease in bio-diversity (plant and animal), water shortages in the southwest and elsewhere, tropical diseases migrating north, and epidemics that spread because of poor nutrition and increased heat affecting people who are otherwise weakened. Electricity will be in much greater demand, and we'll either get more nukes or more solar power and wind power. Either way, power will be much more expensive. People who need it most, won't have it. Some will die from food poisoning—unrefrigerated food—and some will die of the heat more directly. Octavia E. Butler, journal entry, Monday, May 12, 1997, box 57, folder1035, OEB.

30 Octavia E. Butler, journal entry, Tuesday, December 26, 1989, box 57, folder 1020, OEB.

31 Octavia E. Butler, journal entry, undated, box 58, folder 1069, OEB.

32 Octavia E. Butler, journal entry, undated, box 58, folder 1069, OEB.

33 Octavia E. Butler, journal entry, undated, box 58, folder 1069, OEB.

34 Octavia E. Butler, journal entry, February 17, 1998, box 58, folder 1041, OEB.

35 Octavia E. Butler, journal entry, Wednesday, May 24, 1995, box 57, folder 1027, OEB.

36 Octavia E. Butler, journal entry, Wednesday, May 24, 1995, box 57, folder 1027, OEB.

37 Outterson, "Diversity, Change, Violence," 440.

38 Outterson, "Diversity, Change, Violence," 433.

39 Butler, *Clay's Ark*, in Butler, *Seed to Harvest*, 499.

40 Outterson, "Diversity, Change, Violence," 437.

41 Outterson, "Diversity, Change, Violence," 440.

42 In her journal, Butler explains: "Also consider… four novels, TRICKSTER, TEACHER, CHAOS, and CLAY. I could see myself knowingly setting out to do four extraterrestrial novels. Each novel would examine not only how the religion and the people change, but how they change one another. Also, of course, I would be looking at different ways of being human and at what some unacknowledged aspects of our humanity might be. There are those parts of our-

selves that we don't look at—or don't look at intelligently." Although Butler rarely thinks of her stories in racial terms, her first decision to write these sequels is followed by a rare reference to race. "For instance, isn't it amazing that some black people feel ashamed of being the descendants of slaves—just as some white feel proud of being the descendant of those thugs and murderers who were good enough at their thuggary [*sic*] and murder to get themselves a title and/or a fortune. To have ancestors who were victims of crimes is shameful, but to have victims [*sic*] who were successful criminals if good and laudable." Octavia E. Butler, journal entry, Thursday, November 26, 1998, box 58, folder 1054, OEB.

43  Octavia E. Butler, journal entry, May 29, 1989, box 57, folder 1017, OEB.

44  Octavia E. Butler, journal entry, May 29, 1989, box 57, folder 1017, OEB.

45  Octavia E. Butler, journal entry, Saturday, October 10, 1998, box 58, folder 1055, OEB.

46  Octavia E. Butler, journal entry, Wednesday, July 26, 2000, box 59, folder 1092, OEB.

47  Octavia E. Butler, journal entry, undated, box 59, folder 2076, OEB.

48  Alexandro Segade, interview with author, September 27, 2019.

49  Morton, *Ecological Thought*, 30.


CHAPTER 4. SPECULATIVE LIFE

*Abbreviations*

B17   Samuel R. Delany, *Babel 17* (New York: Bantam Books, 1982).

EI    Samuel R. Delany, *The Einstein Intersection* (Middletown, CT: Wesleyan University Press, 1967).


1   Landecker, *Culturing Life*, 140.

2   Macarena Gómez Barris, *Extractive Zone*, 11.

3   Landecker, *Culturing Life*, 235.

4   Bergson, *Creative Evolution*, 10.

5   Bergson, *Creative Evolution*, 14.

6   Bennett, *Vibrant Matter*. Jane Bennett actually prefers the theories of Hans Dreisch over those of Henri Bergson.

7   Agamben, *The Open: Man and Animal*, qtd. in Chen, *Animacies*, 24.

8   Rose, *Politics of Life Itself*.

9   Latour, *We Have Never Been Modern*.

10  Malabou, *What Should We Do?*, 17.

11  Malabou, *What Should We Do?*, 14.

12  Malabou, *What Should We Do?*, 21.

13  Malabou, *What Should We Do?*, 36.

14  Skloot, *Immortal Life of Henrietta Lacks*, 153.

15  Coren, *Invisible Man*, 39.

16 Wells, "Limits of Individual Plasticity," 36.

17 Wells, "Limits of Individual Plasticity," 36.

18 Huxley, *Humanist Frame*, 19.

19 Huxley, *Essays of a Biologist*, viii–ix.

20 Huxley, *Humanist Frame*, 20.

21 Huxley, *Essays of a Humanist*, 222.

22 Chardin, *Phenomenon of Man*, 180.

23 Huxley, *Humanist Frame*, 17.

24 Huxley, "UNESCO," 21.

25 Huxley, "Eugenics in Evolutionary Perspective," 124.

26 Wells, Huxley, and Wells, *Science of Life*, 1465.

27 Huxley, *New Bottles for New Wine*, 16.

28 Huxley, *Essays of a Humanist*, 261.

29 Huxley, "UNESCO," 19.

30 Huxley, "UNESCO," 21.

31 Huxley, *Essays of a Humanist*, 260.

32 H. G. Wells, "Race Prejudice," *Independent* (London), February, 14, 1907, 382.

33 Huxley, *Africa View*, 120. Julian Huxley called himself a proponent of "liberal imperialism" after his trip to East Africa in 1932.

34 Huxley, "UNESCO," 19.

35 Chen, *Animacies*. I owe much to Mel Y. Chen's innovative and insightful work.

36 John Partington, in his essay "The Death of the Static: H. G. Wells and the Kinetic Utopia," is vociferous in his defense of Wells against accusations of racism, calling Wells's critics "biased and selective" in their criticism and distorting of Wells's thought. Yet the copious work of Wells belies Partington's own rather selective use of Wells's oeuvre in his defense. Partington's definition of racism is quite limited. Partington, "Death of the Static," 96.

37 Wells, "Race Prejudice," 383.

38 Wells, "Race Prejudice," 383.

39 Wells, "Race Prejudice," 383.

40 Wells, "Race Prejudice," 384. Whatever had H. G. Wells to do with this penultimate race woman, two years away from founding and becoming president of the National Association of Colored Women? Certainly Wells and Mary Church Terrell seems a strange coupling, but they remained long-term acquaintances. Terrell attended social events at Wells's house when she was in London, and in 1941 Wells wrote the preface to Terrell's autobiography (and in fact helped choose the book's title). Yet Wells is far from glowing in his preface, and his assessment is a rather shallow and simplistic comparison between the English class system and racism in the United States.

41 Wells, *Anticipations*, 104–5.

42 Wells, *Anticipations*, 123, 257.

43 Wells, *Anticipations*, 229.

44 Wells, *Anticipations*, 189–90.

45 Wells, *Anticipations*, 332.

46  Wells, untitled response to Francis Galton's "Eugenics: Its Definition, Scope and Aims," in Galton, Westermarck, Durkheim, Mann, and Branford, *Sociological Papers*, 60.

47  Wells, *Anticipations*, 229.

48  Wells, *Sociological Papers*, 59.

49  Wells, *Modern Utopia*, 266.

50  Wells, *Anticipations*, 323–24.

51  Wells, *Modern Utopia*, 171.

52  Wells, *Anticipations*, 325.

53  Wells, *Modern Utopia*, 142.

54  Wells, *Modern Utopia*, 144.

55  Wells, *Modern Utopia*, 266.

56  Wells's system consists of four classes: the Poetic, the Kinetic, the Dull, and the Base. The Poetic are creative and innovative but lack practicality. The Kinetic are "clever and capable people, but they do not do, and they do not desire to do new things." The Dull are "persons of altogether inadequate imagination, the people who never seem to learn thoroughly, or hear distinctly, or think clearly . . . the stupid people, the incompetent people." The final class, the Base, have "no moral sense." Wells, *Modern Utopia*, 252–59.

57  Wells, *Modern Utopia*, 259.

58  Wells *Modern Utopia*, 285.

59  Wells, *Modern Utopia*, 24.

60  Wells, *Modern Utopia*, 328.

61  Wells, *Modern Utopia*, 338.

62  Wells, *Anticipations*, 304.

63  Wells, *Anticipations*, 304.

64  Wells, *Modern Utopia*, 337–38.

65  Wells, *Modern Utopia*, 339.

66  Wells, *Modern Utopia*, 339.

67  Cole and Frost, *New Materialisms*, 4.

68  Cole and Frost, *New Materialisms*, 2.

69  Chen, *Animacies*, 89.

70  Chen, *Animacies*, 91.

71  Mignolo, "Sylvia Wynter," 106.

72  Wynter, "Unsettling the Coloniality of Being," 329.

73  Wynter, "Unsettling the Coloniality of Being," 329.

74  Wynter, "Unsettling the Coloniality of Being," 326.

75  Wynter, "Unsettling the Coloniality of Being," 328.

76  Wynter, "Unsettling the Coloniality of Being," 328–29.

77  Wynter, "Unsettling the Coloniality of Being," 329.

*Abbreviation*

TT    Samuel R. Delany, *Trouble on Triton* (Hanover, NH: Wesleyan University Press, 1996).

1  Jonathan Beecher's translation in *Charles Fourier: The Visionary and His World*, 297.
2  Butler, *Subjects of Desire*, 205.
3  Butler, *Subjects of Desire*, 213.
4  Butler, *Subjects of Desire*, 209.
5  S. R. Delany, *Longer Views*, 150.
6  Butler, *Subjects of Desire*, 216.
7  Beecher, *Charles Fourier: The Visionary*, 220.
8  Beecher, *Charles Fourier: The Visionary*, 66.
9  Fourier, *Utopian Vision of Charles Fourier*, 101.
10  Beecher, *Charles Fourier: The Visionary*, 226.
11  Beecher, *Charles Fourier: The Visionary*, 227.
12  Beecher, *Charles Fourier: The Visionary*, 228.
13  Fourier, *Theory of the Four Movements*, 82.
14  Fourier, *Utopian Vision of Charles Fourier*, 337.
15  Beecher, *Charles Fourier: The Visionary*, 311.
16  Fourier, *Utopian Vision of Charles Fourier*, 84.
17  Beecher, *Charles Fourier: The Visionary*, 303.
18  Fourier, *Utopian Vision of Charles Fourier*, 337.
19  Fourier, *Utopian Vision of Charles Fourier*, 353.
20  Beecher, *Charles Fourier: The Visionary*, 304.
21  Fourier, *Utopian Vision of Charles Fourier*, 333.
22  Beecher, *Charles Fourier: The Visionary*, 206.
23  Fourier, *Utopian Vision of Charles Fourier*, 334.
24  Beecher, *Charles Fourier: The Visionary*, 305.
25  Fourier, *Utopian Vision of Charles Fourier*, 397.
26  Beecher, *Charles Fourier: The Visionary*, 337.
27  Fourier, *Utopian Vision of Charles Fourier*, 402–3.
28  Beecher, *Charles Fourier: The Visionary*, 340.
29  S. R. Delany, "The Second *Science Fiction Studies* Interview: Of *Trouble on Triton* and Other Matters," in S. R. Delany, *Shorter Views*, 324.
30  S. R. Delany, "Second *Science Fiction Studies* Interview," 328.
31  S. R. Delany, "Second *Science Fiction Studies* Interview," 324.
32  Foucault, "Of Other Spaces," 24.
33  Foucault, "Of Other Spaces," 24.
34  Hetherington, *Badlands of Modernity*, 41.
35  Foucault, "Of Other Spaces," 24.
36  Foucault, "Of Other Spaces," 26.

37 Foucault, "Of Other Spaces," 27.

38 S. R. Delany, "Second *Science Fiction Studies* Interview," 342.

39 Foucault, "Utopian Body," 231.

40 Foucault, "Utopian Body," 233.

41 Foucault, *Order of Things*, xix, qtd. in TT, 292.

42 Fourier, *Utopian Vision of Charles Fourier,* 38.

43 Fourier, *Theory of the Four Movements*, 38.

44 Barthes, *Sade, Fourier, Loyola*, 111.

45 Barthes, *Sade, Fourier, Loyola*, 97.

46 Barthes, *Sade, Fourier, Loyola*, 103–6.

47 Barthes, *Sade, Fourier, Loyola*, 111.

CHAPTER 6. THE FREEDOM NOT TO BE

1 Sun Ra, "State of the Cosmos," in Sun Ra, *This Planet Is Doomed*, 12.

2 Sun Ra, "State of the Cosmos," in Sun Ra, *This Planet Is Doomed*, 12.

3 Sun Ra, "My Music Is Words," in *Sun Ra Collected Works*, 1:xxx.

4 Sun Ra, "State of the Cosmos," in Sun Ra, *This Planet Is Doomed*, 12

5 Szwed, *Space Is the Place*, 5.

6 *Sun Ra Collected Works*, 1:132.

7 Sun Ra, *A Joyful Noise*, directed by Robert Mugge (Philadelphia: Winstar, 1980).

8 Wynter, "Unsettling the Coloniality of Being," 316.

9 Sun Ra, "Omniverse," in *Sun Ra Collected Works*, 1:108.

10 Sun Ra, "My Music Is Words," in *Sun Ra Collected Works*, 1:xxviii.

11 Edwards, "Race for Space," 33.

12 Sun Ra, "In Orbit," in Sun Ra, *This Planet Is Doomed*, 34.

13 Sun Ra, class lecture, "The Black Man on the Cosmos," University of California, 1971. Accessed May 9, 2019. https://ubusound.memoryoftheworld.org/ra_sun /Ra-Sun_Berkeley-Lecture_1971.mp3.

14 Sun Ra, "Omniverse," in *Sun Ra Collected Works*, 1:108.

15 "Sun Ra: Prophet of Music," Interview by Cato Weatherspoon, *Detroit Black Journal*, Detroit, WTVS, 1981. https://www.youtube.com/watch?v=mNgw-zYoKzlM. Accessed July 9, 2020.

16 Sun Ra, "Of the Cosmic Blueprints," in *Sun Ra Collected Works,* 1:103.

17 Sun Ra, "State of the Cosmos," in Sun Ra, *This Planet Is Doomed*, 12.

18 Sun Ra, "State of the Cosmos," in Sun Ra, *This Planet Is Doomed*, 12.

19 Karl Erickson, "Sun Ra—Founding Father of "Psychic Secession," in Corbett, Elms, and Kapsalis, *Traveling the Spaceways*, 83.

20 John Gilmore, in *Sun Ra: Brother from Another Planet*, documentary directed by Don Letts (London: Somethin' Else Sound Directions Limited for BBC, 2005). 60 minutes.

21 Marshall Allen, in *Sun Ra: Brother from Another Planet*.

22 June Tyson, Interview, September 25, 1986. Accessed October 9, 2016. https:// www.youtube.com/watch?v=17EEO6eLzCs. June Tyson has been sorely ne-

glected by music scholars and historians, her story remains untold, her artistic contributions ignored or minimized. This was one of the few pieces of footage I could find. Unfortunately, the interview is no longer available at the link cited.

23  Sun Ra, "This Planet Is Doomed," in *This Planet Is Doomed*, 4.
24  Blavatsky, *Secret Doctrine*, xxiv.
25  Blavatsky, *Secret Doctrine*, xxiv.
26  Blavatsky, *Secret Doctrine*, xxv.
27  "It Knocks on Everybody's Door," interview with Sun Ra by John Sinclair, *Detroit Sun*, 1966, reprinted in *Sun Ra: Interviews and Essays*, 22.
28  Sun Ra, "Jacob in the Land of U.S.," in *Wisdom of Sun Ra*, 77.
29  Sun Ra, "My Music Is Words," in *Sun Ra Collected Works*, 1:xxix.
30  Moten, "Taste, Dissonance, Flavor, Escape," 242.
31  Moten, "Taste, Dissonance, Flavor, Escape," 218.
32  Sun Ra, "The Irrisistible [*sic*]Thought," in *Sun Ra Collected Works*, 1:65.
33  James, *Varieties of Religious Experience*, 32.
34  Sun Ra, "My Music Is Words," in *Sun Ra Collected Works*, 1:xxxii.
35  Bloch, *Principle of Hope*, 3:1072.
36  Sun Ra in *Sun Ra: A Joyful Noise*, directed by Robert Mugge (Philadelphia: Winstar, 1980). 60 mins.
37  Sun Ra, "It Knocks on Everybody's Door," in *Sun Ra: Interviews and Essays*, 24–25.
38  Sun Ra and His Arkestra featuring June Tyson, "I Roam the Cosmos." Accessed May 10, 2019. https://sunramusic.bandcamp.com/track/i-roam-the-cosmos-premiere-release-1.
39  Sun Ra, "It Knocks on Everybody's Door," in *Sun Ra: Interviews and Essays*, 27.
40  Sun Ra, "Of the Day That Died," in *Sun Ra Collected Works*, 1:103.
41  Sun Ra, in *Sun Ra: A Joyful Noise*.
42  Sun Ra, in *Space Is the Place*, directed by John Coney (North American Star System, 1974).
43  Sun Ra, "In Orbit," in Sun Ra, *The Planet Is Doomed*, 34.
44  Bloch, *Principle of Hope*, 1:4.
45  Sun Ra, "It Knocks on Everybody's Door," in *Sun Ra: Interviews and Essays*, 21.
46  Sun Ra, "My Music Is Words," in *Sun Ra Collected Works*, 1:xxxv.
47  Sun Ra, "State of the Cosmos," in Sun Ra, *This Planet Is Doomed*, 12.
48  Sun Ra, "In Orbit," in Sun Ra, *This Planet Is Doomed*, 29.
49  Sun Ra, "My Music Is Words," in *Sun Ra Collected Works*, 1:xxix.
50  Barad, *Meeting the Universe Halfway*, 116.
51  Sun Ra, "In Orbit," in Sun Ra, *This Planet Is Doomed*, 29.
52  Barnard, *Living Consciousness*, 83.
53  Barnard, *Living Consciousness*, 84.
54  Barnard, *Living Consciousness*, 7.
55  Bergson, *Creative Mind*, 160.
56  Eshun, *More Brilliant Than the Sun*, OO [-006].
57  Sun Ra, "It Knocks on Everybody's Door," in *Sun Ra: Interviews and Essays*, 21.

58  Sun Ra, "My Music Is Words," in *Sun Ra Collected Works*, 1:xxx.

59  Wynter, "Unsettling the Coloniality of Being," 257–337.

60  Wynter and Scott, "Re-Enchantment of Humanism," 195.

61  Wynter and Scott, "Re-Enchantment of Humanism," 194.

62  Wynter and Scott, "Re-Enchantment of Humanism," 194.

63  Wynter and Scott, "Re-Enchantment of Humanism," 196.

64  Wynter, "Unsettling the Coloniality of Being," 329.

65  Sun Ra, "The Invented Memory," in *Sun Ra Collected Works*, 1:60–61.

66  Sun Ra, "The Invented Memory," in *Sun Ra Collected Works*, 1:61.

67  Szwed, *Space Is the Place*, 365.

68  Sun Ra, "In Orbit," in Sun Ra, *This Planet Is Doomed*, 30.

69  Sun Ra, "In Orbit," in Sun Ra, *This Planet Is Doomed*, 34.

70  Moten, "Blackness and Nothingness," 751.

71  Sun Ra, "My Music Is Words," in *Sun Ra Collected Works*, 1:xxxii.

72  Sun Ra, "Like a Universe," in Sun Ra, *This Planet Is Doomed*, 109–10.

73  John F. Szwed, in *Sun Ra: Brother from Another Planet*.

# Bibliography

SELECTED DISCOGRAPHY

*Alice Coltrane (Turiyasangitananda) and Flying Lotus*

Coltrane, Alice. *A Monastic Trio*. New York: Impulse! Records, 1968.

Coltrane, Alice. *Huntington Ashram Monastery*. New York: Impulse! Records, 1969.

Coltrane, Alice. *Ptah, the El Dauod*. New York: Impulse! Records, 1970.

Coltrane, Alice. *Journey in Satchidananda*. New York: Impulse! Records, 1970.

Coltrane, Alice. *Universal Consciousness*. New York: Impulse! Records, 1971.

Coltrane, Alice. *Eternity*. Burbank, CA: Warner Bros. Records, 1975.

Coltrane, Alice. *Radha-Krsna Nama Sankirtana*. Burbank, CA: Warner Bros. Records, 1976.

Coltrane, Alice. *Transcendence*. Burbank, CA: Warner Bros. Records, 1977.

Coltrane, Alice. *Transfiguration*. Burbank, CA: Warner Bros. Records, 1978.

Turiyasangitananda, Alice Coltrane. *Divine Songs*. Agoura, CA: Avatar Book Institute, 1987.

Turiyasangitananda, Alice Coltrane. *The Ecstatic Music of Alice Coltrane/ Turiyasangitananda*. New York: Luaka Bop, 2017.

Turiyasangitananda, Alice Coltrane. *Infinite Chants*. Agoura, CA: Avatar Book Institute, 1990.

Turiyasangitananda, Alice Coltrane. *Glorious Chants*. Agoura, CA: Avatar Book Institute, 1995.

Flying Lotus. *1983*. Los Angeles: Plug Research, 2006.

Flying Lotus. *Los Angeles*. London: Warp Records, 2008.

Flying Lotus. *Cosmogramma*. London: Warp Records, 2010.

*Sun Ra and His Arkestra*

Sun Ra. *Angels and Demons at Play*. Chicago: El Saturn Records, 1965.

Sun Ra. *We Travel the Spaceways*. Chicago: El Saturn Records, 1967.

Sun Ra. *The Heliocentric Worlds of Sun Ra*. Vol. 1. ESP-Disk, 1965.
Sun Ra. *The Heliocentric Worlds of Sun Ra*. Vol. 2. ESP-Disk, 1965.
Sun Ra. *Lanquidity*. Conshohocken, PA: Evidence Music, 2000.
Tyson, June, and Sun Ra. *I Roam the Cosmos*. Enterplanetary Koncepts, 2015.


FILMOGRAPHY

Akomfrah, John, dir. *The Last Angel of History*. London: Black Studio Film Collective, 1996.
Coney, John, dir. *Space Is the Place*. North American Star System, 1974.
Letts, Don, dir. *Sun Ra: Brother from Another Planet*. London: Somethin' Else Sound Directions Limited for BBC, 2005.
Mugge, Robert, dir. *A Joyful Noise*. Philadelphia: Winstar, 1980.


WORKS CITED

Agamben, Giorgio. *Homo Sacer: Sovereign Power and Bare Life*. Stanford, CA: Stanford University Press, 1998.
Agamben, Giorgio. *The Open: Man and Animal*. Translated by Kevin Attell. Stanford, CA: Stanford University Press, 2004.
Ahmed, Sara. *The Cultural Politics of Emotion*. New York: Routledge, 2004.
Andrews, William L., ed. *Sisters of the Spirit: Three Black Women's Autobiographies of the Nineteenth Century*. Bloomington: Indiana University Press, 1986.
Ashcroft, Frances. *The Spark of Life: Electricity in the Human Body*. New York: W. W. Norton, 2012.
Bacon, Francis, and Tomasso Campanella. *The New Atlantis and The City of the Sun*. Mineola, NY: Dover Publications, 2003.
Barad, Karen. *Meeting the Universe Halfway: Quantum Physics and the Entanglement of Matter and Meaning*. Durham, NC: Duke University Press, 2007.
Barnard, G. William. *Living Consciousness: The Metaphysical Vision of Henri Bergson*. New York: CUNY Press, 2011.
Barthes, Roland. *Sade, Fourier, Loyola*. Translated by Richard Miller. Berkeley: University of California Press, 1989.
Beecher, Jonathan. *Charles Fourier: The Visionary and His World*. Berkeley: University of California Press, 1983.
Bennett, Jane. *Vibrant Matter: A Political Ecology of Things*. Durham, NC: Duke University Press, 2010.
Bergson, Henri. *Creative Evolution*. Translated by Arthur Mitchell. New York: Henry Holt, 1911.
Bergson, Henri. *The Creative Mind: An Introduction to Metaphysics*. Translated by Mabelle L. Andison. Mineola, NY: Dover Publications, 2007.
Bergson, Henri. "'Phantasms of the Living' and 'Psychical Research.'" Presidential address to the Society for Psychical Research, London, May 23, 1913. In *Mind-*

*Energy: Lectures and Essays*, translated by H. Wildon Carr, 79–103. Westport, CT: Greenwood, 1920.

Bergson, Henri. *Time and Free Will: An Essay on the Immediate Data of Consciousness.* Translated by F. L. Pogson. New York: MacMillan, 1921.

Berkman, Franya. *Monument Eternal: The Music of Alice Coltrane.* Middletown, CT: Wesleyan University Press, 2010. Cited as FB.

Bersani, Leo. "Is the Rectum a Grave?" *October* 43 (Winter 1987): 197–222.

Blavatsky, Helena P. *The Secret Doctrine: The Synthesis of Science, Religion and Philosophy.* Vol. 1, *Cosmogenesis.* London: Theosophical Publishing Society, 1893.

Bloch, Ernst. *Natural Law and Human Dignity.* Translated by Dennis J. Schmidt. Cambridge, MA: MIT Press, 1996.

Bloch, Ernst. *The Principle of Hope.* 3 vols. Translated by Neville Place, Stephen Plaice, and Paul Knight. Cambridge, MA: MIT Press, 1986.

Blount, Herman Poole. *See* Sun Ra.

Braidotti, Rosi. "Posthuman, All Too Human: Towards a New Process Ontology Theory." *Culture and Society* 23, nos. 7–8 (December 2006): 197–208.

Braidotti, Rosi. *Transpositions: On Nomadic Ethics.* Cambridge, UK: Polity, 2006.

Braude, Ann. *Radical Spirits: Spiritualism and Women's Rights in Nineteenth-Century America.* Boston: Beacon Press, 1989.

Brekus, Catherine A. *Strangers and Pilgrims: Female Preaching in America, 1740–1845.* Chapel Hill: University of North Carolina Press, 1998.

Butler, Judith P. *Subjects of Desire: Hegelian Reflections in Twentieth-Century France.* New York: Columbia University Press, 1987.

Butler, Octavia E . *Bloodchild.* New York: Seven Stories, 2005.

Butler, Octavia E . *Clay's Ark.* New York: St. Martin's, 1984.

Butler, Octavia E . *Fledgling.* New York: Grand Central, 2007.

Butler, Octavia E . *Kindred.* Boston: Beacon, 2009.

Butler, Octavia E . *Parable of the Sower.* New York: Warner Books, 1993. Cited as PS.

Butler, Octavia E. *Parable of the Talents.* New York: Seven Stories, 1998. Cited as PT.

Butler, Octavia E. *Seed to Harvest: The Complete Patternist Series.* New York: Grand Central, 2007.

Cayleff, Susan. *Wash and Be Healed: The Water Cure Movement and Women's Health.* Philadelphia: Temple University Press, 1991.

Chalmers, David. *The Conscious Mind: In Search of a Fundamental Theory.* New York: Oxford University Press, 1997.

Chardin, Pierre Teilhard de. *The Phenomenon of Man.* New York: Harper Perennial, 1922.

Chen, Mel Y. *Animacies: Biopolitics, Racial Mattering, and Queer Affect.* Durham, NC: Duke University Press, 2012.

Clark, Christopher, and Kerry W. Buckley. *Letters from an American Utopia: The Stetson Family and the Northampton Association 1843–47.* Amherst: University of Massachusetts Press, 2004.

Cole, Diana, and Samantha Frost, eds. *New Materialisms: Ontology, Agency, and Politics*. Durham, NC: Duke University Press, 2010.

Coltrane, Alice. *See also* Turiyasangitananda, A. C.

Coltrane-Turiyasangitananda, Alice. *Monument Eternal*. Los Angeles: Vedantic Book Press, 1977. Cited as ME.

Corbett, John, Anthony Elms, and Terry Kapsalis, eds. *Traveling the Spaceways: Sun Ra: The Astro Black and Other Solar Myths*. Chicago: WhiteWalls, 2010.

Coren, Michael. *The Invisible Man: The Life and Liberties of H. G. Wells*. New York: Atheneum, 1993.

Cross, Whitney R. *The Burned-over District: The Social and Intellectual History of Enthusiastic Religion in Western New York, 1800–1850*. New York: Octagon Press, 1981.

Darwin, Charles. *On the Origin of Species by Means of Natural Selection or the Preservation of Favoured Races in the Struggle for Life*. Edited by William F. Bynum. New York: Penguin Books, 2009.

Delany, Martin R. "Declaration of Sentiments." In *Proceedings of the National Emigration Convention of Colored People Held at Cleveland, Ohio, 1854*, 23–28. Pittsburgh: A. A. Anderson, 1854.

Delany, Martin R. "Political Destiny of the Colored Race on the American Continent: To the Colored Inhabitants of the United States." In *Proceedings of the National Emigration Convention of Colored People held at Cleveland, Ohio, 1854*, 33–70. Pittsburgh: A. A. Anderson, 1854.

Delany, Samuel R. *Babel 17*. New York: Bantam Books, 1966. Reprint 1982. Cited as B17.

Delany, Samuel R. *The Einstein Intersection*. Middletown, CT: Wesleyan University Press, 1967. Cited as EI.

Delany, Samuel R . *Longer Views: Extended Essays*. Hanover, NH: Wesleyan University Press, 1996.

Delany, Samuel R. *Shorter Views: Queer Thoughts and the Politics of the Paraliterary*. Hanover, NH: Wesleyan University Press, 1999.

Delany, Samuel R. *Silent Interviews: On Language, Race, Sex, Science Fiction, and Some Comics*. Hanover, NH: Wesleyan University Press, 1994.

Delany, Samuel R. *Triton*. New York: Bantam Books, 1976.

Delany, Samuel R. *Trouble on Triton: An Ambiguous Heterotopia*. Hanover, NH: Wesleyan University Press, 1996. Cited as TT.

Dennett, Daniel C. *Consciousness Explained*. Boston: Little, Brown, 1991.

Deveney, John Patrick. *Paschal Beverly Randolph: A Nineteenth-Century Black American Spiritualist, Rosicrucian, and Sex Magician*. New York: State University of New York Press, 1997.

Edelman, Lee. *No Future: Queer Theory and the Death Drive*. Durham, NC: Duke University Press, 2004.

Edwards, Brent Hayes. "The Race for Space: Sun Ra's Poetry." In *Sun Ra: The Immeasurable Equation*, edited by James L. Wolf and Hartmut Geerken, 29–56. Norderstedt, Germany: Waitawhile/Books on Demand, 2005.

Elaw, Zilpha. *Memoirs of a Life, Religious Experience, Ministerial Travels and La-bors of Mrs. Zilpha Elaw*. In Andrews, *Sisters of the Spirit*, 49–160. Cited as ML.

Ellison, Steven. *See* Flying Lotus in Discography.

Eshun, Kodwo. "Further Considerations on Afrofuturism." *CR: The Centennial Review* 3, no. 2 (Summer 2003): 287–302.

Eshun, Kodwo. *More Brilliant Than the Sun: Adventures in Sonic Fiction*. London: Quartet Books, 1998.

Fairfield, Richard, with Timothy Miller, Alan Watts, Nick Tosches, and the Underground Press Syndicate. *The Modern Utopian: Alternative Communities in the '60s and '70s*. Los Angeles: Process, 2010.

Fanon, Frantz. *Black Skin, White Masks*. Translated by Charles Lam Markmann. New York: Grove, 1967.

Foucault, Michel. "Des espaces autres." *Architecture, Mouvement, Continuité* no. 5 (October 1984): 46–49;

Foucault, Michel. "Of Other Spaces" ("Des espaces autres"). Translated by Jay Miskowiec. *Diacritics* 16, no. 1 (Spring 1986): 22–27.

Foucault, Michel. "The Order of Discourse." In *Untying the Text: A Post-Structuralist Reader*, edited by Robert Young. London: Routledge, 1981.

Foucault, Michel . *The Order of Things: An Archaeology of the Human Sciences*. London: Routledge, 1989.

Foucault, Michel. "Utopian Body." Translated by Lucy Allias, with Caroline Jones and Arnold Davidson. In *Sensorium: Embodied Experience, Technology and Contemporary Art*, edited by Caroline Jones, 229–34. Cambridge, MA: MIT Press, 2006.

Fourier, Charles. *Oeuvres Complètes de Charles Fourier*. Charleston, SC: Nabu Press, 2011.

Fourier, Charles. *The Theory of the Four Movements*. Edited by Gareth Stedman Jones and Ian Patterson. Cambridge: Cambridge University Press, 1996.

Fourier, Charles. *The Utopian Vision of Charles Fourier: Selected Texts on Work, Love and Passionate Attraction*. Edited and translated by Jonathan Beecher and Richard Bienvenu. Boston: Beacon Press, 1971.

Galton, Frances, E. Westermarck, P. Geddes, E. Durkheim, Harold H. Mann, and V. V. Branford *Sociological Papers*. London: MacMillan, 1905.

Geoghegan, Vincent. *Ernst Bloch*. London: Routledge, 1996.

Gerona, Carla. *Night Journeys: The Power of Dreams in Transatlantic Quaker Culture*. Charlottesville: University of Virginia Press, 2004.

Geyser, Naomi. "Affective Geographies: Sojourner Truth's *Narrative*, Feminism, and the Ethical Bind of Sentimentalism." *American Literature* 79, no. 2 (2007): 275–305.

Gilbert, Olive. *Narrative of Sojourner Truth: A Bondswoman of Olden Time, with a History of Her Labors and Correspondence Drawn from Her "Book of Life"; also, a Memorial Chapter*. Edited by Nell Painter. New York: Penguin Books, 1998. First published in 1884 by Review and Herald Office (Battle Creek, MI). Cited as NST.

Gómez-Barris, Macarena. *The Extractive Zone: Social Ecologies and Decolonial Perspectives*. Durham, NC: Duke University Press, 2017.

Goodman, Steve. *Sonic Warfare: Sound, Affect, and the Ecology of Fear*. Cambridge, MA: MIT Press, 2010.

Gregg, Melissa, and Gregory J. Seigworth. *The Affect Theory Reader*. Durham, NC: Duke University Press, 2010.

Grosz, Elizabeth *The Nick of Time: Politics, Evolution, and the Untimely*. Durham, NC: Duke University Press, 2004.

Hardinge, Emma. *Modern American Spiritualism: A Twenty Years Record of the Communion Between Earth and the World of the Spirits*. New York: printed by author, 1870.

Hetherington, K. *The Badlands of Modernity: Heterotopia and Social Ordering*. London: Routledge, 1997.

Hodges, Graham Russell Gao. *David Ruggles: A Radical Black Abolitionist and the Underground Railroad in New York City*. Chapel Hill: University of North Carolina Press, 2010.

Huxley, Julian. *Africa View*. London: Chatto & Windus, 1936.

Huxley, Julian. *Essays of a Biologist*. London: Chatto & Windus, 1923.

Huxley, Julian. *Essays of a Humanist*. Middlesex, UK: Pelican Books, 1966.

Huxley, Julian, "Eugenics in Evolutionary Perspective," *The Eugenics Review* 62 (October 1962): 124–41.

Huxley, Julian. *The Humanist Frame*. New York: Harper & Brothers, 1961.

Huxley, Julian. *New Bottles for New Wine*. London: Chatto & Windus, 1957.

Huxley, Julian. *UNESCO: Its Purpose and Philosophy*. Policy document for the UNESCO Preparatory Commission. London: Frederick Printing, 1946.

Jackson, Rebecca Cox. *Gifts of Power: The Writings of Rebecca Cox Jackson, Black Visionary, Shaker Eldress*. Edited by Jean McMahon Humez. Amherst: University of Massachusetts Press, 1981. Cited as GP.

Jackson, Zakiyyah Iman. *Becoming Human: Matter and Meaning in an Antiblack World*. New York: New York University Press, 2020.

James, William. "Address of the President before the Society for Psychical Research." In *Proceedings of the Society for Psychical Research*, 2–10 London: Kegan, Paul, Trench, Trubner, 1897.

James, William. "A Case of Psychic Automatism, Including Speaking in Tongues." In *Proceedings of the Society for Psychical Research*, 277–97 London: Kegan, Paul, Trench, Trubner, 1897.

James, William. *The Varieties of Religious Experience: A Study in Human Nature*. London: Longmans, Green, 1905.

Jameson, Fredric. "Islands and Trenches: Naturalization and the Production of Utopian Discourse." *Diacritics* 7, no. 2 (Summer 1977): 2–21.

Johnson, Paul E., and Sean Wilentz. *The Kingdom of Matthias*. New York: Oxford University Press, 1994.

Landecker, Hannah. *Culturing Life: How Cells Became Technologies*. Cambridge, MA: Harvard University Press, 2007.

Latour, Bruno. *We Have Never Been Modern*. Cambridge, MA: Harvard University Press, 1993.

Lee, Jarena. *Religious Experience and Journal of Mrs. Jarena Lee, Giving an Account of Her Calling To Preach The Gospel*. Philadelphia: printed by the author, 1849. Cited as JL.

Le Guin, Ursula K. *The Dispossessed: An Ambiguous Utopia*. New York: Harper Perennial, 2014.

Levitas, Ruth. *The Concept of Utopia*. Oxford, UK: Peter Lang, 1990.

Mack, Phyllis. *Visionary Women: Ecstatic Prophecy in Seventeenth Century England*. Berkeley: University of California Press, 1992.

Malabou, Catherine. *What Should We Do with Our Brain*? Translated by Sebastian Rand. New York: Fordham University Press, 2008.

Manuel, Frank E., and Fritzie P. Manuel. *Utopian Thought in the Western World*. Cambridge, MA: Belknap, 1979.

Massumi, Brian. "The Autonomy of Affect." Special Issue, *Cultural Critique: The Politics of Systems and Environments*, Part II, no. 31 (Autumn 1995): 83–109.

McGarry, Molly. *Ghosts of Futures Past: Spiritualism and the Cultural Politics of Nineteenth-Century America*. Berkeley: University of California Press, 2008.

McKittrick, Katherine, ed. *Sylvia Wynter: On Being Human as Praxis*. Durham, NC: Duke University Press, 2015.

Mignolo, Walter D. "Sylvia Wynter: What Does it Mean to be Human?" In *Sylvia Wynter: On Being Human as Praxis*, edited by. Katherine McKittrick, 106–123. Durham, NC: Duke University Press, 2015.

Morton, Timothy. *The Ecological Thought*. Cambridge, MA: Harvard University Press, 2010.

Moten, Fred. "Blackness and Nothingness (Mysticism in the Flesh)." *South Atlantic Quarterly* 112, no. 4 (October 2013): 737–80.

Moten, Fred. "Taste, Dissonance, Flavor, Escape: Preface for a Solo by Miles Davis," *Women and Performance: A Journal of Feminist Theory* 17, no. 2 (July 2007): 217–46

Moylan, Tom. "Introduction: Jameson and Utopia." Fredric Jameson Special Issue, ed. Tom Moylan, *Utopian Studies* 9, no. 2 (1998): 1–7.

Moylan, Tom. *Scraps of the Untainted Sky: Science Fiction, Utopia, Dystopia*. Boulder, CO: Westview, 2000.

Muñoz, José Esteban. *Cruising Utopia: The Then and There of Queer Futurity*. New York: New York University Press, 2009.

Outterson, Sarah. "Diversity, Change, Violence: Octavia Butler's Pedagogical Philosophy." Octavia Butler Special Issue, *Utopian Studies* 19, no. 3 (2008): 433–56.

Painter, Nell. *Sojourner Truth: A Life, A Symbol*. New York: Norton, 1996.

Patterson, Orlando. *Slavery and Social Death: A Comparative Study*. Cambridge, MA: Harvard University Press, 2018.

Peterson, Carol L. *Doers of the Word: African American Women Speakers and Writers in the North (1830 1880)*. New Brunswick, NJ: Rutgers University Press, 1995.

Porter, Dorothy B. "David Ruggles, 1810–1849; Hydropathic Practitioner." *Journal of the National Medical Association* 49, no. 1 (Jan. 1957): 67–72.

Randolph, Paschal Beverly. *After Death, the Disembodiment of Man: The World of Spirits, Its Location, Extent, Appearance.* Toledo, OH: Randolph Publishing, 1886.

Randolph, Paschal Beverly. *The Unveiling, or, What I Think of Spiritualism.* Newburyport, MA: William H. Huse, 1860.

Rose, Nicolas. *The Politics of Life Itself: Biomedicine, Power, and Subjectivity in the Twenty-First Century.* Princeton: Princeton University Press, 2007.

Alexandro Segade. "Star Choir: Founding, Dissolution and Reconstitution of the Colonies on Planet 85K: Aurora" (unpublished opera libretto), Microsoft Word file. Quoted with permission of the author.

Sharpe, Christina. *Monstrous Intimacies: Making Post-Slavery Subjects.* Durham, NC: Duke University Press, 2010.

Skloot, Rebecca. *The Immortal Life of Henrietta Lacks.* New York: Crown, 2010.

Smith, Amanda. *An Autobiography: The Story of the Lord's Dealing with Mrs. Amanda Smith, the Colored Evangelist.* Chicago: Meyer & Brother, 1893.

Spillers, Hortense J. "Mama's Baby, Papa's Maybe: An American Grammar Book." *Diacritics* 17, no. 2 (Summer 1987): 64–81.

Sun Ra. *Sun Ra Collected Works.* Vol. 1, *Immeasurable Equation.* Edited by Adam Abraham. Chandler: Phaelos Books, 2005.

Sun Ra. *Sun Ra: The Immeasurable Equation.* Edited by James L. Wolf. and Hartmut Geerken. Norderstedt, Germany: Waitawhile, 2005.

Sun Ra. *This Planet Is Doomed: The Science Fiction Poetry of Sun Ra.* New York: Kick Books, 2011.

Sun Ra. *The Wisdom of Sun Ra: Sun Ra's Polemical Broadsheets and Streetcorner Leaflets.* Edited by John Corbett. Chicago: WhiteWalls, 2006.

Szwed, John. *Space Is the Place: The Lives and Times of Sun Ra.* Boston: Da Capo, 1998.

Taves, Ann. *Fits, Trances and Visions: Experiencing Religion and Explaining Experience from Wesley to James.* Princeton: Princeton University Press, 1999.

Thompson, E. P. *William Morris: Romantic to Revolutionary.* London: Merlin, 1977.

Turiyasangitananda. *See also* Alice Coltrane.

Turiyasangitananda, A. C. *Endless Wisdom*, vol. 1. Agoura, CA: Avatar Book Institute, 1979. Cited as EW.

Turiyasangitananda, A. C.. *Endless Wisdom*, vol. 2. Agoura, CA: Avatar Book Institute, 1998.

Vale, Gilbert. *Fanaticism: Its Source and Influence, Illustrated by the Simple Narrative of Isabella in the Case of Matthias.* 2 parts. New York: published by the author, 1835.

Washington, Margaret. *Sojourner Truth's America.* Chicago: University of Illinois Press, 2009. Cited as ST.

Wegner, Phillip E. "Horizons, Figures, and Machines: The Dialectic of Utopia in the Work of Fredric Jameson." *Utopian Studies* 9, no. 2 (1998): 58–77.

Wegner, Phillip E. *Imaginary Communities: Utopia, the Nation, and the Spatial Histories of Modernity.* Berkeley: University of California Press, 2002.

Wells, H. G. *Anticipations of the Reaction of Mechanical and Scientific Progress Upon Human Life and Thought.* London: Harper & Brothers, 1901.

Wells, H. G. *The Island of Dr. Moreau.* New York: Penguin Classics, 2005.

Wells, H. G. "The Limits of Individual Plasticity." In *H. G. Wells: Early Writing in Science and Science Fiction,* edited by Robert Philmus, 36–39. Berkeley: University of California Press, 1975.

Wells, H. G. *Mankind in the Making.* London: Chapman & Hall, 1903.

Wells, H. G. *A Modern Utopia.* London: Chapman & Hall, 1905.

Wells, H. G. *The Time Machine.* New York: Penguin Classics, 2005.

Wells, H. G., Julian Huxley, and G. P. Wells. *The Science of Life.* Garden City, NY: Doubleday & Doran, 1931.

Wisbey, Herbert A. Jr. *Pioneer Prophetess: Jemima Wilkinson, the Publick Universal Friend.* Ithaca, NY: Cornell University Press, 1964.

Wynter, Sylvia, and David Scott. "The Re-Enchantment of Humanism: An Interview with Sylvia Wynter." *Small Axe: A Caribbean Journal of Criticism* no. 8 (September 2000): 119–207.

Wynter, Sylvia. "Unsettling the Coloniality of Being/Power/Truth/Freedom: Towards the Human, After Man, Its Overrepresentation—An Argument." *New Centennial Review* 3, no. 3 (September 2003): 258–337.

Davis, Andrew Jackson, 53–54

death: Black women mystics on, 48–57; Sun Ra's view of, 167–67

Delany, Martin R., 27; Sun Ra and, 156

Delany, Samuel R., 13–14; heterotopias in fiction of, 138–41; human species construct and work of, 114; malleability of biological matter in fiction of, 126–33

Deleuze, Gilles, 138

Dennett, Daniel, 65

deprivation and suffering, Alice Coltrane's tests involving, 74–76

desire: in Delany's fiction, 138–41; Fourier's sexual utopia and, 141–44; in Fourier's work, 141–44; utopias and fulfillment of, 138–41

devotion, Alice Coltrane and principle of, 73–76

disaster, poverty and, 3–4

discipline: of Black women mystics, 29–30; Sun Ra's concept of, 168–71

*Dispossessed, The* (Le Guin), 144–45

*Divine Songs* (Alice Coltrane cassette), 78

domination, in Butler's *Parable* novels, 89–110

Douglass, Frederick, 33–34

"Dream from Ten Years of Age" (Jackson), 50

"Dream of Slaughter" (Jackson), 50–51

Du Bois, W. E. B., 72

Dumont, John, 34–36, 37

*durée*, Bergson's concept of, 20, 113–14, 171

dystopia, Black condition and, 1–2

Eastern spiritual philosophy: Black religion and, 72; white radicalism and, 70–72

ecstasy, Black women mystics' experience of, 44–48

*Ecstatic Music of Alice Coltrane/Turiyasangitananda, The* (Alice Coltrane album), 79

Edelman, Lee, 15, 17

Edwards, Brent, 159

effort of will, Bloch's concept of, 168–71

Egypt, Sun Ra's reconnection with, 156–57

*Egyptian Book of the Dead, The*, 164

*Einstein Intersection, The* (Delany), 126, 128–33

Elaw, Zilpha, 11, 24–26; camp meetings described by, 45–48; conversion experience of, 29, 48; on death and sickness, 48–57; family relationships of, 36–37; Lee and, 181n3; melting times described by, 25, 45, 91–92; spiritual theater of, 28; utopian vision of, 157; on worship, 46–48

Ellison, Steven, 79–80

*Endless Wisdom* (Alice Coltrane), 62, 73, 75–76

energeia, Jameson's concept of utopia as, 16

Eshun, Kodwo, 17, 171–72

*Essays of a Biologist* (Huxley), 96, 117

estrangement from human species, 137–41

*Eternity* (Alice Coltrane album), 69

Ethiopia, Sun Ra's reconnection with, 156–57

eugenics, 96; Huxley and, 118; Wells and, 118–24, 188n36, 188n40

evolution: in Butler's novels, 97–99; Huxley's concept of, 96–99

extraterrestrial novels, Butler's discussion of, 186n42

"Eyes," Butler's notes for, 106

*Fanaticism* (Vale), 39–40

Fanon, Frantz, 1, 3, 110

feminist theory: Fourier and, 143–44; jazz studies, Alice Coltrane and, 64

*Fledgling* (Butler), 185n10

Flying Lotus. *See* Ellison, Steven

Folger, Ann, 39–40

Folger, Benjamin, 39, 40

Ford, Theodore P., 164–65

Foster, Abby Kelley, 32

Foucault, Michel, 16, 137, 139, 145–46, 149–50, 152–53

Fourier, Charles, 13–14, 138, 141–44, 150–54; Sun Ra and, 156

Freedom Riders, 2

Frost, Samantha, 124

Fruitlands community, 33

Fugitive Slave Act, 26–27, 50

futurism: queer theory and, 17–20; utopia and, 15–20

Gage, Frances, 32

Gaines, Malik, 87, 107–10

Galloway, Catherine, 39